The Sensible Guide to Passing the PfMP^{SM} Exam

Including 400 Practice Exam Questions

First Edition

Dr. Te Wu

(PfMP^{SM}, PgMP®, PMP®, PMI-RMP)

iExperi Press ▪ New York

About This Book

This book is different than other exam preparation guides for two reasons: PfMP^{SM} exam is new and passing the exam requires a significant amount of portfolio management experience. At the time of this book's publication, the PfMP exam is still in pilot. This means that there is very precious little experience about the exam, and PMI® will likely make significant changes over the coming months. Therefore, to create an effective guide to help you, I took a different approach. In addition to providing exam tips, practice questions, and more sample deliverables, this book takes on a more Socratic approach of questions and answers. I hope through thinking and understanding the key challenges and issues, you will be more prepared for the experience-based questions that are prevalent on this exam.

Furthermore, this book does not claim to be an "all in one" guide. It is highly unrealistic for anyone interested in any of the PMI's certifications to go without a thorough understanding of its standards, whether it is the Project Management Body of Knowledge (PMBOK®), the Standard for Program Management®, or in this case, the Standard for Portfolio Management®. Therefore, this book is a companion guide to the Standard for Portfolio Management. It augments the Standard for Portfolio Management with additional clarifications, sample deliverables, and key questions and answers that every portfolio professional needs to know.

In short, this book is designed for busy professionals likely you whose responsibilities have taken them into the realm of coordinating, facilitating, managing, and leading project portfolios. As portfolio managers, you may be the decision maker or at the minimum with a high degree of influence on making sound project and program investment decisions for your organization. This book primarily addresses three concerns:

1. What are the essential concepts, processes, and tools that form the foundation of today's portfolio management?
2. Since portfolio management is still an emerging profession with professionals often working in different ways, what does this mean for a "standard" exam? More specifically, how does that impact your ability to pass the PfMP exam?
3. How best to prepare for the Portfolio Management Professional exam?

On the first concern, this book highlights the underlying rationale for project portfolio management: why it exists in organizations, why it is becoming ever more important, how to think like a portfolio manager (especially important since experience-based exam questions are difficult to predict) and what are the most important concepts, processes, and tools for this profession. This book attempts to simplify complex ideas and communicate them in plain English with relevant examples. The goal is not only to pass the PfMP exam but also to serve as an essential guide to portfolio managers.

On the second concern, this book differs from most other study guides by describing my experience as a portfolio manager and addressing the most pressing questions for each knowledge area in the Standard for Portfolio Management.

To address the third concern, this book provides six mechanisms to prepare for the exam including:

1. Studying for the PfMP exam. This is based on tried and true approaches (after all, the author of this book has passed the PMP, PgMP, and PfMP exam).
2. Practice questions and scenarios. This book contains 400 sample and practice questions.
3. Exam aids. This book contains four exam aids. A pull out is included in Chapter 10. All registered users will be able to receive the exam aids in editable Excel for free.
4. Support Group. All registered user of this book will be invited to a moderated LinkedIn forum dedicated to users of this book and our products. Here, I and my team will regularly monitor the questions and provide answers to your questions. It is my hope that others in the Group will also provide peer support.
5. Discount to additional practice exam and real-time PfMP exam preparation courses.
6. Discount to our PfMP exam preparation course. Please visit us at http://www.pmoadvisory.com/pfmp_prep/ for more details. According to my research, my company is the first to offer extensive training and coaching programs for prospective certified portfolio professionals.

To qualify for the free exam aids in electronic format, support group, and discounts for practice exam and our training course, please complete our short registration form at https://www.surveymonkey.com/s/pmoadvisory. Upon registration, you will receive more information about these services. For more information on the specific discounts, go to the end of this book on "How to Contact the Author" to see the extensive discounts.

Plus, we are also offering our readers an extra bonus. My firm, PMO Advisory, is conducting an ongoing study of "strategic business execution". The survey takes roughly 15 minutes to complete. If you complete our strategic business survey, you will receive even a greater discount code for our online practice exams and PfMP exam preparation course. If you are interested, please complete the survey at www.surveymonkey.com/s/sbe01. Given your role as portfolio managers, I believe you will find the survey and the results fascinating. Please make sure you use the same name, address, and email in the survey as the book registration. Also, on the last question which asks "how did you hear about us", please check "Publication(s) by PMO Advisory or Te Wu". It will take us two business days to process the survey responses. So please be patient.

Core Principles

This book is based on three core principles that underpin all material in this book. These are designed to add tremendous value to you. This book assumes that you are highly intelligent, highly accomplished, and very busy. Therefore, where feasible this book will:

1. Use the simplest language possible to enable greater clarity
2. Provide the basic rationale to encourage deeper understanding
3. Refer to the Standard of Portfolio Management 3rd Edition, henceforth referred to as the "Standard" where this book cannot add significant value.

The last principle assumes an obvious fact. All prospective portfolios managers planning to take the PfMP exam should read and understand The Standard of Portfolio Management – 3rd Edition. The Project Management Institute made substantial improvements to this latest edition, and it is a worthy reference guide. I studied the 1st edition thoroughly back in 2010 when I prepared for the PgMP exam. I am pleasantly surprised at the improvements in the 3rd edition. While I may not necessarily agree with everything in the Standard, it is an excellent guide.

In this sense, this book should be viewed as a companion guide that advances the two concerns stated in the opening paragraph: highlighting of the core concepts and building the required mindset required for the portfolio professionals to pass the PfMP exam

Also, perhaps stating another obvious fact, this book is not designed for geniuses and people with a photographic memory. It is created for mere mortals like me who must struggle to remember and make connections among concepts. Therefore, I hope you find the four exam aids helpful.

Clarification: In common business language, the role of portfolio management can be ambiguous. The term is commonly used by the financial services industry in referring to the management of investment portfolios, which is a group of financial and investment instruments such as equities, bonds, funds, or even target companies. In this book, portfolio management refers solely to project or program portfolios, which are a collection of projects, programs, or other initiatives in which organizations can pursue in advancement of their organization goals. Portfolio management is the art and discipline of making sound investment choices of programs and projects for organizations that maximize the intended benefits and minimize the downside risks. How to best achieve this challenging endeavor is the role of a portfolio manager.

Organization of This Book

This book is presented in eight chapters. Each chapter is written so that they are largely independent, and you can easily jump from one section to another. Chapter 1 provides an overview of PfMP exam and test taking tips. Charter 2 provides the context of portfolio management, discusses a framework to look at the abstract level of organization activities, and starts to develop the necessary mindset of portfolio managers. Chapter 9 contains two full length practice exams. Chapters 3 to 8 are largely aligned with the Standard, and these chapters each contain five sections:

1. Overview
2. Inputs, Tools and Techniques, and Outputs (ITTO)
3. Key concepts and additional explanations (when applicable)
4. Additional example of portfolio management tools, techniques, and other assets
5. Ten practice questions

Chapter 1: Preparing for the PfMP^{SM} Exam

The first part of this chapter discusses the PfMP certification qualification, certification application process, and some of the likely challenges. The second part presents a study plan, exam aids, and test taking tips designed to ease anxiety and aid in the test taking process.

Chapter 2: Portfolio Management – What and Why

This chapter addresses the question of what are portfolio and portfolio management and their relationship between project management, program management, business strategy, and organization. This chapter will also describe the mindset of portfolio managers and how they should think.

Chapter 3: Understanding Portfolio Management Process Groups

PMI's current Portfolio Management Standard (3rd Edition) presents three process groups: defining, aligning, and authorizing. This chapter focuses on these process groups, inputs, outputs, techniques, and tools.

Chapter 4: Understanding Strategic Management

Portfolio strategic management is the first knowledge area in the Standard and it serves as the bridge between strategic planning and portfolio execution. This chapter will cover the major processes and key concepts.

Chapter 5: Understanding Governance

Perhaps what best differentiates program, project, and portfolio management is the emphasis on governance which is essential for decision-making. In addition to covering the key concepts, techniques, and tools, this chapter will discuss some practical examples of its application.

Chapter 6: Understanding Portfolio Performance

Managing portfolio performance is an essential responsibility for all portfolio managers. This chapter highlights the core concepts, tools and examples that help portfolio managers optimize the effectiveness of their portfolios.

Chapter 7: Understanding and Managing Communication

Like program and project management, communication is an important aspect of managing portfolios. But for portfolios, the audience, reports, and intended outcomes can differ. This chapter focuses on the selective key concepts that will help portfolio managers on both the exam and at work.

Chapter 8: Understanding and Managing Risk

From a business execution perspective, the ability to manage risk effectively is perhaps the single most important responsibility of portfolio managers. This is especially true in high stake and turbulent sectors in which the management of "down-side" far outweighs the "up-side". Here, this chapter will introduce the tools, techniques, and concepts essential for portfolio managers.

Chapter 9: Practice Exams

This chapter contains two full-length exams with 170 questions each.

Chapter 10: Pullout of the Four Exam Aids

This chapter contains the four exam aids discussed in this book. The exam aids here are printed on one page, enabling you to make a copy and carry it with you for studying.

About Project Management Institute® and Portfolio Management Professional^{SM}

i. About PMI®

The Project Management Institute (PMI®) is currently the world's large project management professional organization dedicated to advancing the project management profession. According to the June 2014 issue of PMI Today, there are 451,871 members around the world. Its most popular certification is the Project Management Professional (PMP®) with over 615 thousand credential holders. The Project Management Body of Knowledge (PMBOK®) has over 4.5 million copies in circulation today.

PMI currently has seven active certifications plus two certifications in pilot:

#	Certification Name	Number of Active Credential Holders
1	CAPM or Certified Associate in Project Management®	24,404*
2	PMP or Project Management Professional®	615,443*
3	PfMP or Portfolio Management Professional^{SM}	121 (Pilot)**
4	PgMP or Program Management Professional®	1,036*
5	PMI-RMP or Risk Management Professional®	2,696*
6	PMI-SP or Scheduling Professional®	1,167*
7	PMI-ACP or Agile Certified Professional®	5,511*
8	OPM3 or Organization Project Management®	Uncertain
9	PMI-PBA or Professionals in Business Analysis^{SM}	In Pilot

Table 1: PMI® Certifications

* According to PMI Fact File in PMI Today, June 2014 issue.
** According to PMI's Certification Registry, www.certification.pmi.org/registry.aspx on May 15th, 2014.

By becoming a certified professional, you are joining a growing family of project professionals.

ii. About Portfolio Management Professional (PfMP^{SM})

Based on the increasing demand of project professionals, the Project Management Institute developed the new PfMP certification and initiated the PfMP credential process in 2013. The pilot program, which opened to the public in December 2013 and ended in first quarter of 2014, encouraged portfolio management professionals around the world to apply. Pilot participants took the pilot PfMP exam between December 2013 and February of 2014. (The first person who passed the exam took it on the first day in which the PfMP exam was available; I took it on January 4, 2014.) In May 2014, PMI formally informed the pilot participants of their status. I became one of the 121 newly minted PfMPs. (Note: This is an unofficial count derived from PMI's Credential Registry.)

According to the PMI's Credential Library on May 14th, 2014, there are 121 PfMPs. The PfMPs are distributed among 27 countries with the United States in the lead with 59 PfMPs. Of the PfMPs in the United States, Texas has the highest number (6), followed by New Jersey (5), Ohio (5) and Virginia (5). See the table and chart below for details.

Note: The inclusion in the Certification Registry is voluntary. Therefore, not all credential holders are listed. Also, based on this registry, I would be the 8th person in the world achieving the certification. My kudos to the other professionals completing earlier; clearly they spent their holidays studying.

Country	PfMPs
Australia	3
Brazil	4
Canada	7
Colombia	2
Egypt	1
Germany	1
India	11
Israel	1
Italy	2
Japan	1
Kuwait	1
Lebanon	2
Mexico	1
Nigeria	1
Pakistan	1
Peru	1
Philippines	1
Poland	2
Puerto Rico	2
Russian Federation	1
Saudi Arabia	3
South Africa	3
Sweden	1
Taiwan (Republic of China)	1
United Arab Emirates	2
United Kingdom	5
United States	59
(Blank)	1

US State	PfMPs
AK	1
AR	1
AZ	1
CA	2
CO	2
CT	1
FL	4
GA	3
IN	1
MA	1
MD	2
MI	2
MN	1
NC	4
NJ	5
NY	3
OH	5
PA	3
SC	1
TN	2
TX	6
VA	5
WA	2
WI	1

Table 2: PfMPs by Countries

Table 3: PfMPs in the United States

Note: The number of PfMPs is in accordance to PMI's certification registry on May 14, 2014.

The Standard for Portfolio Management (the "Standard") is PMI's latest attempt to institutionalize and formalize the body of knowledge that is integral to project portfolio professionals around the world. Currently in the third edition, it is essential for you to carefully read and assimilate the knowledge and techniques in this guide in order to pass the PfMP exam.

To make this book truly easier for aspiring portfolio professionals, I have worked with PMI and received their permission to use the key concepts including the knowledge areas, process groups, processes, inputs, tools, techniques, and outputs. This is a significant advantage to you, who will be spending many hours studying for the exam. Unlike other guides who may not have the intellectual property rights, this book will use these key terms exactly the same as how would use them on exams. Not only will this save considerable effort, it will also reduce confusion.

The tables below outline the key terms required for passing the PfMP exam:

KA	Processes	Inputs	Tools & Techniques	Outputs
Portfolio Strategic Management	Develop Portfolio Strategic Plan	1. Org strategy and objectives 2. Inventory of work 3. P. Process Assets 4. Org Process Assets 5. Enterprise environmental factors	1. P. Component Inventory 2. Strategic Alignment Analysis 3. Prioritization Analysis	1. P. Strategic Plan 2. Portfolio
	Develop Portfolio Charter	1. P. Strategic Plan 2. P. processes assets 3. Enterprise environmental factors	1. Scenario Analysis 2. Capability and Capacity Analysis	1. P. Strategic Plan Updates 2. P. Charter 3. P. Process Assets Updates
	Define Portfolio Roadmap	1. P. Strategic Plan 2. P. Charter 3. Portfolio	1. Interdependency Analysis 2. Cost/benefit Analysis 3. Prioritization Analysis	1. P. Roadmap
	Manage Strategic Change	1. P. Strategic Plan 2. P. Charter 3. Portfolio 4. P. Roadmap 5. P. Management Plan 6. P. Process Assets	1. Stakeholder Analysis 2. Gap Analysis 3. Readiness Assessment	1. P. Strategic Plan Updates 2. P. Charter Updates 3. P. Updates 4. P. Roadmap Updates 5. P. Management Plan Updates 6. P. Process Assets Updates

KA	Processes	Inputs	Tools & Techniques	Outputs
Portfolio Governance Management	Develop Portfolio Management Plan	1. P. Strategic Plan 2. P. Charter 3. P. Roadmap 4. P. Process Assets 5. Org Process Assets 6. Enterprise environmental factors	1. Elicitation Techniques 2. P. or Org Structure Analysis 3. Integration of P. Management Plans	1. P. Strategic Plan Updates 2. P. Management Plan 3. P. Process Assets Updates
	Define Portfolio	1. P. Strategic Plan 2. P. Charter 3. Portfolio 4. P. Roadmap 5. P. Management Plan 6. P. Process Assets	1. P. Component Inventory 2. P. Component Categorization Techniques 3. Weighted Ranking and Scoring Techniques	1. P. Updates 2. P. Roadmap Updates 3. P. Management Plan Updates
	Optimize Portfolio	1. Portfolio 2. P. Roadmap 3. P. Management Plan 4. P. Reports 5. P. Process Assets	1. Capability and Capacity Analysis 2. Weighted Ranking and Scoring Techniques 3. Quantitative and Qualitative Analysis 4. Graphical Analytical Methods	1. P. Updates 2. P. Roadmap Updates 3. P. Management Plan Updates 4. P. Reports 5. P. Process Assets Updates
	Authorize Portfolio	1. Portfolio 2. P. Management Plan 3. P. Reports	1. P. Authorization Techniques 2. P. Management Information System	1. P. Updates 2. P. Management Plan Updates 3. P. Reports 4. P. Process Assets Updates
	Provide Portfolio Oversight	1. Portfolio 2. P. Roadmap 3. P. Management Plan 4. P. Reports 5. P. Process Assets	1. P. Review Meetings 2. Elicitation Techniques	1. P. Updates 2. P. Management Plan Updates 3. P. Reports 4. P. Process Assets Updates

KA	Processes	Inputs	Tools & Techniques	Outputs
Portfolio Performance Management	Develop Portfolio Performance Management Plan	1. P. Management Plan 2. P. Process Assets 3. Org Process Assets 4. Enterprise Environmental Factors	1. Elicitation Techniques 2. P. management Information System 3. Capability and Capacity Analysis	1. P. Management Plan Updates 2. P. Process Assets Updates
	Manage Supply and Demand	1. Portfolio 2. P. Management Plan 3. P. reports	1. Scenario Analysis 2. Quantitative and Qualitative Analysis 3. Capability and Capacity Analysis	1. P. Updates 2. P. Management Plan Updates 3. P. Reports
	Manage Portfolio Value	1. P. Roadmap 2. P. Management Plan 3. P. Reports	1. Elicitation Techniques 2. Value Scoring and Measurement Analysis 3. Benefits Realization Analysis	1. P. Management Plan Updates 2. P. Reports 3. P. Process Assets Updates
Portfolio Communication Management	Develop Portfolio Communication Management Plan	1. Portfolio 2. P. Roadmap 3. P. Management Plan 4. P. Reports 5. P. Process Assets	1. Stakeholder Analysis 2. Elicitation Techniques 3. Communication Requirement Analysis	1. P. Management Plan Updates 2. P. Process Assets Updates
	Management Portfolio Information	1. Portfolio 2. P. Management Plan 3. P. Reports 4. P. Component Reports 5. P. Process Assets	1. Elicitation Techniques 2. P. Management Information System 3. Communication Requirements Analysis 4. Communication Methods	1. P. Management Plan Updates 2. P. Reports 3. P. Process Assets Updates

KA	Processes	Inputs	Tools & Techniques	Outputs
Portfolio Risk Management	Develop Portfolio Risk Management Plan	1. P. Management Plan 2. P. Process Assets 3. Org Process Assets 4. Enterprise Environmental Factors	1. Weighted Ranking and Scoring Techniques 2. Graphical Analytical Methods 3. Quantitative and Qualitative Analysis	1. P. Management Plan Updates 2. Org Process Assets Updates 3. P. Assets Updates
	Manage Portfolio Risks	1. Portfolio 2. P. Management Plan 3. P. Reports 4. P. Process Assets 5. Org Process Assets 6. Enterprise Environmental Factors	1. Weighted Ranking and Scoring Techniques 2. Quantitative and Qualitative Analysis	1. P. Management Plan Updates 2. P. Reports 3. P. Process Assets 4. Org Process Assets Updates

Legend:	Define (No Shade)	Align (Light Gray)	Authorize & Control (Darker Gray)
Abbreviations used in the above table:	P. = Portfolio	Org = Organizational	KA = Knowledge Area

Table 4: Core Concepts from The Standard for Portfolio Management

Notes:

1. The knowledge areas, process groups, processes, inputs, tools and techniques, and outputs listed used in this document are current as of this book's publication date. Project Management Institute® may change them at any time without prior notice. Please visit the PMI website for the most current information about PMI's Portfolio Management Professional (PfMP[SM]) credentials: http://www.pmi.org.

2. I know the table above is difficult to read as it is split across 3 pages. When you registered for the book, I will send everyone an Excel version of the above table. This way, you can print it on 1 piece of paper and carry it around with you as you study.

Throughout this book, we used abbreviations and acronyms for three reasons:

- Some tables are dense and place a heavy premium on the spacing
- Some concepts and names are long and used frequently
- Some of the acronyms have become a part of the natural language or commonly used by PMI. Therefore, they may appear on exams as acronyms.

Abbreviation or Acronym	Description
CCA	Capability and Capacity Analysis
ET	Elicitation techniques
ITTO	Input, tools and techniques, outputs (of portfolio processes)
PfMP	Portfolio Management Professional
PgMP	Program Management Professional
PMI	Project Management Institute
PMIS	Portfolio management information system
PMP	Project Management Professional
QQA	Quantitative and qualitative analysis
Standard	The Standard for Portfolio Management - 3rd Edition
SWOT	Strength, weakness, opportunity, and threat
WRS	Weighted ranking and scoring techniques

Chapter 1: Preparing for the PfMP^{SM} Exam

In this chapter, you will

- Learn the PfMP qualification, process, and exam details
- Learn a tried and proven approach to studying for the exam
- Customize your own strategy and approach to passing the PfMP exam

1.1. About PfMP Certification

1.1.1. PfMP Certification Requirements

The bar of entry to become a PfMP is set intentionally high. It is designed for current portfolio managers looking to advance their career by solidifying and proving their ability to coordinate, manage, and lead a portfolio of programs and projects. PfMP can be seen as a distinctive differentiator among the professionals and in the eyes of employers.

To qualify for PfMP, applicants must have the following:

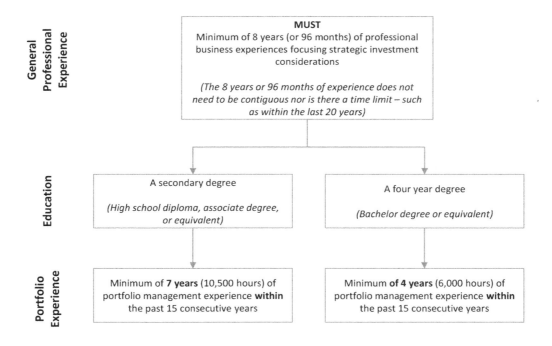

Figure 1: PfMP Minimum Qualifications

Unlike PMP, there is no additional education requirement. However, even for advanced practitioners, it is imperative to read the Standard and this study guide carefully. Similar to PMP and PgMP, it is not sufficient to pass the exam based solely on work experience. The purpose of PMI's PfMP exam is to ensure all PfMPs have similar foundational knowledge.

1.1.2. PfMP Certification Process

The PfMP application occurs in two phases (or evaluations as PMI calls them):

- In Phase 1, the panel will review your completed application. Upon its completion (including audit if PMI randomly selects you for audit), the applicant can proceed to Phase 2.
- Phase 2 is the PfMP examination in which you have one whole year to pass.

To start Phase 1, simply go to www.pmi.org to apply for the PfMP credential. Sign-in to your account or create a new account. In the Certification Program page, click on "Apply for PfMP Credential". PMI also offers the following reference materials to aid in the credential process. These include:

1. PfMP Handbook: www.pmi.org/Certification/~/media/PDF/Certifications/pfmphandbook.ashx
2. PfMP exam guidance: www.pmi.org/en/Certification/Portfolio-Management-Professional-PfMP/PfMP-Exam-Guidance.aspx

My suggestions for you are as follows:

1. Join PMI, if you are not a member already. The cost of the PfMP credential can be expensive (ranging from $700 to $800 USD for members or $900 to $1,000 for non-members at the time of writing). Therefore the discount of $200 more than offsets the cost of PMI membership. Furthermore, included in the annual membership fee, you have access to the three important standards: Project, Program, and Portfolio. The Standard for Portfolio Management – Third Edition costs about $40 at retail.
2. Download the Standard for Portfolio Management – Third Edition and read it carefully. Make sure you gain a working knowledge of the five knowledge areas, by reading the Standard and reviewing Chapter 3 through 8 of this book. This knowledge will help you complete the application.
3. Complete the application process. In addition to developing a working knowledge of the five knowledge areas, make sure you start to document your portfolio management experiences and key contacts who can serve as professional references.

4. After submitting the application, be prepared to be audited. (I had the "pleasure" of being audited on the PgMP and PfMP application process. It was not too painful.)

5. As stated in the handbook, the process time is 10 business days for online application and 20 days for paper applications. Early experience has shown that the turnaround time to be much quicker.

6. Once PMI approves your application, then you have one year to pass the PfMP Exam. Within this one year period, you are allowed to take the exam up to three times. Each of the subsequent exams cost $500 to $600 for members and $700 to $800 for non-members. Given this expense, it is highly recommended to effectively prepare and pass the exam on the first or second attempt. If you fail the PfMP exam three times, you must wait for another year before you may reapply and resubmit your credentials all over again.

7. The exam policies and procedures are extensive. For those who have completed other PMI certifications, the exam policies and procedures are similar. Please re-read the PfMP Handbook to get reacquainted.

8. When scheduling for the exam, my recommendation is to schedule it for late morning, assuming the testing site is within an hour of where you live. The late morning, say 10 or 10:30 AM, gives you the ability to sleep late, eat a larger than usual but healthy meal, avoid morning rush traffic, drive leisurely to the exam site, and finish by a reasonable time in which you can avoid the rush hour drive home.

1.1.3. Some Quick Words on Maintaining PfMP Credential

On the surface, the requirement of 60 PDUs (professional development units) every 3 years to maintain PfMP is similar to PMP and PgMP. However, PfMP Handbook states that the 60 PDUs for portfolio management must be in the specialized area of portfolio management. Since PfMP credential is very new, only time will tell how PMI will enforce this specialization.

Also, similar to PMP and PgMP, PfMP can transfer up to 20 PDUs to the next CCR (continuing certification requirement) cycle.

For more information on maintaining credential status, please refer to the PfMP Handbook.

1.1.4. PfMP Exam

The PfMP examination is similar in format with the PMP and PgMP exam. It is composed of 170 questions of which 20 are pre-test questions and therefore do not affect the test score. These questions are placed randomly throughout the exam to test the validity of future exam questions. But since you do not know which questions are pre-test versus real exam questions, this distinction is largely useful only for PMI. For you as the test taker, your job is to complete 170 questions within the four hours for computer-based testing (CBT). In the next section, this book will present a test taking strategy. It is important to adopt a strategy even before you study. This way, you will develop a helpful routine that should maximize your effectiveness during the actual exam.

Note: Since CBT is the standard method for administering the exam, this book covers only the computer-based testing. PMI does offer a paper-based testing on an exception basis. Please refer to the PfMP Handbook's section on Examination Administration for more details.

1.2. Taking and Preparing for the PfMP Exam

Based on fairly substantial experience with PMI examinations, this book recommends that you plan the major steps backward from the end. While none of us can foresee the future with great accuracy, by envisioning the future state and slowly shifting backwards helps you plan better. Thus, this section covers three major steps, backwards:

    i.   Taking the exam
    ii.   Count down to the exam, five days prior to the exam time
    iii.   You passed Phase 1, Phase 2 starts, and the one year countdown begins.

1.2.1. Taking the exam

Other than the clothing on your back, two perhaps three pencils, blank papers for you to scribble notes, and possibly a pair of earplugs to block out noise, you enter the exam room with nothing else. Depending on the room setup, it may actually feel claustrophobic. So take a deep breath and get ready. Take time to make yourself comfortable like adjusting your seat, placing the keyboard and mouse in the optimal position, adjusting the monitor if necessary. This is where you will spend the next four hours taking the test.

The exam is preceded by an optional 15 minute tutorial on the computer-based training. While it is optional, I highly recommend that you take at least some of the time to get familiar with the environment and the computer setup. Since it will be an intense four hour period, use this time to relax and get comfortable.

Once you exit the tutorial, the four hour countdown begins. Below is my recommendation on how to spend these four hours:

#	Key Objective	Action	Est. Time
1	Download everything you can remember – using the exam aids as an example. Reduce anxiety.	Quickly write down all key concepts that you are afraid of forgetting. This includes inputs, outputs, tools, techniques formulas, and definitions. Writing them down will free your mind from the stress of memorization which reduces anxiety. It will enable you to concentrate on the exam problems.	12-15 minutes
2	Create a simple scoring sheet so you can track your estimated performance. This will help you at the end as you gauge how well you are doing.	See Exam Aid 1: Sample Scoring Sheet below. Create a scoring sheet will allow you to track your progress and estimate your exam performance. Notes: 1. This step is not necessarily for everyone. If you know the materials very well (or very poorly), this step is not going to add value. But for most of us mortals, it is highly desirable to have some guidance. 2. Depending on the number of pieces of paper you are given, you can easily adjust this procedure to fit your preference.	10 minutes
3	Sprint 1. Start taking the exam, and track your performance. Note: See below for a sample score sheet.	Keep your test taking routine simple. Go through the exam questions sequentially. Do not skip and always select an answer even if it is a pure guess. On average, spend 1 minute per question. For answers that 1. You are certain, put a check mark in the 90% column. This assumes you are very sure with the near certainty of being correct. 2. You are able to eliminate two answers but unsure of the remaining two, put a check mark in the 75% column. 3. You are able to eliminate one answer and unsure of the remaining three answers, put a check mark in the 50% column.	90 minutes

#	Key Objective	Action	Est. Time
		4. You are not able to eliminate any answers. Put a check mark in the 25% column. When you complete the first 90 questions, check the time. Ideally the countdown clock should be at around 2:10 hours. If you need to, take a 10 minutes break (which counts toward the countdown). Use this time to stretch, relax, and clear your head.	
4	Sprint 2. Getting to the finish line.	Repeat the steps in #2 for the remaining questions.	80 minutes
5	Estimate your score. The target should be a minimum of 136 (or 80%).	Quickly count the numbers of 25%, 50%, 75%, and 90% in each of the sections. Multiply the count by the probability and add them together to get an estimated total score. For example, let's say you have achieve the following: • 25% -> 5 • 50% -> 10 • 75% -> 110 • 90% -> 45 The estimated score is 129, slightly below the target. Assuming you are objective and realistic about the %, then all you need do is to review a handful of 25% and 50% and convert them to 75% to pass the test.	10 minutes
6	Review and refine 25% and 50% questions.	Spend the remaining time on reviewing and rethinking the exam questions in which you marked 25% and 50%. Even though you may be guessing on the first pass, by going through all the questions in the exam, they may offer new insights to these tough questions. Plus, it is likely that another question can trigger thoughts and memories that can improve your odds on questions with 25% and 50%.	30 minutes
7	Pass the exam and start gloating.	If you are taking the computer-based testing, the exam results should be available almost immediately. Be prepared to gloat with your colleagues!	

Note: Creating and keeping a score sheet can be time intensive. If you are a slow test taker, you may wish to skip these steps and save about 15-20 minutes. But for most people, including myself, I believe keeping a score sheet is immensely helpful. It provides a degree of certainty (and sanity) as you progress through the questions. I was able to gauge my grades on multiple metrics: expected score, relative worst case, and relative best case. Also, remember to practice for test taking starting five days prior to the test.

At this point, PMI does not publish the minimal passing score. It should be assumed to be in the range of other exams such as PMP and PgMP. To be safe, our recommendation is to target for a minimum score of 80% or 136 questions correct – in both the practice and actual exam.

#	25%	50%	75%	90%
1				
2				
3				
4				
5				
6				
7				
8				
9				
10				
11				
12				
13				
14				
15				
16				
17				
18				
19				
20				
21				
22				
23				
24				
25				
26				
27				
28				
29				
30				

#	25%	50%	75%	90%
31				
32				
33				
34				
35				
36				
37				
38				
39				
40				
41				
42				
43				
44				
45				
46				
47				
48				
49				
50				
51				
52				
53				
54				
55				
56				
57				
58				
59				
60				

#	25%	50%	75%	90%
61				
62				
63				
64				
65				
66				
67				
68				
69				
70				
71				
72				
73				
74				
75				
76				
77				
78				
79				
80				
81				
82				
83				
84				
85				
86				
87				
88				
89				
90				

Exam Aid 1: Sample Scoring Sheet

The final five days leading to the exam are especially important, and so use this time wisely. Ideally, you should spend an increasing amount of time to ensure retention of content and gain familiarity with the suggested exam aids. Realistically, however, most of us have to work or have other responsibilities. But please make sure you spend at least a minimum of three to five hours on Days 5 and 4 and then increase it to six hours or more on Days 3 and 2. On the final day before the exam, it is perhaps more important for you to relax and get enough sleep rather than last minute cramming. It is more optimal to have a sharp mind than to remember a bunch of facts but be too tired to process.

Here is my recommendation on how to best maximize the five days leading to the exam.

Day #	Key Objective	Description
5	Complete reading and reviewing of all content including study materials	If you have not done so, please make sure you are familiar with the key concepts in the Standard and this book. You do not need to memorize everything yet, but there should not be any questions about what they are and how they are used. Assuming the above is done, spend at least 1 to 2 hours to review the key concepts, review your study sheets, and manually create the exam aids mentioned throughout this book using paper and pen. Practice makes perfect, and it will save considerable time during the exam. You should also decide on the exam aids that you plan to use. What I offer in this book are my suggestions. You should customize them (or create new ones) so you are comfortable with them.
4	Re-create all the exam aids by heart.	Whether you use the exam aids from this book as-is or if you modify them, make sure you can re-create them manually by heart at this point. The exam aids offered in this book are designed to ease memorization, but feel free to modify them to suit your learning habits. You should also be able to complete most of the exam aids with the PfMP contents by heart. Mistakes at this stage are not ideal but there is still three days left to remedy.

Day #	Key Objective	Description
3	Re-create all of the exam aids and able to fill in the information by heart.	With only three days remaining, it is important to be able to create all of the exam aids by heart and complete them without flaws. If there are minor errors, you still have Day 2 and Day 1 to work on them. Practice taking the sample exam. You should be able to pass the test with 136 correct answers (or 80%). For incorrect answers, it is important to understand why they are wrong and what the correct answers are.
2	Re-create all of the exam aids and able to fill in the information by heart.	The goal is similar to Day 2, but in this case, there is no room for errors. You should be comfortable with the exam process, the recommended exam aids, and the ability to complete them flawlessly. If you have time, my suggestion is to complete the practice test again and make sure you can comfortably pass the test at 80%. While it is still not too late to cram new concepts at this point, it should be avoided. Our human brain works well on repetition. At this point, new concepts may actually cause confusion.
1	Relax, eat right, and sleep well.	At this point, unless you are desperate, it is a bit late to memorize new concepts or learn new ideas. Instead, spend your available time and review the content and re-create the exam aids and fill them in – all in a relaxed fashion. Most importantly, take time to relax, stretch, and even go for 50%-75% of your routine exercise. Exercise is great for the brain. Sleep early at night and make sure you give yourself at least one extra hour of sleep than your routine.

Day #	Key Objective	Description
0	Get ready for the exam	In the morning of the exam, make sure you eat a healthy and nutritious meal (since it will be much harder to concentrate when you are hungry). Drink your favorite beverage but do not drink in excess (as bathroom breaks count against the 4 hour limit). As stated earlier, my recommendation is for scheduling the exam for late morning (between 10 to 11 AM). This may not necessarily work for everyone, so please plan for the time which you know works best for you. Give yourself plenty of time to go to the exam site. You should plan to arrive at least 30 minutes before the start of the exam. Good luck.

Table 6: Exam Preparation - Five Days to Exam!

Note: This book contains two full exams. We also offer additional exams with a greatly reduced fee for owners of this book. For more information, go to the end of the book on "How to Contact the Author".

1.2.3. You passed Phase 1, Phase 2 starts

Congratulations on completing Phase 1 of the PfMP credential process. Now the hard work starts. For the purpose of simplicity, let's assume you plan to start and complete Phase 2 in a one month period with an average study time of 4 hours per day. This is aggressive but realistic. The duration and intensity can obviously be more or less, but not shorter than 2 weeks. Below is our recommended plan of action, but please customize with your preference.

Day #	Key Objective	Description
30 29 28 27 26 25	Becoming familiar with the language and concepts in Portfolio Management	Spend the first week carefully reading the Standard and this book. There may be an urge to skip; my recommendation is do not. Both books are organized for maximum effectiveness.

Day #	Key Objective	Description
24		PMI also recommends an additional set of books. These can be valuable for the profession, but you should only read them if you have sufficient time.
23, 22	Chapter 1	Concentrate on Chapter 1 of both books. From the Standard, be prepared to explain the core concepts. From the Guide, understand the context of Portfolio Management and the recommended testing taking approach. Feel free to customize the approach for your preference and learning style. But once determined, stick to the plan.
21, 20	Chapter 2	Concentrate on Chapter 2 of both books. From the Standard, be prepared to explain the core concepts. From the Guide, spend time going through the practice questions.
19, 18	Chapter 3 on Process Groups	Concentrate on Chapter 3 of both books. From the Standard, be prepared to explain the core concepts. From the Guide, spend time going through the practice questions.
17, 16, 15	Chapter 4 on Portfolio Strategic Management	Concentrate on Chapter 4 of both books. From the Standard, be prepared to explain the core concepts. From the Guide, spend time going through the practice questions.
14, 13	Chapter 5 on Portfolio Governance	Concentrate on Chapter 5 of both books. From the Standard, be prepared to explain the core concepts. From the Guide, spend time going through the practice questions.
12, 11, 10	Chapter 6 on Portfolio Performance Management	Concentrate on Chapter 6 of both books. From the Standard, be prepared to explain the core concepts. From the Guide, spend time going through the practice questions.
9, 8	Chapter 7 on Portfolio Risk Management	Concentrate on Chapter 7 of both books. From the Standard, be prepared to explain the core concepts. From the Guide, spend time going through the practice questions.
7, 6	Chapter 8 on Portfolio Communication Management	Concentrate on Chapter 8 of both books. From the Standard, be prepared to explain the core concepts. From the Guide, spend time going through the practice questions.

Table 7: Suggested 30 Days Study Plan

Note: The study plan above is provided as a template for registered users of this book.

1.3. Important Information from The Standard

1.3.1. Key Tables and Figures to Remember from the Standard

The Standard contains a number of Tables which I believe are essential to passing the exam. You should memorize the following items from the Standard:

- Table 1-1. This table provides a high-level comparison of project, program, and portfolio management across a number of key characteristics.
- Table 3-1. This table is reproduced below with permission from Project Management Institute. This table is essential as it provides an overview of the mapping between Process Groups and Knowledge Areas. You will need to memorize this table; it is a pre-requisite to nearly all other exam aids in this book.
- Table 3-2. This table highlights the key deliverables for selective portfolio management processes. The content (column 3) is extremely useful.
- Ideally, you should remember all process specific Figures, such as Figure 4-2 for creating the portfolio strategic plan. These figures include the Inputs, Tools & Techniques, and Outputs. If you are able to memorize all of them, then your chance of passing the PfMP exam will be extremely high.

If you are like most people, it may be very difficult to remember all of the information for the sixteen processes across the five knowledge areas and three process groups. To aid in the memorization of the Inputs, Tools & Techniques, and Outputs (or ITTO for short), the following sections contain exam aids designed to help you pass the exam.

1.3.2. Map of the Process Groups with Knowledge Area

This table provides an overall map of the process groups and knowledge areas. This is Table 3-1 in the Standard. Remembering this table is critical for passing the exam. I would go further and suggest that if you cannot remember this table three days before the exam, consider rescheduling the exam. There is a small fee for rescheduling, but once you are within 2 days of the exam, you can no longer reschedule (unless you have extraordinary reasons) and you will be forfeiting the entire test fee.

Knowledge Area	Process Groups		
	Defining Process Group (8)	Aligning Process Group (6)	Authorizing & Controlling Process Group (2)
Portfolio Strategy Management (4)	Develop Portfolio Strategic Plan	Manage Strategic Change	
	Develop Portfolio Charter		
	Develop Portfolio Define Roadmap		
Portfolio Governance Management (5)	Develop Portfolio Management Plan	Optimize Portfolio	Authorize Portfolio
	Define Portfolio		Provide Portfolio Oversight
Portfolio Performance Management (3)	Develop Portfolio Performance Management Plan	Manage Supply and Demand	
		Manage Portfolio Value	
Portfolio Communication Management (2)	Develop Portfolio Communication Management Plan	Manage Portfolio Information	
Portfolio Risk Management (2)	Develop Portfolio Risk Management Plan	Manage Portfolio Risk	

Legend:	Define (No Shade)	Align (Light Gray)	Authorize & Control (Darker Gray)

Exam Aid 2: Table 3-1 from the Standard.

Project Management Institute's The Standard for Portfolio Management Third Edition, Project Management Institute, Inc., 2013. Copyrighted and All Rights Reserved. Material from this publication has been reproduced with the permission of PMI.

Hint: You will need to memorize this table. The number in the parenthesis (#) refers to the number of processes in that knowledge area or process group. Here are a few techniques to help you with memorization:

1. Remember there are 3 process groups and 5 knowledge areas.

2. By row (or knowledge area), there are a set number of processes. All knowledge area names start with the word "Portfolio". As listed in the leftmost column, remember the number of processes as follows. The first number is the number of processes in Defining, the second number refers to number of processes in Aligning, and the third number refers to the processes in Authorizing and Controlling.
   a. Strategy: 3, 1
   b. Governance: 2, 1, 2
   c. Performance: 1, 2
   d. Communication: 1, 1
   e. Risk: 1, 1
3. By column (or process group), there are 8 defining processes, 6 aligning processes, and 2 processes for authorizing and controlling.
   a. All processes in Defining process group (2nd column) start with the words "Develop Portfolio" plus the deliverable. The only exception is in Define Portfolio.
   b. All processes in Aligning process group (3rd column) start with the word "Manage" followed by specific action.

1.3.3. Overview of ITTO (Inputs, Tools & Techniques, Outputs)

Ideally, you should remember the ITTO for each process. The exam aid here summarizes all the inputs, tools and techniques, and outputs for each process.

Do not despair if you cannot remember this table. The next exam aid will help my fellow mortals to memorize this table.

From experience, if you are able to memorize Exam Aid 3 below and able to describe it well, you already have achieved about 60% probability of passing the test. This is a good aid to remember well.

KA	Processes	Inputs	Tools & Techniques	Outputs
Strategy Management (4)	Develop Portfolio Strategic Plan	1. Org strategy and objectives 2. Inventory of work 3. P. Process Assets 4. Org Process Assets 5. Enterprise environmental factors	1. P. Component Inventory 2. Strategic Alignment Analysis 3. Prioritization Analysis	1. P. Strategic Plan 2. Portfolio
	Develop Portfolio Charter	1. P. Strategic Plan 2. P. processes assets 3. Enterprise environmental factors	1. Scenario Analysis 2. Capability and Capacity Analysis	1. P. Strategic Plan Updates 2. P. Charter 3. P. Process Assets Updates
	Define Roadmap	1. P. Strategic Plan 2. P. Charter 3. Portfolio	1. Interdependency Analysis 2. Cost/benefit Analysis 3. Prioritization Analysis	1. P. Roadmap
	Manage Strategic Change	1. P. Strategic Plan 2. P. Charter 3. Portfolio 4. P. Roadmap 5. P. Management Plan 6. P. Process Assets	1. Stakeholder Analysis 2. Gap Analysis 3. Readiness Assessment	1. P. Strategic Plan Updates 2. P. Charter Updates 3. P. Updates 4. P. Roadmap Updates 5. P. Management Plan Updates 6. P. Process Assets Updates
Governance Management (5)	Develop Portfolio Management Plan	1. P. Strategic Plan 2. P. Charter 3. P. Roadmap 4. P. Process Assets 5. Org Process Assets 6. Enterprise environmental factors	1. Elicitation Techniques 2. P. or Org Structure Analysis 3. Integration of Portfolio Management Plans	1. P. Strategic Plan Updates 2. P. Management Plan 3. P. Process Assets Updates
	Define Portfolio	1. P. Strategic Plan 2. P. Charter 3. Portfolio 4. P. Roadmap 5. P. Management Plan 6. P. Process Assets	1. P. Component Inventory 2. P. Component Categorization Techniques 3. Weighted Ranking and Scoring Techniques	1. P. Updates 2. P. Roadmap Updates 3. P. Management Plan Updates
	Optimize Portfolio	1. Portfolio 2. P. Roadmap 3. P. Management Plan 4. P. Reports 5. P. Process Assets	1. Capability and Capacity Analysis 2. Weighted Ranking and Scoring Techniques 3. Quantitative and Qualitative Analysis 4. Graphical Analytical	1. P. Updates 2. P. Roadmap Updates 3. P. Management Plan Updates 4. P. Reports 5. P. Process Assets Updates

KA	Processes	Inputs	Tools & Techniques	Outputs
			Methods	
	Authorize Portfolio	1. Portfolio 2. P. Management Plan 3. P. Reports	1. P. Authorization Techniques 2. P. Management Information System	1. P. Updates 2. P. Management Plan Updates 3. P. Reports 4. P. Process Assets Updates
	Provide Portfolio Oversight	1. Portfolio 2. P. Roadmap 3. P. Management Plan 4. P. Reports 5. P. Process Assets	1. P. Review Meetings 2. Elicitation Techniques	1. P. Updates 2. P. Management Plan Updates 3. P. Reports 4. P. Process Assets Updates
Performance Management (3)	Develop Portfolio Performance Management Plan	1. P. Management Plan 2. P. Process Assets 3. Org Process Assets 4. Enterprise Environmental Factors	1. Elicitation Techniques 2. P. management Information System 3. Capability and Capacity Analysis	1. P. Management Plan Updates 2. P. Process Assets Updates
	Manage Supply and Demand	1. Portfolio 2. P. Management Plan 3. P. reports	1. Scenario Analysis 2. Quantitative and Qualitative Analysis 3. Capability and Capacity Analysis	1. P. Updates 2. P. Management Plan Updates 3. P. Reports
	Manage Portfolio Value	1. P. Roadmap 2. P. Management Plan 3. P. Reports	1. Elicitation Techniques 2. Value Scoring and Measurement Analysis 3. Benefits Realization Analysis	1. P. Management Plan Updates 2. P. Reports 3. P. Process Assets Updates
Communication Management (2)	Develop Portfolio Communication Management Plan	1. Portfolio 2. P. Roadmap 3. P. Management Plan 4. P. Reports 5. P. Process Assets	1. Stakeholder Analysis 2. Elicitation Techniques 3. Communication Requirement Analysis	1. P. Management Plan Updates 2. P. Process Assets Updates
	Manage Portfolio Information	1. Portfolio 2. P. Management Plan 3. P. Reports 4. P. Component Reports 5. P. Process Assets	1. Elicitation Techniques 2. P. Management Information System 3. Communication Requirements Analysis 4. Communication Methods	1. P. Management Plan Updates 2. P. Reports 3. P. Process Assets Updates

KA	Processes	Inputs	Tools & Techniques	Outputs
Risk Management (2)	Develop Portfolio Risk Management Plan	1. P. Management Plan 2. P. Process Assets 3. Org Process Assets 4. Enterprise Environmental Factors	1. Weighted Ranking and Scoring Techniques 2. Graphical Analytical Methods 3. Quantitative and Qualitative Analysis	1. P. Management Plan Updates 2. Org Process Assets Updates 3. P. Assets Updates
	Manage Portfolio Risk	1. Portfolio 2. P. Management Plan 3. P. Reports 4. P. Process Assets 5. Org Process Assets 6. Enterprise Environmental Factors	1. Weighted Ranking and Scoring Techniques 2. Quantitative and Qualitative Analysis	1. P. Management Plan Updates 2. P. Reports 3. P. Process Assets 4. Org Process Assets Updates

Legend:	Define (No Shade)	Align (Light Gray)	Authorize & Control (Darker Gray)
Abbreviations:	P. = Portfolio	Org = Organizational	

Exam Aid 3: Master Table of Knowledge Areas, Processes, and Input, Tools & Techniques, and Outputs

1.3.4. ITTO in Context

The inputs, tools, techniques, and outputs are frequently asked on the exam. Questions can be both fact or definitional-based or experience based. Table 8 below summarizes the ITTO and mapped it to the knowledge areas.

Tools & Techniques	# of Use	P. Strategic Mgt				P. Governance Mgt					P. Performance Mgt			P. Comm. Mgt		P. Risk Mgt	
		D.P. Strategic Plan	D.P. Charter	Define P. Roadmap	M. Strategic Change	D.P. Mgt Plan	Define Portfolio	Optimize Portfolio	Authorize Portfolio	Provide P. Oversight	D.P. Performance Mgt Plan	M. Supply and Demand	M. P. Value	D.P. Communication Mgt Plan	Mgt P. Information	D.P. Risk Mgt Plan	M. P. Risks
Benefits Realization Analysis	1												X				
Capability and Capacity Analysis	4		X					X			X	X					
Communication Methods	1														X		
Communication Requirements Analysis	2													X	X		
Cost/benefit Analysis	1		X														
Elicitation Techniques	6						X			X	X			X	X	X	
Gap Analysis	1				X												
Graphical Analytical Methods	2							X								X	
Integration of Portfolio Management Plans	1					X											
Interdependency Analysis	1		X														
Portfolio Authorization Techniques	1								X								
Portfolio Component Categorization Techniques	1						X										

Tools & Techniques	# of Use	P. Strategic Mgt				P. Governance Mgt					P. Performance Mgt			P. Comm. Mgt		P. Risk Mgt	
		D.P. Strategic Plan	D.P. Charter	Define P. Roadmap	M. Strategic Change	D.P. Mgt Plan	Define Portfolio	Optimize Portfolio	Authorize Portfolio	Provide P. Oversight	D.P. Performance Mgt Plan	M. Supply and Demand	M. P. Value	D.P. Communication Mgt Plan	Mgt P. Information	D.P. Risk Mgt Plan	M. P. Risks
Portfolio Component Inventory	2	X					X										
Portfolio Management Information System	3								X		X				X		
Portfolio or Organizational Structure Analysis	1					X											
Portfolio Review Meetings	1									X							
Prioritization Analysis	2	X		X													
Quantitative and Qualitative Analysis	4							X				X				X	X
Readiness Assessment	1				X												
Scenario Analysis	2		X									X					
Stakeholder Analysis	2				X									X			
Strategic Alignment Analysis	1	X															
Value Scoring and Measurement Analysis	1												X				
Weighted Ranking and Scoring Techniques	4						X	X								X	X

Abbreviations:	D.P. = Develop Portfolio	M.P. = Manage Portfolio	Mgt = Management

Table 8: ITTO in Context

For the definitions and descriptions of these tools and techniques, please refer to the Standard. PMI has gone to great lengths to describe them as simply and clearly as possible.

Notes:

1. I do not believe you have to remember this table. Otherwise, I would rename it "Exam Aid" instead of "Table".
2. The Standard introduces 24 tools and techniques, but these should not be seen as exhaustive for two reasons:
   - There are additional tools in the market designed for portfolio planning. For example, business simulation (similar to scenario analysis) but on a grander scale is one such tool.
   - The field of portfolio management is still in its infancy. PMI is constantly updating its test, and it will reflect the latest practices.

1.3.5. Simplifying ITTO

If you closely review the table above, you will quickly realize there are many repetitions. Therefore, to simplify the table, it would be worthwhile to know the frequency of these words. The following tables contain the frequency of Inputs, Outputs, Tools and Techniques.

ID	Deliverables	Input	Output	Total
A	Portfolio	10	7	17
B	Portfolio Charter	4	2	6
C	Portfolio Management Plan	12	13	25
D	Portfolio Reports	8	7	15
E	Portfolio Roadmap	7	4	11
F	Portfolio Strategic Plan	5	4	9
G	Enterprise environmental Factors	6	0	6
H	Organizational Process Assets	5	2	7
I	Portfolio Process Assets	12	12	24

Table 9: Frequency of Input and Output

Abbrev.	Tools and Techniques	Count
CCA	Capability and Capacity Analysis	4
ET	Elicitation techniques	6

Abbrev.	Tools and Techniques	Count
PMIS	P. management information system	3
QQA	Quantitative and qualitative analysis	4
WRS	Weighted ranking and scoring techniques	4

Table 10: High Frequency Tools and Techniques

The above tables demonstrate the high number of repetitions for the common inputs, outputs, tools and techniques. The left column of both tables, ID@ and Abbrev., are important for the next exam aid. Also notice that the inputs and outputs are listed in the process group order.

In addition, for the outputs, most of the deliverables are updates after its first experience. For example, Portfolio is a major output from the Develop Portfolio Strategic Plan process. In all subsequent outputs, the deliverable is Portfolio *Update*. To simplify, I eliminated the term "Update".

Once you understand the above, you can now simplify the ITTO table and combine it with the knowledge areas, process groups, and processes.

KA	Processes	Description	A. Portfolio	B. P. Charter	C. P. Mgmt Plan	D. P. Report	E. P. Roadmap	F. P. Strategic Plan	G. Ent Enviro	H. Org Process	I. P. Proess Assets	Tools and Techniques	Description	A. Portfolio	B. P. Charter	C. P. Mgmt Plan	D. P. Report	E. P. Roadmap	F. P. Strategic Plan	G. Ent Enviro	H. Org Process	I. P. Proess Assets
Strategic Management	D.P. Strategic Plan (3, 2)	GHI * Org strategy & objectives * Inventory of work							x	x	x	1. P. component inventory 2. Strategic alignment analysis 3. Prioritization analysis	A, F	x					x			
	D.P. Charter (3, 3)	FG, I						x	x		x	1. Scenario analysis 2. CCA	B, F, I		x				x			x
	Define Port. Roadmap (3, 1)	AB, F	x	x				x				1. Interdependency analysis 2. Cost/benefit analysis 3. Prioritization analysis	E					x				
	M. Strategic Change (6, 6)	ABC, EF, I	x	x	x		x	x			x	1. Stakeholder analysis 2. Gap analysis 3. Readiness assessment	ABC, EF, I	x	x	x		x	x			x
Governance Management	D.P. Management Plan (6, 3)	B, EFGHI		x			x	x	x	x	x	1. ET 2. P. or Org structure analysis 3. Integration of portfolio management plans	C, F, I			x			x			x
	Define P. (6, 3)	ABC, EF, I	x	x	x		x	x			x	1. P. component inventory 2. P. component categorization techniques 3. WRS	A, C, E	x		x		x				
	Optimize P. (5, 5)	A, CDE, I	x		x	x	x				x	1. CCA 2. WRS 3. QQS 4. Graphical analytical methods	A, CDE, I	x		x	x	x				x
	Authorize P. (3, 4)	A, CD	x		x	x						1. P. authorization techniques 2. PMIS	A, CD, I	x		x	x					x
	Provide P. Oversight (5, 4)	A, CDE, I	x		x	x	x				x	1. P. review meetings 2. ET	A, CD, I	x		x	x					x

KA	Processes	Description	A. Portfolio	B. P. Charter	C. P. Mgmt Plan	D. P. Report	E. P. Roadmap	F. P. Strategic Plan	G. Ent Enviro	H. Org Process	I. P. Proess Assets	Tools and Techniques	Description	A. Portfolio	B. P. Charter	C. P. Mgmt Plan	D. P. Report	E. P. Roadmap	F. P. Strategic Plan	G. Ent Enviro	H. Org Process	I. P. Proess Assets
Performance Management	D.P. Performance Mgmt Plan (4, 2)	C, GHI			x				x	x	x	1. ET 2. PMIS 3. CCA	C, I			x						x
Performance Management	M. Supply and Demand (3, 3)	A, CD	x		x	x						1. Scenario analysis 2. QQS 3. CCA	A, CD	x		x	x					
Performance Management	M. P. Value (3, 3)	CDE			x	x	x					1. ET 2. Value scoring and measurement analysis 3. Benefits realization analysis	CD, I			x	x					x
Communication Management	D.P. Communication Mgmt Plan (5, 2)	A, CDE, I	x		x	x	x				x	1. Stakeholder analysis 2. ET 3. Communication requirement analysis	D, I				x					x
Communication Management	Management P. Information (4, 3)	A, CD, I P. component reports	x		x	x					x	1. ET 2. PMIS 3. Communication requirement analysis 4. Communication methods	CD, I			x	x					x
Risk Management	D.P. Risk Mgmt Plan (4, 3)	C, GHI			x				x	x	x	1. WRS 2. Graphical analytical methods 3. QQS	CD, G			x					x	x
Risk Management	M. P. Risks (6, 4)	A, CD, GHI	x		x	x			x	x	x	1. WRS 2. QQS	CD, G, I			x	x				x	x
	Count:		10	4	12	8	7	5	6	5	12		Count	7	2	13	7	4	4	0	2	12

Exam Aid 4: Comprehensive Aid for all Knowledge Areas, Process Groups, Processes, and ITTO

Explanations:

- KA (Column 1) lists the knowledge area.
- Process (Column 2) lists the name of the portfolio management process.
- Input Description (Column 3) lists the key output deliverables. With minor exceptions, the top 9 deliverables listed are referred to by their letter ID (A-I). The only 3 exceptions are Organization Strategy & Objectives, Inventory of Work, and Portfolio Component Reports.
- The next 9 columns are the common inputs. "X" indicates the presence of this input.
- Tools & Techniques (Column 13) identifies the tools and techniques. The acronyms are identified in Table 10 above. Personally, I found this column to be the most difficult to remember for two reasons:

- There is not much repetition, thus they cannot be easily consolidated.
  - As a portfolio manager, I use a variety of techniques and tools, many of which are not necessarily mentioned by the Standard or listed in the same order.
- Output Description (Column 14) lists the key output deliverables, using the same ID as the input deliverables.
- The next 9 columns are the common outputs. "X" indicates the presence of this output.

The above exam aid may look difficult in the beginning, but it is greatly simplified. With practice, you will see the underlying logic of how the inputs and outputs flow. It is quite feasible to memorize this table. As you are seeking the underlying logic, I am fairly sure most of you will have some disagreements with PMI's attempt at defining the ITTOs. But on the whole, I believe the Standard provided a good and logical flow of these deliverables, tools and techniques.

The exam aid in Excel available to registered users contains a few variations of this table as you progressively memorize more of its content.

Chapter 2: Portfolio Management – What and Why

In this chapter, you will

- Learn a simplified framework for organization and how portfolio management serves to advance organization strategies
- Learn to think like a portfolio manager
- Understand key concepts pertaining to and required for a general understanding of the portfolio management professional

The primary reason that I created this chapter is to help you with the experience-based questions on the PfMP exam. Experience-based questions are difficult as organizations and situations are different. Yet, they are an integral part of the PfMP exam. Based on my experience as a certified portfolio management professional, I believe understanding the context and learning to think like a portfolio manager will be invaluable to tackle those prickly questions.

You can look at the problem in another way. If you are able to remember, describe, and apply the content of Exam Aid 3 on Page 33 very well, you will likely achieve a 60% chance of passing the exam. By assimilating the concepts and theories here, I believe you raise the bar to 80%. The remaining 20% is frankly luck – including good health and plenty of sleep. Thus by following the suggested approaches in Chapter 1, you should be set.

2.1. Context of Portfolio Management

Today's organizations are complex and larger organizations have hundreds of business processes and thousands of activities. Depending on the type and function of the organization, they range from internal processes such as human resources to external or customer facing processes such as sales and marketing. Yet, amidst all these complications, all of these processes and activities can be simplified to just three pillars for *viable* organizations: planning, operating, and changing.

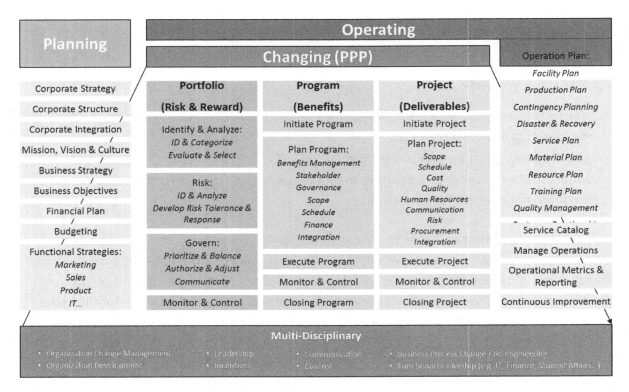

Figure 2: Strategic Business Execution Framework

Planning addresses three essential questions: Who are we, what do we do, where are we going? For smaller organizations, such as a mom and pop grocery store, this can be as simple as deciding what to sell, counting inventory of merchandise and deciding what to replenish, or setting a budget for store operations. For larger organizations, this pillar can be vast ranging from formal strategic planning processes to budget, from visioning to communication, from market research to deciding what product to develop.

Operating has a simple purpose: How to keep the lights on by producing and selling its products and services? For a mom and pop shop, this is selling sufficient merchandise and making sufficient profit to keep on operating. For a manufacturing company, such as a cookie factory, operations include assembling the ingredients, forming the cookies, baking them, and then packaging the finished cookies with minimal damage. For universities, it is preparing and teaching students and hopefully graduating and readying them for the next step of challenges, whether they are finding jobs or furthering their studies. While there are incremental enhancements or continuous improvements, the operating pillar largely focuses on maintaining the existing set of products and services.

If the external world remains static or if the organization itself remains static, then portfolio management is irrelevant. But the world changes and organizations must adopt, evolve, and sometimes revolve to survive and thrive. In the past four decades, the pace of change is ever increasing. For organizations to remain *viable*, they must change. Hence, the ability to change successfully is often more important than planning and operating. For project professionals, change comes in the form of projects and programs that are designed to change the trajectory of the underlying products and services. Changing is often challenging, especially in larger organizations, and it requires a multi-disciplinary approach to ensure its success.

So what is project portfolio management? Project portfolio management (or portfolio management for short) is at the heart of the changing pillar. But it does not exist in isolation; for portfolio management to be successful, portfolios must be aligned with planning and implemented in congruence with operating. Portfolio management is the art and discipline of making sound investment choices of programs and projects for organizations that maximize the intended benefits and minimize the downside risks. How to best achieve this challenging endeavor is the role of a portfolio manager.

Understanding of where portfolio management exists in organizations and how it serves to advance organizational objectives are important to developing the right mindset. On the PfMP exam, it is paramount not only to memorize the core concepts, it is just as important to think like one for experience-based questions. In real life, knowing how to think like a portfolio manager is even more important. In the next section, I will present a simple framework on how to think like a portfolio manager.

2.2. How to Think Like a Portfolio Manager

Portfolio managers are constantly challenged by three key questions:

1. What are the desired business objectives for the portfolio? How do I balance the long-term benefits of the portfolio versus the short-term necessities?
2. How do I maximize the achievement of these objectives (e.g. benefits) by applying the precious and often scarce resources available?
3. How do I minimize the downside risk? What is the "reasonable" worse case (RWC) and can I still claim success when RWC materializes?

The answers to each of these questions vary greatly among organizations, their strategic outlook, internal capabilities, external environment, and their execution capabilities. For portfolio managers to be truly effective, it is not enough that they understand quantitative or qualitative analysis. You need to think like a portfolio manager. Here, based on my experience and knowledge, I highly recommend these four ways of thinking:

1. Think holistic
2. Think economics
3. Think big picture
4. Think practicality

I am sure there are many other ways to think, but I believe these four are foundational, and they go a long way in preparing for the PfMP exam.

2.2.1. Think Holistic

Portfolio managers by role are responsible for achieving a range of company objectives. Depending on the organization and the roles, there may be one or more portfolios in the firm. Regardless of the number of portfolios you manage, the commonalities among them are the intended business objectives. Generally, the greater the clarity and the specificity of the business objectives, the clearer the portfolio strategic plan and roadmap can be.

The competing challenges of meeting short term goals while remaining viable and competitive is perhaps one of the most difficult responsibilities. To be an effective portfolio manager, you must be able to think strategically, implement, and by default, be a change champion. Imagine an abstract scale of one to ten of business activities (see below); portfolio managers must be able to operate comfortably across 7 thorough 6 and at a stretch 8 maybe even 9. Ideally, portfolio managers also have sufficient hands-on skills for 5 and 4.

Level	Pillars			Name	Description
10	Planning			Corporate or Enterprise Strategy	This is the highest level of business strategy and the focus is the entire enterprise. Questions at this level largely pertain to its identity, purpose, and direction.
9				Organization Strategy	Following the corporate or enterprise strategy, organization addresses the question of how an organization needs to evolve over time to meet its business objectives. While mostly internal focused, it is built upon a realistic assessment of external and internal environment.
8				Business Unit Strategy	Depending on the organization, a business unit can be a product line, a geography, or other profit centers. Here, the strategy is less about coordination among the operating units and more about developing and sustaining advantages to advance its products and services.
7		Changing	Operating	Functional Strategy	This is largely the realm of functional strategies including the specific business objectives for sales, marketing, operations, product management, information technology, etc.
6				Portfolio	Even though portfolios can exist at all levels of the organization, I am purposely putting it at Level 6 because this is where abstract planning starts to diminish and the hard work of getting things done starts. In addition, most portfolios exist cross-function and require the clear functional strategy.
5				Program	Programs can be seen as logical constructs of significant work components (other programs, projects, and operational initiatives) that require an organization to change. It is logical because of its relatedness and/or interdependencies. In PMI's definition, program focuses on delivering business benefits.
4				Project	Projects are typically more specific, concentrating on deliverables and outcomes. Portfolio, program, and projects are at the heart of the "changing" pillar.
3				Operational Initiatives	Operational initiatives are generally enhancement activities designed for the continuous improvement of operations. Occasionally, operational initiatives can be large and important to the overall business. In those cases, they are often managed as a part of programs.
2				Tracks	Tracks, are specific work units with specific expertise that is the building block for operational initiatives, projects, or programs. For example, a track in software development can be development, quality assurance, deployment, or business analysis.
1				Tasks and activities	These are specific tasks and activities that operate the business and its routine processes. For example, for Sales, it can be making cold calls. For Developers, it is coding.

Table 11: Organization Operating Level – An Abstract Depiction

2.2.2. Think Economics

There are many great principles of economics, but the two great lessons applicable to portfolio managers are as follows:

1. We are all driven by incentives, especially in the long run. This is true at every level of being: individuals, teams, business units, organizations, and even nations.
2. We all face scarcity. Common scarcity in business includes money, knowledge, physical assets, time, and people.

On incentive, portfolio managers must recognize the true importance of its existence as it is the driving force behind most decisions. For example, if there are two competing projects in a portfolio and the portfolio manager can authorize only one of them. Project A is better for the company, but will likely reward the portfolio manager worse. Project B is the opposite, better for portfolio manager but not as advantageous for the company. Which one will you pick? This time? Next time?

Individuals as well as organizations do rise above personal interests and incentives. For example, there are green initiatives that may not make immediate financial sense now. But how long can organizations sustain purely altruistic endeavors without measurable benefits or incentives to their organization?

For portfolio managers, it is important to recognize that incentive matters, and can be used as a tool to shape motivation. On the above example, Project A is worse for the portfolio manager because the project team responsible for implementation may refuse to work on the project (or more likely drag their feet). Thus, due to poor implementation, the project will likely suffer which would negatively impact the portfolio performance. But the portfolio manager can enhance the incentives by offering more training, more recognition, and perhaps even some bonuses.

On the negative, scarcity often results in a high degree of tension and conflict. On the positive, scarcity also engenders creativity and hard work. For portfolio managers, especially in today's competitive environment, scarcity and sometimes extreme scarcity is a business reality. The responsibility of portfolio managers is to work with senior management as well as the program and project teams to balance the scarcity of everything with feasibility of benefits and execution. This is by no means an easy task, and this is one area in which many portfolio managers spend most of their time negotiating, compromising, facilitating, and deciding.

2.2.3. Think Big Picture

How many executives do you know that DO NOT have their favorite pet projects? Not many. That is why the role of the portfolio manager requires a high degree of objectivity. In most organizations, portfolio managers are the last major process gates before significant investment of time and resources are allocated to programs and projects. If white elephant projects go unchallenged, then the portfolio performance may suffer; worse, the organization is likely to underperform. Yet, is objectivity enough?

Most portfolio managers are mere mortals who do not have all the knowledge. Years ago, as a portfolio manager for a financial service company, I would not have approved one of the CEO's pet projects. The NPV (net present value) was so bad that it would take the project of building an operational unit 15 years to just break even by an objective estimation. Yet, the CEO insisted and the project went ahead. Fast forward ten years, and the market has changed drastically. Thanks to this CEO's vision, the company is still performing precisely because 10 years earlier, it made the investment in that white elephant. This lesson taught me many things: objective analyses have limitations and as intelligent as most of us are, we do not know everything. The CEO's experience demonstrated that industry knowledge can trump all the analysis.

Another aspect of "think big picture" is the concept of optimization of the entire portfolio versus specific components of the portfolio. While we all love wins, in reality, winning 100% is impossible to sustain. For portfolio managers who are responsible for many components in the portfolio, it is important to know when to move on from a failed project or program. As the portfolio manager, your responsibility is toward the "entire" portfolio, not just one or a few projects. Often it is more important to dedicate the right resources and assets to some components while "good enough" is sufficient for others.

2.2.4. Think Practically

My father used to run construction companies, and I learned the key difference between architects and the doers is the art of possible. Architects can come up with beautiful blueprints that are either impossible to implement or too expensive to do; the doers must make do. Portfolio managers play a major role in this balancing act between what's possible and what's feasible. To achieve tangible benefits, execution is paramount. Without execution, the best ideas in the portfolio will remain as mere concepts. Therefore, it is vitally important for portfolio managers to examine the feasibility of getting the projects done.

To be a good portfolio manager and be able to pass the exam, it is important not only to know the inputs, outputs, tools, techniques, and processes. It is important to think like one. A good portfolio of the PfMP exam questions are experience-based questions, and I believe there is no better way to prepare for them than to learn how to think like a portfolio manager.

2.3. Key Concepts from Chapter 1 and 2 of the Standard

The Standard is written and organized as a reference manual. As such, it is neither an easy nor the most enjoyable read. Yet the descriptions and explanations are clear and vital to the profession. Personally, I enjoy all of PMI's standards because they help me organize my thoughts, knowledge, and experiences. Even when I disagree with PMI on some finer points, I relish the knowledge that PMI has done a superb job of advancing the profession.

As mentioned earlier, I will not repeat what PMI has so elegantly presented in the Standard. Therefore I will focus on where I can add additional value, either by ways of clarification or expansion of the concepts in the Standard.

2.3.1. Standard Chapter 1: Introduction to Portfolio Management

Chapter 1 of the Standard serves as an introduction and overview of the portfolio management standard and addresses these key questions:

1. What is a portfolio? (Standard: 1.2)
    a. What is its relationship among operations, projects, programs, and other portfolios? (See #3-#6 in Table 11 above; also read Standard: 1.2.1)
2. What is portfolio management? (Standard: 1.3)
    a. What is its relationship among management of organization endeavors that result in significant change? (this book, Chapter 2.1, the pillar on changing; also read Standard: 1.4)
3. How is portfolio management related to organization strategy? (See #7-#10 in Table 11 above; also read Standard: 1.5)
4. What is business value and how is it attained? (Standard: 1.6)
5. Within a portfolio, there are multiple sub-components. What are their relations and how do they work together? (See #2-#7 in Table 11 above; also read Standard: 1.7.3)
6. What is the role of a portfolio manager and what are their responsibilities? What are the key knowledge and skills? (This book, Chapter 2.2; also read the Standard: 1.8)
7. How is portfolio management managed in most organizations? PMI introduced the concept of PMO (referred to as project, program, or portfolio management office). I will explain the concept of PMO further in the table below. (Standard: 1.9)

This table below contains the two key concepts that are important for portfolio managers from Chapter 1:

#	Concept	Description
1	PMO	Since early 2013, PMI has been making a major push for PMO. Ironically, what PMO stands is anything but stable. In the Standard, it is referred to as "portfolio, program, and project" management office. But there are other industry terms that mean roughly the same thing. For example: PO (stands for project office), SPO (strategic project office), CC (competency center), or even COE (center of excellence). Regardless of the name, and there are variations and nuances among these terms, PMO refers to an organization's attempt to centralize the business execution, specifically projects, programs, portfolios, and operational initiatives. PMO and its equivalent can provide a wide range of services, easily more than 30 processes such as reporting, issue management, change control, governance, process standards, etc. To gain a deeper understanding of PMO and its strategic value, I recommend three sources: 1. PMI Thought Leadership Series: www.pmi.org/Knowledge-Center/PMO-Thought-Leadership.aspx?WT.mc_id=Mar-PMOthoughtL-Googlepmipmo 2. My firm's website (contains a chart of PMO capabilities): www.pmoadvisory.com/pmoplus/ 3. In addition, PMI's PMO Community of Practice published an extensive interview with me in the April 2014 issue of PMO Newsletter. (Issue #3, Volume No 4, April 2014). You will have to be a member to log-in to PMI site and find it. *Tip: For the sake of the PfMP Exam, assume the portfolio management processes are managed by a PMO. Just remember, in reality, this is far more complex.*
2	Portfolio Manager Skills	Portfolio managers play pivotal roles in enabling the efficient and effective decisions on programs and projects. Their primary skills can be simplified into one of these four sets of skills: • Coordinating • Facilitating • Managing • Leading See Figure 4 below for an illustration followed by more detailed discussion.

The figure below provides one illustrative depiction of the potential processes in a strategic PMO.

Figure 3: Comprehensive Map of PMO Processes

The four primary skill sets of portfolio managers are:

- Coordinating – As coordinators, portfolio managers primarily focus on running the portfolio management processes as efficiently as possible. These include organizing activities related to portfolio management, implementing processes, corralling teams and stakeholders, scheduling the various meetings, and communicating to the necessary parties.
- Facilitating – As facilitators, portfolio managers concentrate on solving challenges and driving solutions. This includes engaging experts (e.g. financial experts on a portfolio component's business case), promoting collaborative problem solving, simplifying the complex problems, and managing conflicts and disagreements.
- Managing – As managers, the focus is on ensuring the overall effectiveness of the portfolio management processes and people. Specific activities include allocating resources, establishing process rules and guidelines, motivating teams, and managing stakeholders and their expectations.

- Leading – Portfolio managers can also be leaders. They set directions, maintain alignment with business objectives, ensure portfolio benefits are achieved, determine risk management strategies, and make difficult decisions, especially with the allocation of resources and budget.

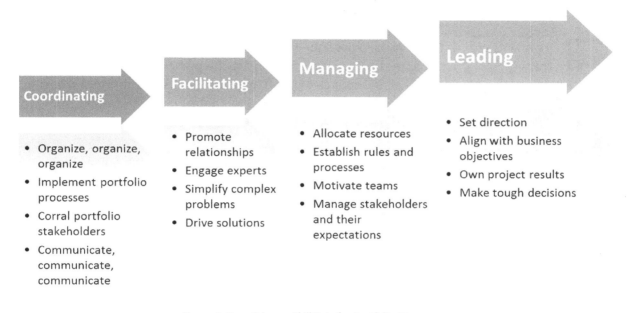

Figure 4: Four Primary Skill Sets for Portfolio Managers

2.3.2. Standard Chapter 2: Overview and Organization of Portfolio Management

Chapter 2 of the Standard provides an overview of portfolio management and how it fits into the organization to help achieve business benefits. To expand on this book's Chapter 2.1, portfolio management is the discipline that enables organization leadership to effectively and efficiently make project and program decisions, allocate resources, align strategies with execution, and manage the upsides (benefits) and downsides (risks).

Chapter 2 of the Standard addresses these key questions:

1. How is portfolio management related to organizational strategy? (Standard: 2.1)
2. What is the process of implementing portfolio management process in organizations? (Standard: 2.2)
3. What is portfolio management information system (PMIS)? (Standard: 2.4)
4. What is portfolio governance and who are the stakeholders? (Standard: 2.5 and 2.6)
5. How does organizational maturity impact portfolio management? (Standard: 2.7)

This table below contains the two key concepts that are important for portfolio managers from Chapter 2:

#	Concept	Description
1	Organization Strategy	The Standard uses the term "organization strategy" extensively, but sometimes inaccurately from the perspective of a strategy expert. Just to be clear, "organization strategy" mentioned in the PMI is equivalent to Level 6-10 of Table 11: Organization Operating Level – An Abstract Depiction described above. Portfolios can exist at all levels of an organization. For a large company, there can be multiple portfolios within a level. For smaller organizations, there may be just a handful such as a portfolio for new products and another portfolio for internal improvements. The number and level of portfolios depend on the organization, its complexity, and its endeavors. *Tip: While an over simplification, for the sake of PfMP exams, treat all strategies as abstract planning that establishes direction and provides guidance for the company.*
2	Organization Maturity	While portfolio management can be implemented in most project-intensive organizations, its relative success requires acceptance that is often more associated with mature organizations. For organizations without stable project management and program management processes, for example, the chance of successfully implementing and sustaining portfolio management is considerably lower. *Tip: Please be aware that when responding to experience-based exam questions, organization maturity can impact the answer.*

Table 13: The Standard Chapter 2 - Additional Concepts

2.4. Practice Questions

This section contains 10 practice questions. While these questions may not appear on the actual PfMP exam (as Chapter 1 and 2 are absent from the examination content outline), I believe having a solid understanding is critical to passing the test. Chapters 1 and 2 are foundational.

2.4.1. Questions

1. How does a portfolio manager address the function of information technology?

   A. Analyzing infrastructure and IT components and ensuring properly trained resources are adequate for support

   B. Not a factor as portfolio managers look at multiple areas

   C. Analyzing infrastructure and IT components

   D. Analyzing infrastructure and IT components and ensuring they are in place

2. How many portfolios may an organization have at any given time?

   A. Any reasonable managed number - one or greater

   B. Only one

   C. Only a few

   D. One per portfolio manager

3. The portfolio manager must have expertise in ALL of the following application and analysis of quantitative and qualitative techniques except:

   A. Prioritization algorithms

   B. Project budgeting

   C. Capability and capacity modeling methods and tools

   D. Project and program auditing techniques

4. How should a portfolio manager maintain portfolio alignment?

   A. By aligning components to the future business objectives

B. By defining the business objectives

C. By aligning one or more components to each strategic objective

D. By aligning only one component per individual strategic objective

5. Which is NOT an assessment activity of the portfolio management process?

   A. Assess the state of the most current project

   B. Identify and evaluate existing portfolio management knowledge

   C. Assess the existing portfolio management process to determine if they support organization mission purpose and vision

   D. Assess the current portfolio management structure and resources for maturity and adequacy

6. Examples of PMIS Tools and Processes include:

   A. Document version control systems

   B. Software tools

   C. Document repository

   D. All of the answer choices

7. Responsibilities of the PMO Include:

   A. Can function on an enterprise-wide level

   B. Provides guidance on the practice or portfolio, project and program management

   C. Involved in project execution

   D. All of the answer choices

8. What is organizational strategy?

   A. A plan that focuses on the profitability

   B. A plan in which the organizations strengths and core competences will be utilized

   C. A plan that incorporates all the elements of a corporate strategy

D. A plan that incorporates the best strengths of the corporation

9. What is project management?

   A. The application of knowledge, skills, tools and techniques to each project

   B. The management of projects

   C. The application of knowledge, skills, tools and techniques to project activities to meet its requirements

   D. The application of knowledge, skills, tools and techniques to project activities to exceed its requirements

10. What is portfolio governance?

   A. Established by a governing body that makes decisions about project status

   B. Established by a governing body that makes decisions about project management

   C. Established by a governing body that makes decisions about HR policy

   D. Established by a governing body that makes decisions about investments and priorities

2.4.2. Practice Questions and Answers

1. How does a portfolio manager address the function of information technology? (Moderate)

   A. Analyzing infrastructure and IT components and ensuring properly trained resources are adequate for support

   B. Not a factor as portfolio managers look at multiple areas

   C. Analyzing infrastructure and IT components

   D. Analyzing infrastructure and IT components and ensuring they are in place

   > The correct answer is **A**. Refer to Section 1.7 of the Standard for Portfolio Management - 3rd Edition. Review the descriptions and definition.

2. How many portfolios may an organization have at any given time? (Easy)

   A. Any reasonable managed number - one or greater

   B. Only one

   C. Only a few

   D. One per portfolio manager

   > The correct answer is **A**. Refer to Section 1.2 of the Standard for Portfolio Management - 3rd Edition. Review the descriptions and definition.

3. The portfolio manager must have expertise in ALL of the following application and analysis of quantitative and qualitative techniques except: (Moderate)

   A. Prioritization algorithms

   B. Project budgeting

   C. Capability and capacity modeling methods and tools

   D. Project and program auditing techniques

   > The correct answer is **B**. Refer to Section 1.8 of the Standard for Portfolio Management - 3rd Edition. Review the descriptions and definition.

4. How should a portfolio manager maintain portfolio alignment? (Moderate)

A. By aligning components to the future business objectives

B. By defining the business objectives

C. By aligning one or more components to each strategic objective

D. By aligning only one component per individual strategic objective

> The correct answer is **C**. Refer to Section 1.5 of the Standard for Portfolio Management - 3rd Edition. Review the descriptions and definition.

5. Which is NOT an assessment activity of the portfolio management process? (Moderate)

A. Assess the state of the most current project

B. Identify and evaluate existing portfolio management knowledge

C. Assess the existing portfolio management process to determine if they support organization mission purpose and vision

D. Assess the current portfolio management structure and resources for maturity and adequacy

> The correct answer is **A**. Refer to Section 2.2 of the Standard for Portfolio Management - 3rd Edition. Review the descriptions and definition.

6. Examples of PMIS Tools and Processes include: (Easy)

A. Document version control systems

B. Software tools

C. Document repository

D. All of the answer choices

> The correct answer is **D**. Refer to Section 2.4 of the Standard for Portfolio Management - 3rd Edition. Review the descriptions and definition.

7. Responsibilities of the PMO Include: (Easy)

A. Can function on an enterprise-wide level

B. Provides guidance on the practice or portfolio, project and program management

C. Involved in project execution

D. All of the answer choices

> The correct answer is **D**. Refer to Section 1.9 of the Standard for Portfolio Management - 3rd Edition. Review the descriptions and definition.

8. What is organizational strategy? (Easy)

   A. A plan that focuses on the profitability

   B. A plan in which the organizations strengths and core competences will be utilized

   C. A plan that incorporates all the elements of a corporate strategy

   D. A plan that incorporates the best strengths of the corporation

> The correct answer is **B**. Refer to Section 1.5 of the Standard for Portfolio Management - 3rd Edition. Review the descriptions and definition.

9. What is project management? (Easy)

   A. The application of knowledge, skills, tools and techniques to each project

   B. The management of projects

   C. The application of knowledge, skills, tools and techniques to project activities to meet its requirements

   D. The application of knowledge, skills, tools and techniques to project activities to exceed its requirements

> The correct answer is **C**. Refer to Section 1.7 of the Standard for Portfolio Management - 3rd Edition. Review the descriptions and definition.

10. What is portfolio governance? (Easy)

   A. Established by a governing body that makes decisions about project status

   B. Established by a governing body that makes decisions about project management

   C. Established by a governing body that makes decisions about HR policy

   D. Established by a governing body that makes decisions about investments and priorities

The correct answer is **D**. Refer to Section 1.9 of the Standard for Portfolio Management - 3rd Edition. Review the descriptions and definition.

Chapter 3: Understanding Portfolio Management Process Groups

3.1. Overview

In the Standard, the portfolio management processes are organized in three groups: Defining, Aligning, and Authorizing & Controlling. Process groups should not be confused with phases, as phases connote a more linear relationship. Since portfolios exist for much greater spans of time, often as long as the existence of the organization unit supporting the underlying endeavor, portfolio management is more like operational management in term of duration.

The process groups provide a logical construct for the individual processes. In the Standard, there are 16 processes organized within the three process groups: Defining, Aligning, and Authorizing & Controlling.

3.2. Process Group Overview

The three process groups defined in the Standard are as follows:

1. Defining Process Group – Consists of eight processes across all five knowledge areas whose primary purpose is to thoroughly plan how the portfolio will be managed. This includes the development of a base set of assets as shown in Table 3-2 of the Standard.
2. Aligning Process Group – Consists of six processes across all five knowledge groups whose primary purpose is to ensure the continual support of the organizational strategy. Unlike Defining Process Group whose end goals are developing specific portfolio assets, Aligning Process Group focuses on achieving results. Some of the results are updated in the portfolio assets.
3. Authorizing & Controlling Process Group – Consists of only two processes of the Portfolio Governance Management knowledge area. But do not let the two processes beguile the importance and intensity of these processes. In reality, portfolio managers are likely to spend most of their time on providing portfolio supervision to the implementation team.

Knowledge Area	Process Groups		
	Defining Process Group (8)	Aligning Process Group (6)	Authorizing & Controlling Process Group (2)
Portfolio Strategy Management (4)	Develop Portfolio Strategic Plan	Manage Strategic Change	
	Develop Portfolio Charter		
	Develop Portfolio Define Roadmap		
Portfolio Governance Management (5)	Develop Portfolio Management Plan	Optimize Portfolio	Authorize Portfolio
	Define Portfolio		Provide Portfolio Oversight
Portfolio Performance Management (3)	Develop Portfolio Performance Management Plan	Manage Supply and Demand	
		Manage Portfolio Value	
Portfolio Communication Management (2)	Develop Portfolio Communication Management Plan	Manage Portfolio Information	
Portfolio Risk Management (2)	Develop Portfolio Risk Management Plan	Manage Portfolio Risk	

Legend:	Define (No Shade)	Align (Light Gray)	Authorize & Control (Darker Gray)

Table 14: Map of Portfolio Management Process Group and Knowledge Area (Table 3-1 from the Standard)

3.3. Key Concepts

Even though Chapter 3 itself is not officially on the exam, the key concepts here permeate the rest of the book. Below are the key concepts: Please review the Standard for their definitions and description. (As stated in the beginning of the book, I will only elaborate on areas of confusion or where I can add more value. I am not re-describing them with the potential of creating confusion.)

- Remember the process groups and its processes. See Table 14 above.
- Understand the interactions between the process groups and processes. They are tightly connected with the business and organizational processes, from developing business strategies to implementing and monitoring progress of portfolio decisions. (See Standard 3.2)
- The Standard's Section 3.2.1 describes the common inputs and outputs, which commonly appears on the exam. Specifically, you should have a good understanding of the following:
  - Portfolio process assets – appears 24 times in Exam Aid 3 (See Standard: 3.2.1.1)
  - Portfolio reports – appears 15 times in Exam Aid 3 (See Standard: 3.2.1.2)
  - Organizational process assets – appears 7 times in Exam Aid 3 (See Standard: 3.2.1.3)
  - Enterprise environment factors – appears 6 times in Exam Aid 3 (See Standard: 3.2.1.4)

- There are five key deliverables across the portfolio management process. Figure 3-2 of the Standard provides an executive summary. Below they are listed in the reverse order of frequency:
  - Portfolio management plan - appears 25 times in Exam Aid 3
  - Portfolio - appears 17 times in Exam Aid 3
  - Portfolio roadmap - appears 9 times in Exam Aid 3
  - Portfolio strategic plan - appears 9 times in Exam Aid 3
  - Portfolio charter - appears 6 times in Exam Aid 3

3.4. Practice Questions

According to the PfMP Exam Outline, there is officially zero questions from this chapter. However, I believe the core concepts in this chapter, as well as chapter 1 and 2 are foundational and hence critical to the successful preparation of the exam. Below are some sample questions for you to practice.

3.4.1. Questions

1. The Defining Process Group is most active:

    A. At the time the organization identifies and updates its goals

    B. At the time the organization identifies and updates its strategic goals

    C. At the time the organization identifies and updates its near term budgets

    D. All of the answer choices

2. How many portfolio management knowledge areas are there?

    A. Three

    B. Six

    C. Five

    D. Four

3. All of the following are process assets except:

    A. Portfolio reports

    B. Project Plan

    C. Lessons learned

    D. Information on tools and models

4. The portfolio management plan contains which of the following?

    A. Portfolio risk management planning

    B. Portfolio performance reporting and review

C. Communication model

D. All of the answer choices

5. The Strategic Plan contains all of the following except:

A. Corporate tactics

B. Initiatives to be appraised and prioritized

C. Strategic objectives to be optimized

D. Key assumptions, constraints, dependencies and risks

6. Which of the following is NOT a key deliverable needed for the portfolio management process?

A. Portfolio Roadmap

B. Portfolio charter

C. Portfolio

D. Projects lifecycle

7. What are Enterprise Environmental Factors?

A. External conditions not under the control of the portfolio organization

B. Internal conditions not under the control of the portfolio organization

C. Internal or external conditions not under the control of the portfolio organization which influence, constrain or direct the success of the portfolio

D. Internal or external conditions that are under the control of the portfolio organization which influence, constrain or direct the success of the portfolio

8. What is/are the process(es) in both the knowledge area "Portfolio Communication Management" and the Aligning Process Group:

A. Manage portfolio information

B. None of the answer choices

C. Manage financial information

D. Manage project plan

9. What is contained in Portfolio Reports?

    A. Portfolio component recommendations

    B. Portfolio risks and issues

    C. Governance recommendations and decisions

    D. All of the answer choices

10. Portfolio process groups are independent of:

    A. Business objectives

    B. Application areas and industry focus

    C. Budget

    D. Human resources

1. The Defining Process Group is most active: (Moderate)

    A. At the time the organization identifies and updates its goals

    B. At the time the organization identifies and updates its strategic goals

    C. At the time the organization identifies and updates its near term budgets

    D. All of the answer choices

    > The correct answer is **D**. Refer to Section 3.1 of the Standard for Portfolio Management - 3rd Edition. Review the descriptions and definition.

2. How many portfolio management knowledge areas are there? (Easy)

    A. Three

    B. Six

    C. Five

    D. Four

    > The correct answer is **C**. Refer to Section 3.1 of the Standard for Portfolio Management - 3rd Edition. Review the descriptions and definition.

3. All of the following are process assets except: (Difficult)

    A. Portfolio reports

    B. Project Plan

    C. Lessons learned

    D. Information on tools and models

    > The correct answer is **A**. Refer to Section 3.2 of the Standard for Portfolio Management - 3rd Edition. Review the descriptions and definition.

4. The portfolio management plan contains which of the following? (Easy)

    A. Portfolio risk management planning

    B. Portfolio performance reporting and review

C. Communication model

D. All of the answer choices

> The correct answer is **D**. Refer to Section 3.2 of the Standard for Portfolio Management - 3rd Edition. Review the descriptions and definition.

5. The Strategic Plan contains all of the following except: (Moderate)

  A. Corporate tactics

  B. Initiatives to be appraised and prioritized

  C. Strategic objectives to be optimized

  D. Key assumptions, constraints, dependencies and risks

> The correct answer is **A**. Refer to Section 3.2 of the Standard for Portfolio Management - 3rd Edition. Review the descriptions and definition.

6. Which of the following is NOT a key deliverable needed for the portfolio management process? (Easy)

  A. Portfolio Roadmap

  B. Portfolio charter

  C. Portfolio

  D. Project lifecycle

> The correct answer is **D**. Refer to Section 3.2 of the Standard for Portfolio Management - 3rd Edition. Review the descriptions and definition.

7. What are Enterprise Environmental Factors? (Difficult)

  A. External conditions not under the control of the portfolio organization

  B. Internal conditions not under the control of the portfolio organization

  C. Internal or external conditions not under the control of the portfolio organization which influence, constrain or direct the success of the portfolio

  D. Internal or external conditions that are under the control of the portfolio organization which influence, constrain or direct the success of the portfolio

> The correct answer is **C**. Refer to Section 3.2 of the Standard for Portfolio Management - 3rd Edition. Review the descriptions and definition.

8. What is/are the process(es) in both the knowledge area "Portfolio Communication Management" and the Aligning Process Group: (Moderate)

   A. Manage portfolio information

   B. None of the answer choices

   C. Manage financial information

   D. Manage project plan

   > The correct answer is **A**. Refer to Section 3.1 of the Standard for Portfolio Management - 3rd Edition. Review the descriptions and definition.

9. What is contained in Portfolio Reports? (Easy)

   A. Portfolio component recommendations

   B. Portfolio risks and issues

   C. Governance recommendations and decisions

   D. All of the answer choices

   > The correct answer is **D**. Refer to Section 3.2 of the Standard for Portfolio Management - 3rd Edition. Review the descriptions and definition.

10. Portfolio process groups are independent of: (Moderate)

    A. Business objectives

    B. Application areas and industry focus

    C. Budget

    D. Human resources

    > The correct answer is **B**. Refer to Section 3.1 of the Standard for Portfolio Management - 3rd Edition. Review the descriptions and definition.

Chapter 4: Understanding Portfolio Strategic Management

4.1 Overview

The goal of the Portfolio Strategic Management knowledge area is to ensure the portfolio management processes and activities are in support of the organization strategy, not just at the beginning of the portfolio, but also sustained throughout the entire lifecycle of a portfolio.

To achieve this goal, PMI introduced four processes, of which three are in the Defining Process Group and one in the Aligning Process Group as illustrated in Table 15 below.

Knowledge Area	Process Groups		
	Defining (3)	Aligning (1)	Authorizing & Controlling (0)
Portfolio Strategic Management (4)	Develop Portfolio Strategic Plan	Manage Strategic Change	
	Develop Portfolio Charter		
	Define Roadmap		

Legend:	Define (No Shade)	Align (Light Gray)	Authorize & Control (Darker Gray)

Table 15: Processes in Portfolio Strategy Management

The three most important questions that the Portfolio Strategic Management address are the following:

1. How to best align organization strategies with business execution?
2. What are the ideas that are worth investing in, now and in the future?
3. How to adjust and change course when necessary?

4.1.1. How to best align organization strategies with business execution?

For organizations to remain viable and thrive in the ever more competitive environment, they must change and change successfully to achieve real and meaningful value. See Chapter

2.1. Context of Portfolio Management on page 41 for the fuller discussion on the three pillars of organizational activities.

The most sensible approach to convert ideas into action and to manage this change is through portfolio, program, and project management.

- Portfolio to ensure close alignment with business objectives and to achieve business value at an acceptable risk.
- Program to manage large initiatives with other programs and projects to achieve tangible benefits.
- Project to manage specific deliverables and outcomes.

Therefore as a portfolio manager, your job is to make sure the organization is investing in the right initiatives and making sure these initiatives are achieving the planned value. As portfolios can contain many projects and programs, it is not likely all of them will be successful. The balance and threshold depends on the organization's risk appetite and investment resources.

4.1.2. What are the ideas that are worth investing in, now and in the future?

To determine the right initiatives, portfolio managers are responsible for identifying and nurturing ideas that are aligned with the portfolio strategy and worth investing. Therefore, it is essential for portfolio managers to create a robust pipeline of ideas and opportunities for their organizations. A healthy portfolio will contain programs and projects in various stages of implementation, from pre-initiation to operations.

4.1.3. 3. How to adjust and change course when necessary?

In today's hyper competitive market, organization strategies rarely remain static for long. As organization strategies change, it is imperative that this change is reflected in its project investments. Portfolio managers play this pivotal role in organizations.

In the Standard, it appears that change is distilled from organization strategy to portfolio strategy. This is often true, but the reverse can also happen. For example, in a portfolio that invests in innovation, a portfolio manager can come across ideas that can change the organization strategy – for example, invest in a new market segment due to technology changes.

Regardless of the direction of the change, portfolio managers are responsible for the *continual* alignment between strategy and execution.

4.2. Inputs, Tools & Techniques, Outputs

In conjunction with the discussion on the Portfolio Strategy Management, this chapter presents details of the process's ITTO. Remember the table below:

Processes	Inputs	Tools & Techniques	Outputs
Develop Portfolio Strategic Plan	1. Org strategy and objectives 2. Inventory of work 3. Portfolio Process Assets 4. Org Process Assets 5. Enterprise environmental factors	1. Portfolio Component Inventory 2. Strategic Alignment Analysis 3. Prioritization Analysis	1. Portfolio Strategic Plan 2. Portfolio
Develop Portfolio Charter	1. Portfolio Strategic Plan 2. Portfolio processes assets 3. Enterprise environmental factors	1. Scenario Analysis 2. Capability and Capacity Analysis	1. Portfolio Strategic Plan Updates 2. Portfolio Charter 3. Portfolio Process Assets Updates
Define Portfolio Roadmap	1. Portfolio Strategic Plan 2. Portfolio Charter 3. Portfolio	1. Interdependency Analysis 2. Cost/benefit Analysis 3. Prioritization Analysis	1. Portfolio Roadmap
Manage Strategic Change	1. Portfolio Strategic Plan 2. Portfolio Charter 3. Portfolio 4. Portfolio Roadmap 5. Portfolio Management Plan 6. Portfolio Process Assets	1. Stakeholder Analysis 2. Gap Analysis 3. Readiness Assessment	1. Portfolio Strategic Plan Updates 2. Portfolio Charter Updates 3. Portfolio Updates 4. Portfolio Roadmap Updates 5. Portfolio Management Plan Updates 6. Portfolio Process Assets Updates

Legend:	Define (No Shade)	Align (Light Gray)	Authorize & Control (Darker Gray)

Table 16: ITTO for Portfolio Strategic Management

Hint: Notice that all outputs contain the term "updates" when it appears in the subsequent time. For example, in Develop Portfolio Strategic Plan process, the outputs are Portfolio Strategic Plan and Portfolio. In all subsequent processes, the corresponding outputs are Portfolio Strategic Plan *Updates* and Portfolio *Updates*.

4.3. Key Concepts for Portfolio Strategic Management

Chapter 4 of the Standard contains a number of key concepts that are important for portfolio managers. Most of these are well explained in the Standard. Here are a few concepts that require further elaboration and/or clarification.

#	Concept	Description
1	Portfolio	A portfolio is a logical collection of projects, programs, and sometimes, operational initiatives. The exact logic depends on organizations and their business objectives. For example, a small financial services company may develop two portfolios: • Revenue generating – products and services whose primary goal is creating new revenue • Operational effectiveness – internal projects, programs, and operational initiatives designed to optimize the organization On the exam, remember that there is no right number of portfolios in organizations; it is highly dependent on the environmental considerations, organization structure, geographic scope, and culture.
2	Portfolio Charter	The portfolio charter is a contract (can be formal or informal) of the structure, people, and processes that will be used to manage the portfolio. Once approved, it serves as an organization's commitment to the purpose and resources for managing the portfolio. Questions with regards to portfolio charters are very likely on the PfMP exam. (Remember, PMI loves charter.)
3	Portfolio Roadmap	The roadmap is a high-level schedule showing the specific components of the portfolio and how these components achieve the overall portfolio goals. The schedule can also show dependencies, gaps, conflicts, resources, and risks. Since roadmaps can exist at project, program, and portfolio levels, it can be confusing on exams. If this question comes up on the exam, remember that portfolio roadmap has the greatest duration, often with a span of multiple years.

#	Concept	Description
4	Portfolio Strategic Plan	This plan defines the guidelines and direction of the portfolio for the purpose of making investment decisions. The plan should support the overall organization strategy (See levels of 6 to 10 in Table 11 above) with specific programs and projects. Figure 4-4 of the Standard provides an illustration of the portfolio roadmap. For another illustration, see Figure 5 below.

Table 17: Key Concepts from the Standard Chapter 4 on Portfolio Strategic Management

4.4. Examples of Portfolio Strategic Management Tools and Techniques

The Standard provides many good examples of portfolio tools and techniques for Portfolio Strategic Management. This section provides a few additional ones that may appear on the PfMP exam. Remember, the PfMP exam is more than the Standard; it is designed to encompass the common project portfolio management practices in use currently.

4.4.1. Capability Maturity Heat Map

The example below is a capability-based portfolio. For example, an organization may wish to create a new business capability, and the capabilities include three components: foundational, operational, and project management. The illustration below highlights the planned approach to creating this capability over a five year period.

The heat map demonstrates the progressive maturity (and gaps) of a business' capability over the coming years. The numbers (0, 1, 2, 3, 4, and 5) refer to the maturity level of the capabilities. See Table 18 below for a description of these levels.

ID	Capabilities	Year 0	Year 1	Year 2	Year 3	Year 4	Year 5
Foundational							
F-01	Benefits Management	0	1	2	2	3	3
F-02	Communication & Stakeholder	0.5	1.5	2	2.5	3	3
F-03	Contract Strategy / Management	To be determined					
F-04	Financial Management	1	1.5	2	2	2	2
F-05	Governance	To be determined					
F-06	Performance Metrics	0.5	1	1.5	2	2.5	3
F-07	Reporting	0.5	1	2	3	4	5
F-08	Resource Management	1	2	2	2	2	2
Operational							
O-01	In-Take and Triage	1	2	2.5	2.5	3	3
O-02	Defect Management	1	2	2.5	2.5	3	3
O-03	Service Request	1	2	2.5	2.5	3	3
O-04	Change Request	1	2	2.5	2.5	3	3
O-05	Release Management	0.5	1	2	3	4	5
O-06	Landscape / Environment Mgmt	0.5	1	2	2	2	2
O-07	Code Management	2	2	3	3	3	3
O-08	Quality Assurance	0.5	1	2	3	3	3
Project							
P-01	Project In-Take Process	0	1	2	2	2	2
P-02	Project Planning	0.5	1.5	2	2	3	3
P-03	Technical Spec	1	2	2	3	4	4
P-04	Development	2	2	3	4	4	4
P-05	Quality Assurance	1	2	3	4	4	4
P-06	Deployment	1	1.5	2	2.5	3	3.5
P-07	Project Management	2	2.5	3	3.5	4	4

Figure 5: Sample Portfolio Strategy Overview Based on Capability Maturity

Level	Name	Description
0	Not Present / Ad Hoc	This capability or process has not been formally introduced
1	As-is / Basic	**Either No change** from the current situation or basic concept introduced
2	Improved	Improved capabilities strive toward **standardization** and **clarity** of capability or process definition
3	Efficiency	Building upon improved capabilities, efficiency is gained through **consistent adoption** and **execution** across the regions
4	Effectiveness	After attaining efficiency, the goal is to achieve greater effectiveness as defined by **consistency and repeatability of results**
5	Continuous Improvement	The processes and capabilities are mature and stable; continue to seek for **continuous improvements**

Table 18: Capability Maturity Level – A Sample

4.5. Practice Questions for Portfolio Strategic Management

4.5.1. Questions

1. The development of the Portfolio Strategic Plan process includes the following inputs:

    A. Inventory of work

    B. Portfolio process assets

    C. Enterprise environmental factors

    D. All of the answer choices

2. Which of the following should happen when doing a capability and capacity analysis?

    A. A variety of portfolio scenarios using difference combinations of potential and current components are evaluated

    B. Internal resource capacity should be measured and external resource availability is required to be established to complete the portfolio structure

    C. Organizational, environmental, and governmental variables that may constrain the charter are evaluated

    D. External resource capacity should be measured and internal resource availability is required to be established to complete the portfolio structure

3. Interdependency analysis is a technique for defining a portfolio roadmap.   What is its benefit?

    A. Identifies the dependencies the portfolio may have in relationship to other organizations

    B. Identifies the dependencies the portfolio may have in relationship to other projects

    C. Identifies the dependencies the portfolio may have in relationship to other portfolios

    D. None of the answer choices

4. Phillip comes to you and is very concerned about the level of change in his new portfolio. He explains that he has a strategic plan and has aligned it to organizational strategy but that various factors have caused his portfolio to change. How would you advise him?

A. I would advise him not to worry as his portfolio in its early stages when portfolios tend to evolve as more details are provided

B. I would advise him to be concerned as his portfolio should not experience a large amount of change

C. I would advise him not to be concerned as even established portfolios experience large amounts of change on a regular basis

D. I would advise him to be concerned as the organization strategies may have changed

5. Patrick is meeting with Rob about managing strategic change. Rob suggests to Patrick that he needs to update the portfolio management plan. Patrick asks Rob why it needs to be updated. How should Rob respond?

A. Rob should explain to Patrick that the portfolio management plan should have been updated during the Develop Portfolio Strategic Plan process

B. Rob should explain to Patrick that there have been some changes in management approach that need to be reflected in the plan

C. Rob should explain to Patrick that he should have discovered this when he performed a strategic alignment analysis

D. Rob should explain to Patrick that he should have discovered this when he performed a prioritization analysis

6. What does the portfolio charter provide?

A. Formal and informal plans, policies, procedures, and guidelines, which may need to be updated

B. It serves as a guide for developing the portfolio strategic plan

C. The portfolio structure including the hierarchy and organization of the portfolio, subportfolios, programs, projects, and operations

D. None of the answer choices

7. What information should the portfolio roadmap provide?

A. High-level strategic direction, information in a chronological view, and enabled dependencies within the portfolio to be established and evaluated

B. Highly detailed strategic information in a chronological view along with dependency information

C. Highly detailed strategic information at different time increments across the last month

D. None of the answer choices

8. What is the purpose of a prioritization analysis?

    A. To identify new or changing organizational strategy and objectives

    B. To understand the objectives, expected benefits, performance, and prioritization criteria

    C. To guide ongoing decisions as to which portfolio components should be added, terminated, or changed

    D. All of the answer choices

9. What type of information is referenced from the portfolio when defining the portfolio roadmap?

    A. Cost, investment risks, and dependencies

    B. Portfolio charter, organizational strategy, portfolio component inventory

    C. Prioritization analysis, strategic alignment analysis, cost-benefit analysis

    D. Prioritization, dependencies, and organization areas

10. Portfolios or inventory of work should be:

    A. Validated against organization strategy updates

    B. Validated against organization strategy updates to ensure consistency with the evolving organization mission, goals and objectives

    C. Validated against organization strategy updates to ensure consistency

    D. Validated against organization strategy updates to ensure consistency with a stable organization mission, goals and objectives

1. The development of the Portfolio Strategic Plan process includes the following inputs: (Moderate)

    A. Inventory of work

    B. Portfolio process assets

    C. Enterprise environmental factors

    D. All of the answer choices

    > The correct answer is **D**. Refer to Section 4.1 of the Standard for Portfolio Management - 3rd Edition. Review the descriptions and definition.

2. Which of the following should happen when doing a capability and capacity analysis? (Difficult)

    A. A variety of portfolio scenarios using difference combinations of potential and current components are evaluated

    B. Internal resource capacity should be measured and external resource availability is required to be established to complete the portfolio structure

    C. Organizational, environmental, and governmental variables that may constrain the charter are evaluated

    D. External resource capacity should be measured and internal resource availability is required to be established to complete the portfolio structure

    > The correct answer is **B**. Refer to Section 4.2.2.2 of the Standard for Portfolio Management - 3rd Edition. Review the descriptions and definition.

3. Interdependency analysis is a technique for defining a portfolio roadmap. What is its benefit? (Moderate)

    A. Identifies the dependencies the portfolio may have in relationship to other organizations

    B. Identifies the dependencies the portfolio may have in relationship to other projects

    C. Identifies the dependencies the portfolio may have in relationship to other portfolios

    D. None of the answer choices

The correct answer is **C**. Refer to Section 4.3 of the Standard for Portfolio Management - 3rd Edition. Review the descriptions and definition.

4. Phillip comes to you and is very concerned about the level of change in his new portfolio. He explains that he has a strategic plan and has aligned it to organizational strategy but that various factors have caused his portfolio to change. How would you advise him? (Difficult)

 A. I would advise him not to worry as his portfolio in its early stages when portfolios tend to evolve as more details are provided

 B. I would advise him to be concerned as his portfolio should not experience a large amount of change

 C. I would advise him not to be concerned as even established portfolios experience large amounts of change on a regular basis

 D. I would advise him to be concerned as the organization strategies may have changed

The correct answer is **A**. Refer to Section 4.1.3.2 of the Standard for Portfolio Management - 3rd Edition. Review the descriptions and definition.

5. Patrick is meeting with Rob about managing strategic change. Rob suggests to Patrick that he needs to update the portfolio management plan. Patrick asks Rob why it needs to be updated. How should Rob respond? (Difficult)

 A. Rob should explain to Patrick that the portfolio management plan should have been updated during the Develop Portfolio Strategic Plan process

 B. Rob should explain to Patrick that there have been some changes in management approach that need to be reflected in the plan

 C. Rob should explain to Patrick that he should have discovered this when he performed a strategic alignment analysis

 D. Rob should explain to Patrick that he should have discovered this when he performed a prioritization analysis

The correct answer is **B**. Refer to Section 4.4.3.5 of the Standard for Portfolio Management - 3rd Edition. Review the descriptions and definition.

6. What does the portfolio charter provide? (Easy)

A. Formal and informal plans, policies, procedures, and guidelines, which may need to be updated

B. It serves as a guide for developing the portfolio strategic plan

C. The portfolio structure including the hierarchy and organization of the portfolio, subportfolios, programs, projects, and operations

D. None of the answer choices

> The correct answer is **C**. Refer to Section 4.2.3.1 of the Standard for Portfolio Management - 3rd Edition. Review the descriptions and definition.

7. What information should the portfolio roadmap provide? (Easy)

A. High-level strategic direction, information in a chronological view, and enabled dependencies within the portfolio to be established and evaluated

B. Highly detailed strategic information in a chronological view along with dependency information

C. Highly detailed strategic information at different time increments across the last month

D. None of the answer choices

> The correct answer is **A**. Refer to Section 4.3.3.1 of the Standard for Portfolio Management - 3rd Edition. Review the descriptions and definition.

8. What is the purpose of a prioritization analysis? (Easy)

A. To identify new or changing organizational strategy and objectives

B. To understand the objectives, expected benefits, performance, and prioritization criteria

C. To guide ongoing decisions as to which portfolio components should be added, terminated, or changed

D. All of the answer choices

> The correct answer is **C**. Refer to Section 4.1.2.3 of the Standard for Portfolio Management - 3rd Edition. Review the descriptions and definition.

9. What type of information is referenced from the portfolio when defining the portfolio roadmap? (Moderate)

   A. Cost, investment risks, and dependencies

   B. Portfolio charter, organizational strategy, portfolio component inventory

   C. Prioritization analysis, strategic alignment analysis, cost-benefit analysis

   D. Prioritization, dependencies, and organization areas

   > The correct answer is **D**. Refer to Section 4.3.1.3 of the Standard for Portfolio Management - 3rd Edition. Review the descriptions and definition.

10. Portfolios or inventory of work should be: (Difficult)

    A. Validated against organization strategy updates

    B. Validated against organization strategy updates to ensure consistency with the evolving organization mission, goals and objectives

    C. Validated against organization strategy updates to ensure consistency

    D. Validated against organization strategy updates to ensure consistency with a stable organization mission, goals and objectives

    > The correct answer is **B**. Refer to Section 4.1 of the Standard for Portfolio Management - 3rd Edition. Review the descriptions and definition.

Chapter 5: Understanding Portfolio Governance Management

5.1. Overview

The goal of Portfolio Governance Management knowledge area is to provide the proper portfolio oversight including defining, categorizing, optimizing and changing, and authorizing portfolio components for execution.

The knowledge area contains five processes across the three process groups as shown below.

Knowledge Area	Process Groups		
	Defining (2)	Aligning (1)	Authorizing & Controlling (2)
Portfolio Governance Management (5)	Develop Portfolio Management Plan	Optimize Portfolio	Authorize Portfolio
	Define Portfolio		Provide Portfolio Oversight

Legend:	Define (No Shade)	Align (Light Gray)	Authorize & Control (Darker Gray)

Table 19: Processes in Portfolio Governance Management

The three most important questions addressed by Portfolio Governance Management are as follows:

1. What is the best approach to portfolio governance?
2. How to select and optimize portfolio components?
3. How to provide ongoing management of the portfolio?

5.1.1. What is the best approach to portfolio governance?

The Portfolio Governance Management knowledge area of the Standard provides an excellent framework for managing portfolios. The framework includes five processes as shown in Table 19 above.

But the question on the actual implementation depends on many factors. The art of management is finding what works at a minimum cost and risk. For portfolio management, it is relatively simple to suggest a thorough process of managing portfolios, programs, and projects. But is the expense and overhead of establishing a heavy process worth the benefits? You can examine this problem in another way, should a $10 million portfolio have the same process and rigor as a $100 million portfolio?

The above is important to remember on certain experience-based questions. Remember, PMI is not dictating the details of how much sophistication or automation is required for the proper functioning of portfolio management.

5.1.2. How to select and optimize portfolio components?

Portfolio managers are investors, and one of their key roles is to determine the best mix of components in a portfolio. The Standard provides multiple ways to define, categorize, evaluate, and optimize portfolio components. On the exam, it is important to follow the process order in the order that they are defined in the Standard.

5.1.3. How to provide ongoing management of the portfolio?

The key for portfolio management is not the establishment of the processes initially, but rather, it is the sustainment of the portfolio management processes. There are only two processes in the PfMP framework that deals with the ongoing management and they are Authorize Portfolio and Provide Portfolio Oversight process. Remember to understand the processes here thoroughly.

5.2. Inputs, Tools & Techniques, Outputs

In conjunction with the discussion on the Portfolio Governance Management, this chapter presents the details of the process's ITTO. Remember the table below:

	Processes	Inputs	Tools & Techniques	Outputs
Governance Management (5)	Develop Portfolio Management Plan	1. P. Strategic Plan 2. P. Charter 3. P. Roadmap 4. P. Process Assets 5. Org Process Assets 6. Enterprise environmental factors	1. Elicitation Techniques 2. P. or Org Structure Analysis 3. Integration of Portfolio Management Plans	1. P. Strategic Plan Updates 2. P. Management Plan 3. P. Process Assets Updates
	Define Portfolio	1. P. Strategic Plan 2. P. Charter 3. Portfolio 4. P. Roadmap 5. P. Management Plan 6. P. Process Assets	1. P. Component Inventory 2. P. Component Categorization Techniques 3. Weighted Ranking and Scoring Techniques	1. P. Updates 2. P. Roadmap Updates 3. P. Management Plan Updates
	Optimize Portfolio	1. Portfolio 2. P. Roadmap 3. P. Management Plan 4. P. Reports 5. P. Process Assets	1. Capability and Capacity Analysis 2. Weighted Ranking and Scoring Techniques 3. Quantitative and Qualitative Analysis 4. Graphical Analytical Methods	1. P. Updates 2. P. Roadmap Updates 3. P. Management Plan Updates 4. P. Reports 5. P. Process Assets Updates
	Authorize Portfolio	1. Portfolio 2. P. Management Plan 3. P. Reports	1. P. Authorization Techniques 2. P. Management Information System	1. P. Updates 2. P. Management Plan Updates 3. P. Reports 4. P. Process Assets Updates
	Provide Portfolio Oversight	1. Portfolio 2. P. Roadmap 3. P. Management Plan 4. P. Reports 5. P. Process Assets	1. P. Review Meetings 2. Elicitation Techniques	1. P. Updates 2. P. Management Plan Updates 3. P. Reports 4. P. Process Assets Updates

Legend:	Define (No Shade)	Align (Light Gray)	Authorize & Control (Darker Gray)

Table 20: ITTO for Portfolio Governance Management

Hint: On the output, it is important to note that aside from Portfolio Management Plan and Portfolio Reports, all other outputs from all Governance Management processes are "updates" (e.g. portfolio strategic plan updates, portfolio updates, portfolio asset updates, etc.)

5.3. Key Concepts for Portfolio Governance Management

Chapter 5 of the Standard contains a number of key concepts that are important for portfolio managers. Most of these are well explained in the Standard. Here are a few additional concepts that require further elaboration and/or clarification.

#	Concept	Description
1	Change, control and management	In the Standard, change is discussed at two levels which can cause confusion. Change Control and Management is very tactical and is defined as the process of managing portfolio component changes which can include changes to scope, requirements, schedules, and resources. It can also include changes to portfolio management processes. This should not be confused with Strategic Change.
2	Change, strategic	In the Standard, change is discussed at two levels which can cause confusion. On the Managing Strategic Change, this process focuses on responding to changes in organizational strategy and objectives. These changes can be a consequence of both internal and external change. Note: In the Standard, while not explicitly stated, it is assumed that Portfolio Management is the recipient of strategic change, not the cause. In reality, the relationship is much fuzzier and likely to be bi-directional.
3	Compliance	Since portfolios are larger constructs with programs and projects, compliance with regulations are often taken more significantly especially in highly regulated industries such as pharmaceutical, financial services, and utility industries. In addition, with the emerging sensitivity of data privacy and confidentiality, data security is gaining renewed attention. Compliance related questions on PfMP require experience to properly answer. The correct answers are more often focused on "doing the right thing" and not on the "practicalities."

#	Concept	Description
4	Dependencies	For portfolio managers managing large portfolio of projects and programs, defining and managing dependencies among the portfolio components can be challenging. When questions related to dependencies come up, focus on these three aspects: what is the strategic direction, what are the priorities, and how to mitigate risks of action or inaction.
5	Governance	In PfMP, the governance management is organized in five processes: 1. Define how to govern (Develop Portfolio Management Plan) 2. Create portfolio (Define Portfolio) 3. Maximize benefits and minimize risks (Optimize Portfolio) 4. Approve components (Authorize Portfolio) 5. Provide ongoing management (Provide Portfolio Oversight) Questions on the exam are often related to two aspects of governance: doing the right thing and providing the optimal balance. But remember not to skip a step.
6	Provide Portfolio Oversight	Key activities in the Provide Portfolio Oversight process are predominantly monitoring, reviewing, reporting and communication. Portfolio managers do not make component-level changes, which may be the case in reality. Portfolio managers must work with program and project managers to make actual component changes.

Table 21: Key Concepts from the Standard Chapter 5 on Portfolio Governance Management

5.4. Examples of Portfolio Governance Tools and Techniques

The Standard provides many good examples of portfolio tools and techniques for Portfolio Governance Management. This section provides a few additional ones that may appear on the PfMP exam. Remember, the PfMP exam is more than the Standard; it is designed to encompass the common project portfolio management practices in use currently.

5.4.1. Sample Portfolio Bubble Chart

Below is an example of a portfolio with ten projects. The analysis in the bubble chart shows three dimensions: initial investment (x-axis), probability of success (y-axis), and net present value (bubble size).

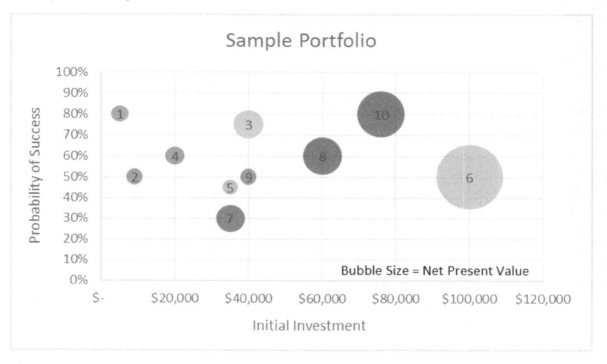

Figure 6: A Sample Portfolio in Graphical Representation - Bubble Chart

1. How is the portfolio roadmap used when developing the portfolio management plan?

    A. It is used to reference portfolio policies, processes and procedures, and portfolio knowledge bases

    B. It provides the portfolio structure, scope, resources, timeline, stakeholder communication requirements, and performance expectations

    C. It uses the high-level strategic direction and extended timelines to define the low-level schedule and timelines for portfolio components

    D. None of the answer choices

2. Kim is working on developing the portfolio management plan. She wants to make sure that dependencies between portfolio components are defined as they have been elsewhere. Where would they have been previously defined?

    A. Portfolio roadmap

    B. Portfolio charter

    C. Enterprise environmental factors

    D. Portfolio strategic plan

3. The weight in a scoring model can be:

    A. Percentage only

    B. None of the answer choices

    C. Score only

    D. Percentage and score

4. Sandy has been asked to develop a portfolio management plan. Sandy has never done this before and wants to know what a good starting point would be to begin this process. What does she need to get started?

    A. Portfolio charter, portfolio roadmap, portfolio strategic plan, portfolio process assets, organizational process assets, enterprise environmental factors

B. Elicitation techniques, portfolio organizational structure analysis, integration of portfolio management plans

C. Elicitation techniques, portfolio organizational structure analysis, integration of portfolio management plans, enterprise environmental factors

D. Portfolio charter, portfolio roadmap, portfolio strategic plan, portfolio process assets, elicitation techniques

5. Corey has been informed that several planned portfolio components have been postponed due to new legislation. What plan within the portfolio management plan should Corey consult?

A. Balancing portfolio and managing dependencies

B. Procurement planning

C. Portfolio oversight

D. Managing compliance

6. Cliff is working on developing a portfolio management plan. He has all of the initial information he needs to begin the process and has evaluated and reviewed it. What would be an appropriate next step?

A. Perform elicitation techniques

B. All of the answer choices

C. Conduct portfolio organizational structure analysis

D. Conduct integration of portfolio management plans

7. Myron is currently applying facilitation techniques, survey techniques, and collaboration techniques for the first time in the Defining process group. What is the most likely process that Myron is currently involved in?

A. Develop Portfolio Charter

B. Authorize Portfolio

C. Develop Portfolio Management Plan

D. Define Portfolio

8. Jessica is about to start working on the Provide Portfolio Oversight process. She is trying to find historical performance information as well as open issues. Where can she find this information?

    A. Portfolio component inventory

    B. Portfolio process assets

    C. Portfolio charter

    D. Portfolio reports

9. Portfolio Reports support Portfolio Oversight in all of the following ways except:

    A. Maximize benefits provided to the organization

    B. Minimize risk delivered to the organization

    C. Level of performance and alignment with all financial projections

    D. Level of performance and alignment with organizational strategy

10. In the Authorize Portfolio process, which is not a key activity?

    A. Allocating resources to authorized portfolio components

    B. Allocating resources to new portfolio components

    C. Reallocating funding and resources from deactivated to activated portfolio components

    D. Reallocating funding and resources from terminated to activated portfolio components

5.5.2. Questions and Answers

1. How is the portfolio roadmap used when developing the portfolio management plan? (Moderate)

   A. It is used to reference portfolio policies, processes and procedures, and portfolio knowledge bases

   B. It provides the portfolio structure, scope, resources, timeline, stakeholder communication requirements, and performance expectations

   C. It uses the high-level strategic direction and extended timelines to define the low-level schedule and timelines for portfolio components

   D. None of the answer choices

   > The correct answer is **C**. Refer to Section 5.1.1.3 of the Standard for Portfolio Management - 3rd Edition. Review the descriptions and definition.

2. Kim is working on developing the portfolio management plan. She wants to make sure that dependencies between portfolio components are defined as they have been elsewhere. Where would they have been previously defined? (Difficult)

   A. Portfolio roadmap

   B. Portfolio charter

   C. Enterprise environmental factors

   D. Portfolio strategic plan

   > The correct answer is **A**. Refer to Section 5.1.1.3 of the Standard for Portfolio Management - 3rd Edition. Review the descriptions and definition.

3. The weight in a scoring model can be: (Easy)

   A. Percentage only

   B. None of the answer choices

   C. Score only

   D. Percentage and score

4. Sandy has been asked to develop a portfolio management plan. Sandy has never done this before and wants to know what a good starting point would be to begin this process. What does she need to get started? (Difficult)

   A. Portfolio charter, portfolio roadmap, portfolio strategic plan, portfolio process assets, organizational process assets, enterprise environmental factors

   B. Elicitation techniques, portfolio organizational structure analysis, integration of portfolio management plans

   C. Elicitation techniques, portfolio organizational structure analysis, integration of portfolio management plans, enterprise environmental factors

   D. Portfolio charter, portfolio roadmap, portfolio strategic plan, portfolio process assets, elicitation techniques

   The correct answer is **A**. Refer to Section 5.1 of the Standard for Portfolio Management - 3rd Edition. Review the descriptions and definition.

5. Corey has been informed that several planned portfolio components have been postponed due to new legislation. What plan within the portfolio management plan should Corey consult? (Difficult)

   A. Balancing portfolio and managing dependencies

   B. Procurement planning

   C. Portfolio oversight

   D. Managing compliance

   The correct answer is **D**. The key word here is legislation so it is clearly a compliance related issue.

   Refer to Section 5.1.3.2 of the Standard for Portfolio Management - 3rd Edition. Review the descriptions and definition.

6. Cliff is working on developing a portfolio management plan. He has all of the initial information he needs to begin the process and has evaluated and reviewed it. What would be an appropriate next step? (Difficult)

    A. Perform elicitation techniques

    B. All of the answer choices

    C. Conduct portfolio organizational structure analysis

    D. Conduct integration of portfolio management plans

    > The correct answer is **B**. Refer to Section 5.1 of the Standard for Portfolio Management - 3rd Edition. Review the descriptions and definition.

7. Myron is currently applying facilitation techniques, survey techniques, and collaboration techniques for the first time in the Defining process group. What is the most likely process that Myron is currently involved in? (Difficult)

    A. Develop Portfolio Charter

    B. Authorize Portfolio

    C. Develop Portfolio Management Plan

    D. Define Portfolio

    > The correct answer is **C**. Refer to Section 5.1.2.1 of the Standard for Portfolio Management - 3rd Edition. Review the descriptions and definition.

8. Jessica is about to start working on the Provide Portfolio Oversight process. She is trying to find historical performance information as well as open issues. Where can she find this information? (Moderate)

    A. Portfolio component inventory

    B. Portfolio process assets

    C. Portfolio charter

    D. Portfolio reports

    > The correct answer is **B**. Refer to Section 5.5.1.5 of the Standard for Portfolio Management - 3rd Edition. Review the descriptions and definition.

9. Portfolio Reports support Portfolio Oversight in all of the following ways except: (Moderate)

    A. Maximize benefits provided to the organization

    B. Minimize risk delivered to the organization

    C. Level of performance and alignment with all financial projections

    D. Level of performance and alignment with organizational strategy

    > The correct answer is **C**. Refer to Section 5.5.1 of the Standard for Portfolio Management - 3rd Edition. Review the descriptions and definition.

10. In the Authorize Portfolio process, which is not a key activity? (Moderate)

    A. Allocating resources to authorized portfolio components

    B. Allocating resources to new portfolio components

    C. Reallocating funding and resources from deactivated to activated portfolio components

    D. Reallocating funding and resources from terminated to activated portfolio components

    > The correct answer is **B**. Refer to Section 5.4 of the Standard for Portfolio Management - 3rd Edition. Review the descriptions and definition.

Chapter 6: Understanding Portfolio Performance Management

6.1. Overview

The goal of Portfolio Performance Management knowledge area is to deliver the desired business value of the portfolio. This is achieved by finding the best mix of portfolio components, determining their sequence of implementation, and applying the optimal level of resources.

This knowledge area contains three processes across the Defining and Aligning process groups.

Knowledge Area	Process Groups		
	Defining (1)	Aligning (2)	Authorizing & Controlling (0)
Portfolio Performance Management (3)	Develop Portfolio Performance Management Plan	Manage Supply and Demand	
		Manage Portfolio Value	

Legend:	Define (No Shade)	Align (Light Gray)	Authorize & Control (Darker Gray)

Table 22: Processes in Portfolio Performance Management

The three essential questions for this knowledge area are as follows:

1. What are the desired performance goals?
2. How to best utilize the resources available?
3. How to measure and report on the portfolio value (at an acceptable risk level)?

6.1.1. What are the desired performance goals?

Most portfolios have a mixture of performance goals, whether they are related to economic, quality, customer service, innovation, or security values. PMI's approach is always systemic and collaborative. It is systemic as the portfolio performance metrics should be determined through a process of inquiry and validation. It is collaborative because the portfolio manager should not develop the performance goals in isolation; it requires leveraging existing knowledge assets such as portfolio and organizational process assets, stakeholder inputs and factors from the external environment.

It is important to remember that once the performance goals are defined, there must be a deliberate and systemic process of updating them.

In this book, I also recommend a variation of the SMART system on defining metrics. See 6.4.2. The SMARTIE System below; this is the system I use for designing performance metrics.

6.1.2. How to best utilize the resources available?

One of the key steps to value maximization is finding the optimal utilization of resources. This includes funding, people and skills, knowledge, computing resources, physical assets, and other scarce organizational assets. For portfolio managers, the four ways of thinking as described in Section 2.2. How to Think Like a Portfolio Manager on page 44 is crucial.

Also, it is important to invest the unused capacity wisely as well. An optimal portfolio management system allocates all of its resources working on the entire lifecycle of portfolio activities from pre-initiation to program and project implementation and ongoing operation.

6.1.3. How to measure and report on the portfolio value?

The Standard provides a number of tools and techniques on managing portfolio value including illustrations on component value. Any number of charts such as "cost-benefit" and "portfolio efficient frontier" can provide insightful illustrations. However, what is missing and not widely discussed in the Standard is the ideation. As stated earlier, it is important to manage the entire lifecycle of a portfolio, starting with ideation. See Table 27: Sample Portfolio Lifecycle Report below for an example of a portfolio performance report across the entire lifecycle.

6.2. Inputs, Tools & Techniques, Outputs

In conjunction with the discussion on the Portfolio Performance Management, this chapter presents the details of the process's ITTO. Remember the table below:

	Processes	Inputs	Tools & Techniques	Outputs
Performance Management (3)	Develop Portfolio Performance Management Plan	1. P. Management Plan 2. P. Process Assets 3. Org Process Assets 4. Enterprise Environmental Factors	1. Elicitation Techniques 2. P. management Information System 3. Capability and Capacity Analysis	1. P. Management Plan Updates 2. P. Process Assets Updates
	Manage Supply and Demand	1. Portfolio 2. P. Management Plan 3. P. reports	1. Scenario Analysis 2. Quantitative and Qualitative Analysis 3. Capability and Capacity Analysis	1. P. Updates 2. P. Management Plan Updates 3. P. Reports
	Manage Portfolio Value	1. P. Roadmap 2. P. Management Plan 3. P. Reports	1. Elicitation Techniques 2. Value Scoring and Measurement Analysis 3. Benefits Realization Analysis	1. P. Management Plan Updates 2. P. Reports 3. P. Process Assets Updates

Legend:	Define (No Shade)	Align (Light Gray)	Authorize & Control (Darker Gray)

Table 23: ITTO for Portfolio Performance Management

Chapter 6 of the Standard contains a number of key concepts that are important for portfolio managers. Most of these are well explained in the Standard. Here are a few additional concepts that require further elaboration and/or clarification.

#	Concept	Description
1	Benefits and Values	The ultimate goal of a portfolio is to achieve its planned benefits and value. Often, the organization benefits and value are beyond economic value such as value to the society, customers, employees, and shareholders. For instance, Table 25 below shows a set of benefit categories for a portfolio of data management projects. Being certified in project, program, and portfolio, I can see the nuances in choice of words. I believe PMI emphasizes the following associations: • Value is related to portfolio management • Benefit is related to program management • Deliverable is related to project management But since the concept of "benefit" is so general and broad, the term "benefits" is used generically. Remember this association as it is important for the exam to avoid confusion. If an exam question discusses deliverables, for example, then the correct answer is related to project management. If the question uses the word "value" sometimes in addition to the word "benefit", then it is portfolio management related.

#	Concept	Description
2	Performance metrics	Portfolio performance metrics is a complex topic. The PMI exams often trick you in focusing on the common metrics such as financial (ROI, BCR, NPV), customer satisfaction, etc. But performance metrics can also be based on innovation, sustainability, and corporate responsibility. On the exam, remember that metrics can be tangible and intangible. But more important, portfolio metrics focus on the entire portfolio, not just program and project successes. The Standard also discusses the SMART guideline: **S**pecific, **M**easurable, **A**ttainable, **R**ealistic, and **T**imely. But in my experience, we use the SMARTIE guideline with "IE" stands for **I**ntegrated and **E**ssential. See Table 26 below for a full description.
3	Portfolio efficient frontier	Portfolio efficient frontier is a portfolio optimization tool. The efficient frontier is a curve (rather than linear line) in which the portfolio achieves the highest expected return for a defined level of risk. Portfolios that lie below the efficient frontier are sub-optimal. This is considered an advanced topic, and the exam will likely have a question on this topic. See Figure 6-13 of the Standard for an example of the Portfolio Efficient Frontier.
4	Portfolio management information system (PMIS)	Portfolio management information system (PMIS) is a tool or collection of tools that is designed to support portfolio management processes. The PMIS may include tools for managing resources, change, risks, costs, and performance metrics. The system can be highly sophisticated with automations and workflows, but it can also be simple and manual. Microsoft Excel, for example, is likely the most popular PMIS. On the exam, remember that PMIS does not need to be sophisticated, but it should be formally agreed upon and used by the portfolio management team.

#	Concept	Description
5	Supply and demand	Manage Supply and Demand is the process of allocating, balancing, and optimizing resources or supply or capacity (e.g. human capital, funding, and other scarce resources) with the portfolio components or demand (e.g. programs, projects, and other operational initiatives). On the exam, supply and demand questions are likely to be experience-based. It is important to remember that resource allocation is iterative and requires careful planning. Also, it is as important to keep unused capacity or resources to a minimum.

Table 24: Key Concepts from the Standard Chapter 6 on Portfolio Performance Management

6.4. Examples of Portfolio Performance Tools and Techniques

The Standard provides many good examples of portfolio tools and techniques for Portfolio Performance Management. This section provides a few additional ones that may appear on the PfMP exam. Remember, the PfMP exam is more than the Standard; it is designed to encompass the common project portfolio management practices in use currently.

6.4.1. Sample Benefit Categories for a Data Management Portfolio

Below is an example of a portfolio benefit realization category for a strategic data management portfolio. The value achieved can be both qualitative and quantitative. Furthermore, while economic value is typical, portfolio value can be much more.

#	Benefit Category	Description
1	Data Quality: General	General improvement in quality of data, including data cleanup
1.1	Data Quality: Risk Mitigation	Improve controls of our applications and environment via authentication and access
1.2	Data Quality: Workflow	Improve controls of workflow capability in applications
1.3	Data Quality: Reporting	Improve quality of reports by improving the underlying data
1.4	Data Quality: Intelligence	Enhance relevance of data via reporting to bring out intelligence and insights; becoming a decision support system
2	Data Consistency	Improve how data is structured between global and local sources that enables both globalization and localization
3	Process Quality	Process improvement as mainly defined by consistency and also simplification
4	Provisioning	Availability of data for provisioning by local, regional, and global applications
5	Change Catalyst	Leveraging MDM applications as a conduit for change
6	Critical Asset	Establishes the importance of data and the discipline of data management to view data as a strategic differentiator
7	Ease of Implementation	This is a minimization of a negative – or headache - of implementation. This is used to indicate the ease of implementing the initiative.

Table 25: Sample Portfolio Benefit Categories

6.4.2. The SMARTIE System

A common system for defining performance metrics is the SMART system (Section 6.1.2.1 of the Standard). But my experience has shown that for portfolio management, SMART is not sufficient. There are two additional variables plus some changes to the original SMART system. Here is how I use the SMARTIE system:

Concept	Description
Specific	5 W's (who, what, where, when, and why)
Measurable	Preferably quantitative and objective
Attainable	(Internal evaluation) Do we have the capability, resources, and drive to achieve this?
Realistic	(External evaluation) Are there precedents? Have others within similar resources and constraints achieved this?
Timely	Does the goal change over time?
Integrated	How well does this metric align and integrate with the overall organization objectives? Are there areas of conflicts?
Essential	Is this objective really essential and relevant to the project success?

Table 26: SMARTIE System

6.4.3. Portfolio Lifecycle Report

The Standard provides some excellent insights and tools on managing portfolio value. But I believe an important missing component is the management of ideas as well as operational initiatives. Below is a simple but illustrative table showing the distribution of a $100 million portfolio in Year 2:

Phase#	Sub-Phase	# of Components	Success Rate*, %
Planning	New Ideas	50	27%
	Completed Business Cases	15	73%
	Approved, Waiting to Start	4	89%
Execution	Initiation	4	82%
	Development	8	84%
	Testing & QA	5	78%
	Deployment	4	91%
Operational	Operational / Live	12	99%
	Sunset / Terminated	4	

Table 27: Sample Portfolio Lifecycle Report

* Success rate is defined as the ability to move to the next stage with the acceptable threshold.

1. Tom has recently started working on the Manage Portfolio Value process. He is looking for a burn-up chart that would show the delivery of a component over time. Where would Tom find this?

    A. Portfolio charter

    B. Portfolio reports

    C. Portfolio roadmap

    D. Portfolio management plan

2. Organizations can further facilitate alignment by strengthening these organizational enablers:

    A. Structural, cultural, technological and asset management practices

    B. Structural, religious, technological and staff management practices

    C. Structural, cultural, technological and human resource practices

    D. None of the answer choices

3. Kathryn is working on portfolio performance management. She is currently measuring the degree to which portfolio and organizational risks have been adequately managed by undertaking the portfolio components. What type of measure is Kathryn applying?

    A. Quantitative measures

    B. Value measures

    C. Qualitative measures

    D. All of the answer choices

4. During the optimization process, component proposals provide initial assessments of:

    A. Expected business value

    B. Estimated project cost

    C. Expected marketing value

D. Estimated financial value

5. Denise is currently applying a tool within the benefits realization analysis which allows her to estimate the potential portfolio outcomes with respect to success criteria. What tool is Denise using?

   A. Value scoring and measurement analysis

   B. Outcome probability analysis of the portfolio

   C. Prioritization analysis

   D. Results chain

6. Carl is currently working on the Manage Portfolio Value process. He is currently defining performance indicators based on assessed value and is going to use them to measure and report portfolio performance. What type of technique is Carl applying?

   A. Progress measurement techniques

   B. Portfolio authorization techniques

   C. Elicitation techniques

   D. Value measurement techniques

7. Scenario Analysis looks at what would happen if all of the following were increased or decreased except:

   A. Equipment Funding

   B. Human Funding

   C. Financial Funding

   D. Project Funding

8. Vinnie is ready to start the Manage Supply and Demand process. He has the portfolio reports, but doesn't have anything else. What is he missing that he needs to start this process?

   A. Portfolio roadmap, organizational process assets

B. Portfolio, portfolio management plan

C. Enterprise environmental factors, portfolio process assets

D. Portfolio management plan, enterprise environmental factors

9. What are the inputs to the Manage Supply and Demand process?

    A. Portfolio reports, organizational process assets, enterprise environmental factors

    B. Portfolio management plan, portfolio process assets, organizational process assets, enterprise environmental factors

    C. Portfolio, portfolio management plan, portfolio reports

    D. Portfolio management plan, portfolio reports, enterprise environmental factors

10. What is an example of a Resource Schedule?

    A. A listing of detailing forecasts and ongoing resource supply and demand

    B. Histograms combining and detailing forecasts and ongoing resource supply and demand

    C. A table combining and detailing forecasts and ongoing resource supply and demand

    D. All of the answer choices

1. Tom has recently started working on the Manage Portfolio Value process. He is looking for a burn-up chart that would show the delivery of a component over time. Where would Tom find this? (Difficult)

   A. Portfolio charter

   B. Portfolio reports

   C. Portfolio roadmap

   D. Portfolio management plan

   > The correct answer is **B**. Burn-up charts over time can be found in portfolio reports.
   >
   > Refer to Section 6.3.1.3 of the Standard for Portfolio Management - 3rd Edition. Review the descriptions and definition.

2. Organizations can further facilitate alignment by strengthening these organizational enablers: (Moderate)

   A. Structural, cultural, technological and asset management practices

   B. Structural, religious, technological and staff management practices

   C. Structural, cultural, technological and human resource practices

   D. None of the answer choices

   > The correct answer is **C**. Refer to Section 6 of the Standard for Portfolio Management - 3rd Edition. Review the descriptions and definition.

3. Kathryn is working on portfolio performance management. She is currently measuring the degree to which portfolio and organizational risks have been adequately managed by undertaking the portfolio components. What type of measure is Kathryn applying? (Moderate)

   A. Quantitative measures

   B. Value measures

   C. Qualitative measures

   D. All of the answer choices

> The correct answer is **C**. The situation describe a qualitative measure as per Ch.6/Pg 85 in the Standard.
>
> Refer to Section 6 of the Standard for Portfolio Management - 3rd Edition. Review the descriptions and definition.

4. During the optimization process, component proposals provide initial assessments of: (Moderate)

   A. Expected business value

   B. Estimated project cost

   C. Expected marketing value

   D. Estimated financial value

   > The correct answer is **A**. Refer to Section 6.3 of the Standard for Portfolio Management - 3rd Edition. Review the descriptions and definition.

5. Denise is currently applying a tool within the benefits realization analysis which allows her to estimate the potential portfolio outcomes with respect to success criteria. What tool is Denise using? (Moderate)

   A. Value scoring and measurement analysis

   B. Outcome probability analysis of the portfolio

   C. Prioritization analysis

   D. Results chain

   > The correct answer is **B**. The situation describes the definition on a results chain per the Standard 6.3.2.3.
   >
   > Refer to Section 6.3.2.3 of the Standard for Portfolio Management - 3rd Edition. Review the descriptions and definition.

6. Carl is currently working on the Manage Portfolio Value process. He is currently defining performance indicators based on assessed value and is going to use them to measure and report portfolio performance. What type of technique is Carl applying? (Moderate)

   A. Progress measurement techniques

B. Portfolio authorization techniques

C. Elicitation techniques

D. Value measurement techniques

> The correct answer is **D**. The situation described reflects the definition of value measurement technique from the Standard.
>
> Refer to Section 6.3.2.2 of the Standard for Portfolio Management - 3rd Edition. Review the descriptions and definition.

7. Scenario Analysis looks at what would happen if all of the following were increased or decreased except: (Moderate)

   A. Equipment Funding

   B. Human Funding

   C. Financial Funding

   D. Project Funding

   > The correct answer is **D**. Refer to Section 6.2.2.1 of the Standard for Portfolio Management - 3rd Edition. Review the descriptions and definition.

8. Vinnie is ready to start the Manage Supply and Demand process. He has the portfolio reports, but doesn't have anything else. What is he missing that he needs to start this process? (Moderate)

   A. Portfolio roadmap, organizational process assets

   B. Portfolio, portfolio management plan

   C. Enterprise environmental factors, portfolio process assets

   D. Portfolio management plan, enterprise environmental factors

   > The correct answer is **B**. Inputs to the Manage Supply and Demand process.
   >
   > Refer to Section 6/Figure 6-1 of the Standard for Portfolio Management - 3rd Edition. Review the descriptions and definition.

9. What are the inputs to the Manage Supply and Demand process? (Moderate)

A. Portfolio reports, organizational process assets, enterprise environmental factors

B. Portfolio management plan, portfolio process assets, organizational process assets, enterprise environmental factors

C. Portfolio, portfolio management plan, portfolio reports

D. Portfolio management plan, portfolio reports, enterprise environmental factors

> The correct answer is **C**. Refer to Section 6/Figure 6-1 of the Standard for Portfolio Management - 3rd Edition. Review the descriptions and definition.

10. What is an example of a Resource Schedule? (Moderate)

A. A listing of detailing forecasts and ongoing resource supply and demand

B. Histograms combining and detailing forecasts and ongoing resource supply and demand

C. A table combining and detailing forecasts and ongoing resource supply and demand

D. All of the answer choices

> The correct answer is **D**. Refer to Section 6.1.2.4 of the Standard for Portfolio Management - 3rd Edition. Review the descriptions and definition.

Chapter 7: Understanding Portfolio Communication Management

7.1. Overview

The goal of Portfolio Communication Management knowledge area is to ensure the proper and systemic communication of the portfolio information to the key stakeholders. According to the Standard, there are only two processes in Portfolio Communication Management as shown below.

Knowledge Area	Process Groups		
	Defining (1)	Aligning (1)	Authorizing & Controlling (0)
Portfolio Communication Management (2)	Develop Portfolio Communication Management Plan	Manage Portfolio Information	

Legend:	Define (No Shade)	Align (Light Gray)	Authorize & Control (Darker Gray)

Table 28: Processes in Portfolio Communication Management

The top three questions addressed by this knowledge area are as follows:

1. Who should the portfolio management team communicate with? Who are the portfolio stakeholders?
2. What is the optimal communication plan to support the portfolio management processes?
3. How to manage the portfolio information – collection, storage, and dissemination?

7.1.1. Who to communicate with? Who are my stakeholders?

There are two major challenges with portfolio communication plans: who and what. On who, portfolios can be large with many stakeholders. For example, should the project team members be included in portfolio decision-related communications? There may be dependencies that project team members can readily identify but missed at a portfolio level. On the other hand, project team members may receive so much other communication already that they tune out.

As you prepare for the exam, remember that the Standard tackles this problem in a process-oriented way. Stakeholders are the ones identified in the Portfolio Communication Plan, which itself is created using a combination of stakeholder analysis, elicitation techniques, and communication requirement analysis.

7.1.2. What is the optimal communication plan to support the portfolio management processes?

Based on experience, there are four major criteria for an optimal communication plan. The four criteria are as follows:

1. Include the required stakeholders (Standard's Table 7-2 provides a good framework for stakeholder analysis).
2. Create a communication matrix that the stakeholders agree to (Standard's Table 7-3 Communication Matrix provides a good start)
3. Make sure the portfolio management team has adequate resources to sustain the communication plan. Often, portfolio managers establish a highly robust communication plan at the beginning, but then scale back or miss deadlines as the volume of work grows.
4. Communication consistency is paramount.

7.1.3. How to manage the portfolio information – collection, storage, and dissemination?

The process required to manage portfolio information includes the collection, analysis, storage, dissemination, and eventual removal of portfolio information. The basic requirements include accessibility, timeliness, and adequate security to prevent improper communication.

Unless you already have a defined and consistently applied communication management process, it will likely be more efficient to use basic tools like Excel, PowerPoint, Word, and SharePoint. Manual tools can change readily, but automated tools with workflow may be required for more complex portfolios. For the PfMP exam, remember that PMI does not endorse one solution over another. The exam questions focus on processes.

In Section 7.2.2.4, the Standard provides a number of examples including a Portfolio Dashboard. Also see Figure 7: Sample Portfolio Dashboard below for another example of a portfolio dashboard that provides both historical and current information.

7.2. Inputs, Tools & Techniques, Outputs

In conjunction with the discussion on Portfolio Performance Management, this chapter presents the details of the process's ITTO. Remember the table below:

	Processes	Inputs	Tools & Techniques	Outputs
Communication Management (2)	Develop Portfolio Communication Management Plan	1. Portfolio 2. P. Roadmap 3. P. Management Plan 4. P. Reports 5. P. Process Assets	1. Stakeholder Analysis 2. Elicitation Techniques 3. Communication Requirement Analysis	1. P. Management Plan Updates 2. P. Process Assets Updates
	Manage Portfolio Information	1. Portfolio 2. P. Management Plan 3. P. Reports 4. P. Component Reports 5. P. Process Assets	1. Elicitation Techniques 2. P. Management Information System 3. Communication Requirements Analysis 4. Communication Methods	1. P. Management Plan Updates 2. P. Reports 3. P. Process Assets Updates

Legend:	Define (No Shade)	Align (Light Gray)	Authorize & Control (Darker Gray)

Table 29: ITTO for Portfolio Communication Management

7.3. Key Concepts for Portfolio Communication Management

Chapter 7 of the Standard contains a number of key communication management concepts that are important for portfolio managers. Most of these are well explained in the Standard. Here are a few additional concepts that require further elaboration and/or clarification.

#	Concept	Description
1	Communication and stakeholder management	If you already have PMP or PgMP, you would quickly realize that the Portfolio Communication Management process is very similar. The differences are more in the scope, level and timing of communication. For portfolio, the scope is at a portfolio level, often directly associated with organization strategy. The target audience is more likely to include a broader constituent of executives, and the timing is well established in advance. On exam questions, it can be confusing to differentiate whether the question is related to project, program, or portfolios. Remember the following: • The portfolio Standard describes Communication Management as a knowledge area, with stakeholder analysis as a tool and technique. • In the third edition of the program management standard, there is a performance domain named in stakeholder engagement. There is also a program support process for communication management. • In PMBOK (Project Management Body of Knowledge 5th Edition), communication and stakeholder management are separate and distinct knowledge areas.
2	Portfolio Information Management System (PMIS)	In the Standard (see 7.2.2.2), PMIS is described as a "technology-based" method of capturing and managing information. But based on my experience managing portfolios of over $100 million in projects, it is often more important for the PMIS to be process-based as well. For example, analysis of information, how it should be organized, and reported are all process-based activities, not just technology. This distinction is important as the PfMP asks process-based questions about the PMIS.

#	Concept	Description
3	Stakeholder matrix	Stakeholder matrix (See Table 7-2). This table provides a concise overview of the key considerations in the development of a stakeholder analysis. It is important for you to know that this Table is illustrative and not comprehensive or exhaustive. For example, here are some additional stakeholder groups that should be considered: • Business executives who are sponsors of portfolio components but who may not be a member of the portfolio governance team. • Other portfolio managers who may have dependencies and integration areas • Similar to Contract Management Team, there may be other supporting teams such as Risk Management and Human Resources who are required to assist with managing resources and risks.

Table 30: Key Concepts from the Standard Chapter 7 on Portfolio Communication Management

7.4. Examples of Portfolio Communication Tools and Techniques

The Standard provides many good examples of portfolio tools and techniques for Portfolio Communication Management. This section provides a few additional ones that may appear on the PfMP exam. Remember, the PfMP exam is more than the Standard; it is designed to encompass the common project portfolio management practices in use currently.

7.4.1. Portfolio Dashboard for Active Components

The best portfolio dashboards provide both descriptive and prescriptive abilities. I used the following portfolio dashboard for one of my client's product portfolios (names are fictitious). The components are mainly projects and programs designed to improve the product.

Example of Portfolio Dashboard of Active Components

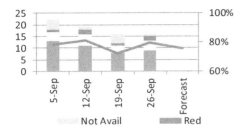

Health	5-Sep	12-Sep	19-Sep	26-Sep
Green	13	11	8	9
Yellow	4	5	3	4
Red	1	2	1	2
Not Avail	4	1	4	1
Total	22	19	16	16
Overall Health	79%	81%	73%	79%

Portfolio Component Name	Portfolio ID	Primary Category	Project Manager	Status	5-Sep	12-Sep	19-Sep	26-Sep
Program: Content Restructure								
Redefining Copy Editing Process	10	Content	Cyndy O'Neill	Active	75% (P2)	75% (P2)	75% (P2)	95% (P2)
Persona	97	Content	Bryan Clark	Active	60%	60%	60%	60%
Search Engine Optimization	98	Content	Cyndy O'Neill	Active	35%	35%		40%
Digital Facts	99	Content	Tom Eccles	Active		20%	20%	20%
Master Template for Content	107	Content	Tom Eccles & Dana	Active		15%	15%	15%
Restructure for Post-Prod	106	Content	Cyndy O'Neill	Active		15%	20%	40%
Individual Projects								
Notification	14	Process Improvement	Jim Joseph	Active	92%	93%	93%	95%
Dashboard Reporting	21	Reporting / Dashboards	Larry Levine	Active	Ongoing	Ongoing	Ongoing	Ongoing
Post Launch Content	29	Process	David Koch	Completed				
Web Hosting	42	Product	Kumar Chakaborty	Terminated				
Feature Migration from Legacy SEO	44	Product	Alex Smith	On Hold				
... about 15 more projects								

Legend:

Project not started
Did not receive status

Project Closed (which can be duplicate, on hold, terminated, post review, or completed)

Figure 7: Sample Portfolio Dashboard

Dashboards are an effective way of communicating often complex messages on portfolio status and their trends. More importantly, I also believe historical information can be highly pertinent to future decisions. Some key features of this dashboard report include:

1. Upper left: Summary of the of the portfolio health. The full dashboard shows all 30 weeks of health.

2. Upper right: This dashboard quickly shows the number of active projects and their relative health. Furthermore, an overall portfolio health is determined. This dashboard also provides a historical account of the project health.
3. The body of the report contains the weekly progress of the portfolio components. This example only showed one program and five individual reports. Naturally the full report shows much more.
4. The historical information combined with overall health trend analysis provides a degree of prescriptive ability to portfolio managers.

7.5.1. Questions

1. Which of the following is not an input to the Develop Portfolio Communication Management Plan?

    A. Portfolio Charter

    B. Portfolio

    C. Portfolio Roadmap

    D. Portfolio Reports

2. Which of the following provides a technology-based method of capturing and managing all portfolio-related communication needs?

    A. Portfolio management plan

    B. Elicitation techniques

    C. Portfolio management information system

    D. Portfolio component reports

3. Dave has just started working on the Develop Portfolio Communication Management Plan process. He is trying to find level of effort and point of contact information for a few portfolio components. Where can Dave find this information?

    A. Portfolio

    B. Portfolio roadmap

    C. Portfolio management plan

    D. Portfolio reports

4. During the Manage Portfolio Information process, what type of changes would cause there to be a need to update the portfolio management plan?

    A. New delivery mechanisms

    B. New information management needs

    C. New information management guidelines

D. All of the answer choices

5. As it relates to the Develop Portfolio Communication Management Plan, what plays a role in determining if reports should be distributed electronically or via paper copies?

    A. Cost is the only factor considered

    B. Organization's culture and comfort level with technology

    C. The only factor considered what the senior executives prefer

    D. None of the answer choices

6. A communication calendar:

    A. Represents all of the communication for the portfolio and its respective stakeholders

    B. Represents all of the communication for the portfolio

    C. Represents all of the communication for the portfolio and their frequency over a period of time

    D. Represents all of the communication for the portfolio and the follow-ups

7. What are the outputs of the Manage Portfolio Information process?

    A. Portfolio management plan updates, portfolio reports, portfolio roadmap updates

    B. Portfolio management plan updates, portfolio roadmap updates

    C. Portfolio charter updates, portfolio management plan updates

    D. Portfolio management plan updates, portfolio reports, portfolio process assets updates

8. What is a resource histogram?

    A. A graphical representation of how changing organizational priorities including realigning resource efforts, altering the work force, and modifying the cost structure of resources impact the portfolio

    B. It is an effective way to communicate multiple messages on portfolio status and trending simultaneously

C. A graphical representation of all of the communication for the portfolio and their frequency over a period of time

D. None of the answer choices

9. Portfolio communication facilitates effective two-way dialogue between which group of stakeholders?

A. Governing bodies

B. Executive managers

C. Operations managers

D. All of the answer choices

10. Insufficient communication results in all of the following except:

A. Failure to identify risks

B. Improved stakeholder confidence

C. Failure to accomplish portfolio objectives

D. Increase in duplication of efforts

1. Which of the following is not an input to the Develop Portfolio Communication Management Plan ? (Moderate)

   A. Portfolio Charter

   B. Portfolio

   C. Portfolio Roadmap

   D. Portfolio Reports

   > The correct answer is **A**. Refer to Section 7.1 of the Standard for Portfolio Management - 3rd Edition. Review the descriptions and definition.

2. Which of the following provides a technology-based method of capturing and managing all portfolio-related communication needs? (Easy)

   A. Portfolio management plan

   B. Elicitation techniques

   C. Portfolio management information system

   D. Portfolio component reports

   > The correct answer is **C**. Refer to Section 7.2.2.2 of the Standard for Portfolio Management - 3rd Edition. Review the descriptions and definition.

3. Dave has just started working on the Develop Portfolio Communication Management Plan process. He is trying to find level of effort and point of contact information for a few portfolio components. Where can Dave find this information? (Moderate)

   A. Portfolio

   B. Portfolio roadmap

   C. Portfolio management plan

   D. Portfolio reports

   > The correct answer is **A**. The portfolio contains level of effort and POC information as specified in the Standard in 7.1.1

4. During the Manage Portfolio Information process, what type of changes would cause there to be a need to update the portfolio management plan? (Moderate)

    A. New delivery mechanisms

    B. New information management needs

    C. New information management guidelines

    D. All of the answer choices

> The correct answer is **B**. Guidelines are part of portfolio process assets and delivery mechanisms are part of portfolio reports
>
> .
>
> Refer to Section 7.2.3.1 of the Standard for Portfolio Management - 3rd Edition. Review the descriptions and definition.

5. As it relates to the Develop Portfolio Communication Management Plan, what plays a role in determining if reports should be distributed electronically or via paper copies? (Moderate)

    A. Cost is the only factor considered

    B. Organization's culture and comfort level with technology

    C. The only factor considered what the senior executives prefer

    D. None of the answer choices

> The correct answer is **B**. Refer to Section 7.1.2.3 of the Standard for Portfolio Management - 3rd Edition. Review the descriptions and definition.

6. A communication calendar: (Moderate)

    A. Represents all of the communication for the portfolio and its respective stakeholders

    B. Represents all of the communication for the portfolio

    C. Represents all of the communication for the portfolio and their frequency over a period of time

    D. Represents all of the communication for the portfolio and the follow-ups

7. What are the outputs of the Manage Portfolio Information process? (Moderate)

   A. Portfolio management plan updates, portfolio reports, portfolio roadmap updates

   B. Portfolio management plan updates, portfolio roadmap updates

   C. Portfolio charter updates, portfolio management plan updates

   D. Portfolio management plan updates, portfolio reports, portfolio process assets updates

   The correct answer is **D**. Refer to Section 7/Figure 7-1 of the Standard for Portfolio Management - 3rd Edition. Review the descriptions and definition.

8. What is a resource histogram? (Easy)

   A. A graphical representation of how changing organizational priorities including realigning resource efforts, altering the work force, and modifying the cost structure of resources impact the portfolio

   B. It is an effective way to communicate multiple messages on portfolio status and trending simultaneously

   C. A graphical representation of all of the communication for the portfolio and their frequency over a period of time

   D. None of the answer choices

   The correct answer is **A**. Refer to Section 7.2.2.4 of the Standard for Portfolio Management - 3rd Edition. Review the descriptions and definition.

9. Portfolio communication facilitates effective two-way dialogue between which group of stakeholders? (Moderate)

   A. Governing bodies

   B. Executive managers

   C. Operations managers

   D. All of the answer choices

The correct answer is **D**. Refer to Section 7.1 of the Standard for Portfolio Management - 3rd Edition. Review the descriptions and definition.

10. Insufficient communication results in all of the following except: (Moderate)

A. Failure to identify risks

B. Improved stakeholder confidence

C. Failure to accomplish portfolio objectives

D. Increase in duplication of efforts

The correct answer is **B**. Refer to Section 7.1.3.1 of the Standard for Portfolio Management - 3rd Edition. Review the descriptions and definition.

Chapter 8: Understanding Portfolio Risk Management

8.1. Overview

The goal of Portfolio Risk Management knowledge area is to manage the portfolio within the acceptable tolerance of the portfolio. From a risk management perspective, all uncertainties, even positive ones, result in surprises. The goal is to convert positive risks into known opportunities and maximize them when possible and to minimize negative risks.

The Portfolio Risk Management contains two processes as outlined below.

Knowledge Area	Process Groups		
	Defining (1)	Aligning (1)	Authorizing & Controlling (0)
Portfolio Risk Management (2)	Develop Portfolio Risk Management Plan	Manage Portfolio Risk	

Legend:	Define (No Shade)	Align (Light Gray)	Authorize & Control (Darker Gray)

Table 31: Processes in Portfolio Risk Management

The three most pressing questions for Portfolio Risk Management are as follows:

1. How to determine portfolio risks?
2. How to manage them on a sustainable basis?
3. How to deal with low probability but high impact risks (black swans)?

8.1.1. How to determine portfolio risks?

Consistent with other PMI approaches, the Standard advocates a structured process for evaluating portfolio risks with the goal of capitalizing on the positive risks (called opportunities) and minimizing the negative risks (called threats). In portfolios, risks often exist at the points of interaction such as integration between portfolio components and handoff areas in which work from one component is required for another component. But portfolio risks can also be external to the portfolio and even external to the organization. Regulatory, compliance, and politics are just some of these risks.

The Standard proposes a three steps approach to develop a risk management approach. This includes risk planning, assessment, and response. As a part of risk planning, portfolio managers should determine the risk tolerance of the portfolio, design processes to manage risks, identify risks themselves, and assign owners. However, not all portfolio risks are readily identified. Therefore, it is important for portfolio managers to establish resource boundaries to determine the amount of resources dedicated to risk identification. See Section "8.1.3. How to deal with low probability but high impact risks (black swans)?" below on how to manage black swan risks.

8.1.2. How to manage them on a sustainable basis?

One of the biggest challenges with risk management is to find the right balance of dedicating resources to risks that is commensurate with the risk tolerance. The right balance depends on many factors. More importantly, risk management is typically not a one-time activity and it requires continual resource investments.

From my experience, it is important to determine the risk tolerance at the beginning, then push the organizational boundaries to test its tolerance. Use 70% of the agreed resources to manage the day-to-day activities of portfolio risk management and use 30% of the remaining resources to manage true surprises.

8.1.3. How to deal with low probability but high impact risks (black swans)?

Black swan theory, develop by Nassim Nicholas Taleb, is used to explain the disproportionate role of high profile, low probability or rare events, often with catastrophic consequences. Phrases such as "100 Year Flood" is often used to describe these rare outliers.

Since portfolio often involves much greater organization resources than program or project level risks, black swan risks also have great impact on the organizations. According to Taleb, there is no easy way to predict black swan events as it is outside the normal awareness. Rather, organizations should develop their ability to come back from such negative consequence. While organization resiliency is important, I propose that portfolio managers can do a much better job of anticipating the unknown. That's why in Section 8.1.2. How to manage them on a sustainable basis? (See above), I recommend dedicating 30% of the resources to manage surprises.

The secret to managing surprises is to raise the awareness of the portfolio risk management team. This is predominantly to increase the flow of information among the portfolio teams, examine outlying events and issues such as increasing the peripheral vision, reducing the tendency to downplay other people's ideas and views, and encouraging the team to question. By raising the team's ability to sense, the team is more likely to identify "unknown unknowns" and convert them progressively to "known unknowns".

8.2. Inputs, Tools & Techniques, Outputs

In conjunction with the discussion on the Portfolio Performance Management, this chapter presents the details of the process's ITTO. Remember the table below:

Processes	Inputs	Tools & Techniques	Outputs
Develop Portfolio Risk Management Plan	1. P. Management Plan 2. P. Process Assets 3. Org Process Assets 4. Enterprise Environmental Factors	1. Weighted Ranking and Scoring Techniques 2. Graphical Analytical Methods 3. Quantitative and Qualitative Analysis	1. P. Management Plan Updates 2. Org Process Assets Updates 3. P. Assets Updates
Manage Portfolio Risk	1. Portfolio 2. P. Management Plan 3. P. Reports 4. P. Process Assets 5. Org Process Assets 6. Enterprise Environmental Factors	1. Weighted Ranking and Scoring Techniques 2. Quantitative and Qualitative Analysis	1. P. Management Plan Updates 2. P. Reports 3. P. Process Assets 4. Org Process Assets Updates

Legend:	Define (No Shade)	Align (Light Gray)	Authorize & Control (Darker Gray)

Table 32: ITTO for Portfolio Risk Management

8.3. Key Concepts for Portfolio Risk Management

Chapter 8 of the Standard contains a number of key risk management concepts that are important for portfolio managers. Most of these are well explained in the Standard. Here are a few additional concepts that require further elaboration and/or clarification.

#	Concept	Description
1	Portfolio Risk Management	Similar to project and program, Portfolio Risk Management deals with uncertain events or conditions, which can be both positive and negative. But unlike project and program risks, portfolio risk management often has greater strategic maneuverability as well as implications. For example, at a portfolio level, organizations can decide to invest in a very high risk component but make sure that it is balanced with other lower risk investments. Also, unlike project and program risks where most of the concerns arise internal to the specific programs and projects, the major portfolio risks are often external to the portfolio, whether they are changes to organization strategies or external environment. For the exam, it is important to remember portfolio risk management is a structured process for managing the portfolios, dealing with interdependencies among its components, and optimizing outcomes for the short, medium, and long term.
2	Risk Manager	Risk management is an integral part of the portfolio standard. With its own knowledge area, the importance of managing risk is self-evident. However, I would like to make a distinction between a "project portfolio manager managing portfolio risk" versus "risk managers or officers" in selective industries such as financial services and information technology. In risk adverse industries, organizations often have specialized risk management functions, just like contract management.

#	Concept	Description
2	Risk Manager (Continued)	Regardless of whether your organization has risk managers, it is important to categorize risks. This way, the boundaries of who should manage the risks become clearer. (See Standard 8.1.3.1 for a sample list of risk categories.) Note: I do not believe this distinction is important for the exam, but it is important in practice. Portfolio managers focus only on the risks affecting the portfolio, and they may need to work with dedicated risk managers to tackle risks at an organizational level.
3	Sensitivity analysis	While sensitivity analysis is also utilized for projects and programs, this analysis is likely to be more important for portfolio management because of the broader organizational impact. The Standard provides an illustration of a tornado diagram (Figure 8-10) as an illustrative output of the sensitivity analysis. Other concepts that may appear on the exam include simulation and the Monte Carlo technique.

Table 33: Key Concepts from the Standard Chapter 8 on Portfolio Risk Management

8.4. Examples of Portfolio Risk Tools and Techniques

The Standard provides many good examples of portfolio tools and techniques for Portfolio Risk Management. This section provides a few additional ones that may appear on the PfMP exam. Remember, the PfMP exam materials come from not just the Standard; the exam is designed to encompass the current and common project portfolio management practices.

8.4.1. Risk Levels

Risks are prevalent in portfolios, and they have the tendency to shift across different levels of organization (as discussed in Table 11: Organization Operating Level – An Abstract Depiction on page 45).

To properly manage portfolio risks, it is important to understand this dynamic of shifting across levels. It is therefore important for portfolio managers to develop a framework to evaluate, prioritize, and manage risks by its appropriate level within the organization.

Below is an example indicating the organization level in which certain risks should be managed.

#	Level	Description
1	Organizational / Inter-portfolios	Responsible for the overall culture of managing risks in organizations. Organizational assets from this level are primary inputs to portfolio management. Business executives and leadership may be required to manage risks across multiple portfolios, naturally with input from the portfolio managers.
2	Portfolio	Responsible for customizing and configuring the organization risk management approach to the portfolio, which will likely contain unique elements. Portfolio managers should be prepared to address risks between programs and projects.
3	Inter-component	Risks that are shared between multiple portfolio components may be more effectively managed at the portfolio level.
4	Intra-component	Program, project, and operational risks are typically more effectively managed within the respective teams. Portfolio managers may need to be involved to make sure of the agreement with the risk management approach.

1. For Operations Management, what are example(s) of risk?

    A. Processes needed to support change

    B. Product / project development

    C. Organization products and services

    D. All of the answer choices

2. What tools and techniques can be applied during the Develop Portfolio Risk Management Plan process?

    A. Elicitation techniques, graphical analytical methods, quantitative and qualitative analysis

    B. Feasibility study, scenario analysis, portfolio component inventory

    C. Elicitation techniques, portfolio management information system, communication requirements analysis, communication methods

    D. Weighted ranking and scoring techniques, graphical analytical methods, quantitative and qualitative analysis

3. Blue Fox Technologies is developing a new smartphone which has some features that have never been implemented before by another smartphone manufacturer. The executives at the company realize that being the first to market is a huge advantage and decide to go forward with releasing their smartphone despite many risks including the fact that the market may not accept the new product. What is this an example of?

    A. Risk probability assessment

    B. The difference between portfolio level risk and program or project level risk

    C. Mitigating risk

    D. Outcome probability analysis

4. Kate has nearly finished the Manage Portfolio Risks process. During the process, there were a series of governance recommendations made. What does Kate need to do to reflect these recommendations?

    A. Portfolio process assets

    B. Enterprise environmental factors

    C. Portfolio management plan

    D. Portfolio reports

5. Project risk is defined as:

    A. An uncertain event or condition, that if it occurs, the corresponding effects may have a positive or negative impact on one or more portfolio success criteria

    B. An uncertain event or condition, that if it occurs, the corresponding effects can be catastrophic one or more portfolio success criteria

    C. An uncertain event or condition , that if it occurs, the corresponding effects may have a negative impact on multiple portfolio success criteria

    D. An uncertain event or condition , that if it occurs, the corresponding effects may have a positive or negative impact on multiple portfolio success criteria

6. Becky is working on the Develop Portfolio Risk Management Plan process. She is currently using a tool which provides her with an outcome probability analysis of the portfolio. What tool is Becky using?

    A. Status analysis

    B. Rebalancing methods

    C. Portfolio risk exposure chart

    D. Trade-off analysis

7. Kelly is about to start working on the Develop Portfolio Risk Management Plan process. She has the portfolio management plan and portfolio process assets. What is she missing?

    A. Portfolio roadmap, portfolio

    B. Organization process assets, enterprise environmental factors

C. Enterprise environmental factors, portfolio reports

D. Portfolio, organization process assets

8. Which of the following are considered key elements in portfolio risk management?

    A. Risk response

    B. Risk Planning

    C. Risk assessment

    D. All of the answer choices

9. In the process which of the following is not a tool or technique?

    A. SWOT

    B. Weighted ranking and scoring techniques

    C. Quantitative analysis

    D. Qualitative analysis

10. Heather is working on the Develop Portfolio Risk Management Plan process. She is currently determining the likelihood of occurrence for each specific risk along with the potential effect. What analysis tool is Heather applying?

    A. Status analysis

    B. Probability and impact matrix

    C. Trend analysis

    D. Watch list

1. For Operations Management, what are example(s) of risk? (Easy)

    A. Processes needed to support change

    B. Product / project development

    C. Organization products and services

    D. All of the answer choices

> The correct answer is **D**. Refer to Section 8 of the Standard for Portfolio Management - 3rd Edition. Review the descriptions and definition.

2. What tools and techniques can be applied during the Develop Portfolio Risk Management Plan process? (Moderate)

    A. Elicitation techniques, graphical analytical methods, quantitative and qualitative analysis

    B. Feasibility study, scenario analysis, portfolio component inventory

    C. Elicitation techniques, portfolio management information system, communication requirements analysis, communication methods

    D. Weighted ranking and scoring techniques, graphical analytical methods, quantitative and qualitative analysis

> The correct answer is **D**. Refer to Section 8/Figure 8-1 of the Standard for Portfolio Management - 3rd Edition. Review the descriptions and definition.

3. Blue Fox Technologies is developing a new smartphone which has some features that have never been implemented before by another smartphone manufacturer. The executives at the company realize that being the first to market is a huge advantage and decide to go forward with releasing their smartphone despite many risks including the fact that the market may not accept the new product. What is this an example of? (Difficult)

    A. Risk probability assessment

    B. The difference between portfolio level risk and program or project level risk

    C. Mitigating risk

    D. Outcome probability analysis

> The correct answer is **B**. Per the Standard, the situation described illustrates that at the portfolio level organizations may choose to actively embrace risk in anticipation of high rewards
>
> .
>
> Refer to Section 8 of the Standard for Portfolio Management - 3rd Edition. Review the descriptions and definition.

4. Kate has nearly finished the Manage Portfolio Risks process. During the process, there were a series of governance recommendations made. What does Kate need to do to reflect these recommendations? (Difficult)

   A. Portfolio process assets

   B. Enterprise environmental factors

   C. Portfolio management plan

   D. Portfolio reports

   > The correct answer is **D**. Governance recommendations are part of portfolio reports.
   >
   > Refer to Section 8.2.3.2 of the Standard for Portfolio Management - 3rd Edition. Review the descriptions and definition.

5. Project risk is defined as: (Moderate)

   A. An uncertain event or condition, that if it occurs, the corresponding effects may have a positive or negative impact on one or more portfolio success criteria

   B. An uncertain event or condition, that if it occurs, the corresponding effects can be catastrophic one or more portfolio success criteria

   C. An uncertain event or condition , that if it occurs, the corresponding effects may have a negative impact on multiple portfolio success criteria

   D. An uncertain event or condition , that if it occurs, the corresponding effects may have a positive or negative impact on multiple portfolio success criteria

   > The correct answer is **A**. Refer to Section 8 of the Standard for Portfolio Management - 3rd Edition. Review the descriptions and definition.

6. Becky is working on the Develop Portfolio Risk Management Plan process. She is currently using a tool which provides her with an outcome probability analysis of the portfolio. What tool is Becky using? (Difficult)

A. Status analysis

B. Rebalancing methods

C. Portfolio risk exposure chart

D. Trade-off analysis

> The correct answer is **C**. Outcome probability analysis of the portfolio is gleaned from the portfolio risk exposure chart
> .
>
> Refer to Section 8.1.2.3 of the Standard for Portfolio Management - 3rd Edition. Review the descriptions and definition.

7. Kelly is about to start working on the Develop Portfolio Risk Management Plan process. She has the portfolio management plan and portfolio process assets. What is she missing? (Difficult)

A. Portfolio roadmap, portfolio

B. Organization process assets, enterprise environmental factors

C. Enterprise environmental factors, portfolio reports

D. Portfolio, organization process assets

> The correct answer is **B**. Inputs to Develop Portfolio Risk Management Plan
> .
>
> Refer to Section 8/Figure 8-1 of the Standard for Portfolio Management - 3rd Edition. Review the descriptions and definition.

8. Which of the following are considered key elements in portfolio risk management? (Moderate)

A. Risk response

B. Risk Planning

C. Risk assessment

D. All of the answer choices

> The correct answer is **D**. Refer to Section 8 of the Standard for Portfolio Management - 3rd Edition. Review the descriptions and definition.

9. In the Manage Portfolio Risksprocess which of the following is not a tool or technique? (Moderate)

   A. SWOT

   B. Weighted ranking and scoring techniques

   C. Quantitative analysis

   D. Qualitative analysis

> The correct answer is **A**. Refer to Section 8.2 of the Standard for Portfolio Management - 3rd Edition. Review the descriptions and definition.

10. Heather is working on the Develop Portfolio Risk Management Plan process. She is currently determining the likelihood of occurrence for each specific risk along with the potential effect. What analysis tool is Heather applying? (Easy)

   A. Status analysis

   B. Probability and impact matrix

   C. Trend analysis

   D. Watch list

> The correct answer is **B**. Refer to Section 8.1.2.2 of the Standard for Portfolio Management - 3rd Edition. Review the descriptions and definition.

Chapter 9: Practice Exams

This chapter contains two full exams of 170 questions each. To simulate the testing environment, please provide yourself with 4 full hours. You are allowed only blank paper and pencil or pen.

9.1. Practice Exam 1

9.1.1. Questions

1. The Aligning Process Group:

    A. How portfolio components will be evaluated in the portfolio

    B. How portfolio components will be categorized in the portfolio

    C. How portfolio components will be selected for inclusion in the portfolio

    D. All of the answer choices

2. You are currently engaged in working with focus groups and brainstorming activities to develop the portfolio management plan. What best describes what you are doing?

    A. Facilitation techniques

    B. Portfolio organizational structure analysis

    C. Survey techniques

    D. Collaboration techniques

3. The Authorizing and Controlling Process Group:

    A. Consists of the processes for determining how to authorize the portfolio

    B. Consists of processes for selecting components to the portfolio

    C. Consists of the processes for determining how to authorize the portfolio and providing ongoing oversight of the portfolio

    D. Consists of the processes for providing ongoing portfolio oversight

4. Ben comes to you for advice. He understands that there is a strategic management process but is unsure of what stage in the process he is in. He is currently doing a strategic alignment analysis. What phase is he in?

    A. Define Portfolio Roadmap

    B. Develop Portfolio Charter

    C. Manage Strategic Change

    D. Develop Portfolio Strategic Plan

5. The development of the Portfolio Strategic Plan process includes the following outputs:

    A. Portfolio strategic plan

    B. Portfolio charter

    C. Portfolio Roadmap

    D. None of the answer choices

6. How does a portfolio manager address the function of marketing?

    A. Analyzing resources and budget

    B. Not a factor as portfolio managers look at multiple areas

    C. Analyzing Market opportunity

    D. Analyzing Market opportunity and competitive advantage

7. The following are all examples of categories that the portfolio component along with its key descriptors can be assigned to except:

    A. Efficiency improvement

    B. Strategic improvement

    C. Process improvement

    D. Continuous improvement

8. Rob has just started working on the Develop Portfolio Risk Management Plan process. He is trying to find information on roles and responsibilities for conducting risk management. Where can Rob find this information?

    A. Portfolio management plan

    B. Enterprise environmental factors

    C. Organizational process assets

    D. Portfolio process assets

9. You have been asked to complete a portfolio roadmap. What do you need to start the process?

    A. Portfolio strategic plan, portfolio charter, portfolio management plan

    B. Portfolio process assets, portfolio charter, readiness assessment

    C. Portfolio charter, portfolio, portfolio process assets

    D. Portfolio strategic plan, portfolio charter, portfolio

10. How is success measured for portfolio management?

    A. Just generically in terms of how successful the portfolio is

    B. In terms of the aggregate investment performance and benefit realization of the portfolio

    C. Whether it satisfies the needs and benefits for which the portfolio was initially undertaken

    D. As measured by the success of the managers

11. How is the portfolio strategic plan used within the Define Portfolio process?

    A. It is used to describe the approach and intent of management in identifying, approving, and procuring portfolio components

    B. It is not used in this process

    C. It is used to align the portfolio with organizational strategy and objectives including the use of the prioritization model

D. It is used to identify and categorize qualified portfolio components

12. How is portfolio value defined?

    A. It is defined as the aggregate value delivered by the portfolio components

    B. It is defined only by quantitative metrics

    C. It is defined by the implementation success of its components

    D. It is defined only in terms of financial value such as revenue growth and increased operating margins

13. How is SWOT analysis used within the Manage Portfolio Value process?

    A. It is used to score and measure organizational value

    B. It is used to measure revenue growth and operating margins

    C. It is used to show the cause and effect relationships between portfolio components

    D. It is used to elicit information to ensure benefits are comprehensively and holistically taken into consideration

14. Lee is working on the Develop Portfolio Communication Management Plan process. He is trying to determine the optimal type of communication for the stakeholders. Which process involved in a stakeholder analysis will help Lee make this assessment?

    A. Assigning stakeholders into groups and classifying them as external or internal

    B. Assigning stakeholders into groups and classifying them as critical or non-critical

    C. Assigning stakeholders into groups and classifying them as influential or non-influential

    D. Assigning stakeholders into groups and classifying them as key or executive

15. All of the following are key descriptors of portfolio components that a portfolio manager may make use of except:

    A. Portfolio component description

    B. Portfolio component number

    C. Portfolio component code

D. Portfolio component list

16. The portfolio of operational projects links a subset of recurring activities managed as projects to the organizations':

    A. Tactics

    B. Finances

    C. Planning

    D. Strategy

17. The portfolio manager must have expertise in ALL of the following application and analysis of quantitative and qualitative techniques except:

    A. Opportunity management

    B. Internal risk management

    C. Managing profit and loss

    D. External risk management

18. The portfolio management plan contains which of the following?

    A. Managing compliance

    B. Procurement procedures

    C. Portfolio prioritization model

    D. All of the answer choices

19. The portfolio strategic plan key contents are:

    A. High level prioritization

    B. Portfolio prioritization model

    C. Decision making framework

    D. All of the answer choices

20. The portfolio strategic plan:

   A. Is a key source to ensure the organization will meet its objectives

   B. Has nothing to do with the portfolio

   C. Is a key source to ensure the organization will meet its project demands

   D. Is a key source to ensure the organization will meet its financial obligations

21. The portfolio performance management plan is a subsidiary plan. What is it a subsidiary plan of?

   A. Portfolio process assets

   B. Portfolio roadmap

   C. Portfolio management plan

   D. Enterprise environmental factors

22. The portfolio management plan defines all of the following for the risk management plan except:

   A. Process asset risk

   B. Risk categories

   C. Stakeholder risk tolerances

   D. Definition of probability and impact

23. The risk management plan can be a component of which of the following?

   A. Portfolio management plan

   B. Project management plan

   C. Program management plan

   D. All of the answer choices

24. Tina has recently started working on the Manage Supply and Demand process. She is trying to find the guidelines for reporting delays due to a constraint on resources. Where can Tina find this information?

    A. Portfolio reports

    B. Portfolio roadmap

    C. Portfolio

    D. Portfolio management plan

25. Gina is ready to apply tools and techniques within the Optimize Portfolio process. What tools and techniques are typically applied during this process?

    A. Weighted ranking and scoring techniques, portfolio component inventory, graphical analytical methods

    B. Portfolio component categorization techniques, readiness assessment, enterprise environmental factors

    C. Portfolio component categorization techniques, portfolio component inventory, weighted ranking and scoring techniques

    D. Capability and capacity analysis, weighted ranking and scoring techniques, quantitative and qualitative analysis, graphical analytical methods

26. In a simple prioritization model, what can scoring elements be based on?

    A. Strategic alignment, financial costs, risks, and dependencies

    B. Enterprise environmental factors, portfolio process assets, portfolio strategic plan

    C. Financial costs, risks, scenario analysis

    D. All of the answer choices

27. A sample of risk categories in the risk management plan includes all of the following except:

    A. Financial/Budget and Resource risk

    B. Portfolio component risk

    C. Market and Regulatory risk

D. Risk impact

28. Brianna comes to you for advice and believes she has completed the Manage Portfolio Information process. She shows you that she has completed portfolio reports. What is she missing?

    A. Portfolio management plan updates, portfolio process assets updates

    B. Portfolio charter updates, portfolio process assets updates

    C. Portfolio charter updates, portfolio management plan updates

    D. Portfolio roadmap updates, portfolio process assets updates

29. Negative risks not identified and treated become:

    A. Measurable

    B. Worse

    C. Impacts

    D. Issues

30. Vince comes to you for advice. He recently started working on his portfolio roadmap but he is noticing that not all of his portfolio components are identified. How would you advise Vince?

    A. That roadmaps may not provide details of all identified portfolio components, but can be used to build details later

    B. That roadmaps focus on the detailed aspects of the portfolio components and that all components should be clearly detailed

    C. That roadmaps show components at a high level and very few portfolio components have any detail

    D. None of the answer choices

31. Bryce has been tasked to develop a portfolio strategic plan. Bryce is struggling with where to start. What should Bryce use as a good starting point?

A. Enterprise environmental factors, portfolio component inventory, organizational process assets

B. Portfolio charter, portfolio roadmap, organizational strategy and objectives

C. Prioritization analysis, portfolio process assets, portfolio roadmap

D. Organizational strategy and objectives, inventory of work, portfolio process assets

32. Process Assets include which of the following:

A. Information on Integrated Schedules

B. Information on component proposals

C. Information on risk and performance data

D. All of the answer choices

33. Which best describes risk tolerance?

A. Organization's willingness to develop comprehensive risk management plan

B. Organization's willingness to accept risk

C. Threshold or attitude of the organization towards the positive or negative effects of risk on the portfolio

D. Threshold or attitude of the organization towards the negative effects of risk on the portfolio

34. Which of the following does not impact strategy relative to a portfolio plan?

A. Allocating human and financial resources

B. Maintaining portfolio alignment

C. Managing risk

D. Evaluation of a project or program manager

35. Which of the following services does a portfolio management office NOT provide to a program or project management office:

A. Define portfolio management standards

B. Define portfolio management best practices

C. Formulating project and program management standards

D. Formulate organizational standards

36. Which of the following is an interaction with a portfolio management process group?

A. Organizational strategy and objectives

B. Organization financial plan

C. Organization Tactics

D. None of the answer choices

37. Process Assets include which of the following:

A. Information on techniques, models and tools

B. Information on techniques

C. Information on models

D. None of the answer choices

38. Which of the four Portfolio Strategic Management processes enables the portfolio manager to make changes in organizational strategy and to enhance the ability to accept and and act on significant strategic change that impacts portfolio planning and management?

A. Manage Portfolio Change

B. Manage Strategic Change

C. Manage Strategic Planning

D. Manage Portfolio Strategy

39. Which of the following is the least important evaluation criterion that a portfolio manager should use?

A. External risks

B. Internal risks

C. Legal/regulatory compliance

D. Subjective risks

40. Which of the following is not an example of a portfolio report?

    A. Project status report

    B. Value or benefits report

    C. Portfolio status report

    D. Capability report

41. Which of the following quantitative or qualitative tools and techniques are applicable for optimizing a portfolio?

    A. Business value analysis

    B. Cost-benefit analysis

    C. Market/competitor analysis

    D. All of the answer choices

42. Which of the following can be a Portfolio Management Information System?

    A. Enterprise portfolio systems

    B. Excel-based tools

    C. Resource database

    D. All of the answer choices

43. Which of the following activities are performed during the Provide Portfolio Oversight process?

    A. Conducting recurring and nonrecurring governance meetings for reviews and decision making

B. Reporting portfolio changes and information on resources, risks, performance, and financials

C. Reviewing information on portfolio resources, risks, performance, and financial information

D. All of the answer choices

44. Which of the following is a Portfolio Performance Management process?

A. Manage supply and demand

B. Manage the portfolio progress

C. Manage portfolio assets

D. Manage portfolio financials

45. Which of the following are examples of resource capability and capability management analysis?

A. Finite capacity planning and reporting

B. Resource types

C. Resource schedules

D. All of the answer choices

46. Dashboards are:

A. Effective way to communicate multiple messages on portfolio risk and trending simultaneously

B. Effective way to communicate multiple messages on portfolio communication and trending simultaneously

C. Effective way to communicate multiple messages on portfolio plan and trending simultaneously

D. Effective way to communicate multiple messages on portfolio status and trending simultaneously

47. Which of the following are examples of value scoring and measurement analysis?

    A. Value measurement techniques

    B. Cost-benefit analysis

    C. Scoring models

    D. All of the answer choices

48. Which of the following is not a Tool or Technique for the Develop Portfolio Communication Management Plan?

    A. SWOT

    B. Stakeholder analysis

    C. Communication requirements analysis

    D. Elicitation techniques

49. Which of the following is a classification of stakeholders?

    A. Critical, non-critical

    B. Key, non-key

    C. Influential, non-influential

    D. Internal, external

50. Which of the following is not a tool or technique for the Manage Portfolio Information process?

    A. Elicitation techniques

    B. SWOT

    C. Portfolio management information system

    D. Communication methods and requirements analysis

51. Which of the following are examples of risk conditions that may exist in an organization's environment that may contribute to portfolio risk?

A. Integrated management systems

B. Poor management practices

C. Excessive number of concurrent projects

D. All of the answer choices

52. Which of the following Enterprise Environmental Factors as inputs to planning for risk management is least relevant?

   A. Market research

   B. Academic studies

   C. Benchmarking

   D. None of the answer choices

53. Which of the following are investment choice tools?

   A. Market-payoff variability

   B. Trade-off analysis

   C. Performance variability analysis

   D. All of the answer choices

54. Which process within portfolio communication management executes the communication plan by collecting data, translating data into meaningful information, and supplying it to identified stakeholders in a timely manner?

   A. Manage Communication

   B. Provide Communication Oversight

   C. Develop Portfolio Communication Management Plan

   D. Manage Portfolio Information

55. Mitchell is a portfolio manager and is currently working on the Develop Portfolio Management Plan. He comes to you for advice. Mitchell knows that he needs to plan to

develop and report on predefined and preapproved metrics. However, Mitchell isn't sure what these metrics are used to monitor. How would you advise him?

A. I would tell Mitchell that the metrics are used to monitor strategic goal achievement, financial contribution, stakeholder satisfaction, risk profile, and resource utilization

B. I would tell Mitchell that the metrics are mainly used to monitor profitability

C. I would advise Mitchell that the metrics are mainly used to determine if portfolio components are having a positive or negative influence on the portfolio

D. I would advise Mitchell that the metrics are used almost exclusively to monitor resource utilization

56. In creating a Stakeholder Matrix for use in Stakeholder Analysis, which of the following is not analyzed?

A. Stakeholder interests

B. Stakeholder roles

C. Stakeholder assets

D. Stakeholder expectations

57. To define the management of strategic change the following inputs are needed:

A. Portfolio

B. Portfolio strategic plan

C. Portfolio charter

D. All of the answer choices

58. What role does the portfolio charter play in the Manage Strategic Change process?

A. The original charter should only be consulted to ensure that the strategic goals are still in alignment with the original charter

B. The charter does not play a role in this process

C. The charter does not get updated and is static once it is created

D. The original or revised charter should be reviewed to ensure that the charter and portfolio remain in alignment are updated as required

59. Dwayne is currently working on the Manage Supply and Demand process. He is currently in the process of studying skill sets and certifications and trying to match them up against the portfolio's objectives and goals to try to meet the portfolio demands as much as possible. What type of analysis is Dwayne performing?

    A. Quantitative and qualitative analysis

    B. Trend analysis

    C. Scenario analysis

    D. Capability and capacity analysis

60. In developing the portfolio for the Portfolio Governance Model, which of the following is not a tool or technique?

    A. Portfolio process assets

    B. Weighted ranking and scoring techniques

    C. Portfolio component inventory

    D. Component categorization

61. In developing the process for Optimize the Portfolio, which of the following is not a tool or technique?

    A. Graphical analytic methods

    B. Capability and capacity analysis

    C. Quantitative and qualitative analysis

    D. Mathematical modeling

62. Cindy is working on developing the portfolio charter. As she is working on the charter, she keeps finding different constraints in the form of corporate and government policies. What is Cindy describing?

    A. The impact of portfolio process assets

B. The impact of a portfolio roadmap

C. The impact of a scenario analysis

D. The impact of enterprise environmental factors

63. Some examples of internal risks include all of the following except:

    A. Funding reallocation

    B. Natural events

    C. Bankruptcy

    D. Corporate / organizational realignments

64. Once the Portfolio Strategic Plan is developed, it should contain which of the following key contents?

    A. Key assumptions, resources required, measurable goals, scenario analysis

    B. Resources required by type and quantity, risk tolerance, portfolio strategic plan update, portfolio process assets updates

    C. Portfolio strategic plan, risk tolerance, capability and capacity analysis

    D. Portfolio prioritization model, portfolio benefits, allocation of funds to different types of initiatives, organizational structure and organization areas

65. Jeremy is working on developing a portfolio strategic plan. He is trying to find a tool or technique that will focus on the changing the organizational strategy and objectives and showing where gaps in focus, investment, or alignment exist within the portfolio. What tool and technique should Jeremy use?

    A. Portfolio current inventory

    B. Enterprise environmental factors

    C. Prioritization analysis

    D. Strategic alignment analysis

66. Karen comes to you for advice. She is about to start working on the Manage Portfolio Information process. She has the portfolio and the portfolio management plan. What is Karen missing that she will need to start this process?

A. Portfolio reports, portfolio component reports, portfolio process assets

B. Portfolio charter, organizational process assets, enterprise environmental factors

C. Portfolio component reports, portfolio roadmap, portfolio process assets

D. Enterprise environmental factors, portfolio reports, portfolio charter

67. James has been advised that organization strategy has changed. He understands that he needs to manage this strategic change. What should James ensure that the portfolio remains in alignment with?

A. Portfolio component inventory

B. Stakeholder analysis

C. Readiness assessment

D. Portfolio Strategic Plan

68. Ernest is currently involved in reporting portfolio changes and information on resources, risks, performance, and financials. He is also ensuring compliance with organizational standards. Which portfolio governance process is Ernest involved in?

A. Authorize Portfolio

B. Define Portfolio

C. Optimize Portfolio

D. Provide Portfolio Oversight

69. Performance metrics are the mechanism used for targeting areas of measurement for assessing how the mix or portfolio components are performing. Quantitative measures include all of the following except:

A. NPV

B. CPI

C. ROI

D. IRR

70. Maggie is working on the performance management plan. She knows that there are three key things that she needs to document regarding how the organization plans to measure, monitor, control, and report on them. What are they?

   A. Portfolio performance, resource management, portfolio value

   B. Portfolio management, portfolio value, portfolio status

   C. Portfolio value, portfolio value planning, portfolio management

   D. Resource management, portfolio value, portfolio status

71. Michael is developing a portfolio strategic plan. He is having difficulty understanding the objectives, expected benefits, performance, and prioritization criteria. What tool and technique would you recommend to Michael?

   A. Strategic alignment analysis

   B. Enterprise environmental factors

   C. Prioritization analysis

   D. Portfolio component inventory

72. Perhaps the most common tool used to demonstrate progress is a:

   A. Portfolio Roadmap

   B. Portfolio charter

   C. Portfolio management plan

   D. Portfolio dashboard

73. Which of the following are examples of resource capability and capacity management analysis?

   A. Resource types

   B. What-if scenarios

   C. Resource management tools

D. All of the answer choices

74. Within the Manage Portfolio Risks process, which of the following are fallback plans a risk owner would consider should the originally selected risk strategy not be successful?

    A. Risk methodology, risk roles and responsibilities, risk frequency

    B. Response strategy selection, strategies for both threats and opportunities, scenario analysis

    C. Risk methodology, strategies for both threats and opportunities

    D. Response strategy selection, strategies for both threats and opportunities, risk frequency

75. Within the portfolio strategic plan, what is useful as a decision framework to structure the portfolio components?

    A. Portfolio roadmap

    B. Prioritization model

    C. Scenario analysis

    D. Interdependency analysis

76. Within portfolio performance management, what does portfolio reporting provide?

    A. It enables the portfolio sponsors to quickly understand the status of a portfolio's progress

    B. It provides stakeholders and the governing body with metrics to determine where the portfolio is meeting the organization strategy

    C. It provides those responsible for executing portfolio components with meaningful information on the status of the respective portfolio components in the context of other components and the overall portfolio

    D. All of the answer choices

77. Anthony has come to you for advice. He believes that he has completed the Optimize Portfolio process. However, he doesn't appear to have any of the normal outputs for the process. What should he have?

   A. Portfolio updates, portfolio charter updates, portfolio management plan updates, portfolio reports, portfolio process asset updates

   B. Portfolio charter, portfolio roadmap, portfolio management plan

   C. Portfolio updates, portfolio roadmap updates, portfolio management plan updates

   D. Portfolio updates, portfolio roadmap updates, portfolio management plan updates, portfolio reports, portfolio process asset updates

78. Business value may be created by:

   A. The effective change in present operations

   B. The better costing of projects

   C. The effective management of finances

   D. The effective management of ongoing operations

79. During the alignment of the organizational strategy and objectives, the portfolio manager refers to and is guided by the portfolio's plans, policies, procedures, and guidelines. What is the portfolio manager referencing?

   A. Enterprise environmental factors

   B. Portfolio component inventory

   C. Organizational process assets

   D. Portfolio process assets

80. During the Provide Portfolio Oversight process, Keith holds regular meetings to review the current status of the portfolio and determine if any changes are necessary. What tool and technique is Keith utilizing?

   A. Portfolio authorization process

   B. Business value analysis

   C. Portfolio review meetings

D. Elicitation techniques

81. Christy is working on defining a portfolio roadmap. She needs to use a tool which will identify portfolio dependencies as it relates to other portfolios. What tool and technique should be used?

A. Prioritization analysis

B. Cost-benefit analysis

C. Scenario analysis

D. Interdependency analysis

82. As it relates to the Authorize Portfolio process, what information does the portfolio management plan provide?

A. It describes the process to authorize the portfolio components to allow and reallocate resources and funding and to define the key communication needs within the portfolio management process

B. It is used to describe the approach and intent of management in identifying, approving, and procuring portfolio components

C. It contains relevant data, tools, and templates regarding the portfolio

D. None of the answer choices

83. Ricardo has all of the inputs for the Develop Portfolio Communication Plan. He comes to you for advice as he is overwhelmed with the information and isn't sure where to start in terms of analyzing it. How would you advise Ricardo to proceed in terms of applying tools and techniques?

A. Communication methods, communication requirements analysis

B. Gap analysis, communication methods, portfolio component reports

C. Elicitation techniques, portfolio management information system, communication requirements analysis, communication methods

D. Stakeholder analysis, elicitation techniques, communication requirements analysis

84. Hank runs the portfolio management office within his organization. He is currently working on the Develop Portfolio Management Plan process. Some stakeholders have identified metrics that they believe no longer support organizational strategy. What should Hank do as director of the PMO?

   A. He should eliminate the metrics the stakeholders identified but not add any new ones at this time

   B. He should develop new metrics which better match organizational strategy

   C. He should develop a very large number of new metrics to show the stakeholders that he is trying to create metrics that are better aligned with organizational strategy

   D. He should explain to the stakeholders that the metrics cannot be changed at this point in the process

85. Becky is working on the process of managing strategic change. She has all of the inputs to the process but is unfamiliar with the tools and techniques typically used. What should she be using?

   A. Readiness assessment, stakeholder analysis, prioritization analysis

   B. Stakeholder analysis, gap analysis, readiness assessment

   C. Portfolio process assets, portfolio charter, gap analysis

   D. Stakeholder analysis, gap analysis, capability and capacity analysis

86. Bill is working on the Manage Portfolio Information process. He has all of the inputs to the process. What tools and techniques would Bill typically apply during this process?

   A. Elicitation techniques, portfolio management information system, communication requirements analysis, communication methods

   B. Stakeholder analysis, elicitation techniques, communication requirements analysis

   C. Portfolio management information system, elicitation techniques, communication requirements analysis

   D. Portfolio management information system, communication requirements analysis, communication methods, stakeholder analysis

87. Stella has nearly finished the Manage Portfolio Information process. She knows that she needs to make note of the announcement of an upcoming stakeholder meeting as well as a portfolio manager meeting. Where would Stella document this information?

   A. Portfolio process assets

   B. Portfolio charter

   C. Portfolio management plan

   D. Portfolio reports

88. Kelly has nearly finished the Manage Portfolio Value process. During the process, there were some cost savings forecasted. Kelly knows she needs to document this. Where should she document it?

   A. Portfolio process assets

   B. Portfolio charter

   C. Portfolio management plan

   D. Portfolio reports

89. In Managing Supply and Demand, the term "Demand" refers to:

   A. Resource requirements from the portfolio components and from the component proposals requesting resources

   B. Resource from the component proposals requesting resources

   C. Resource requirements from the portfolio components

   D. Resource requirements from the portfolio components and from the component proposals requesting only financial funding

90. Examples of PMS Tools and Processes include:

   A. Communication management processes and tools

   B. Earned value management processes and tools

   C. Knowledge management tools and processes

   D. All of the answer choices

91. Examples of Portfolio Process Assets used as inputs to plan for risk management include all of the following except:

    A. Portfolio issue register

    B. Portfolio risk register

    C. Portfolio change management register

    D. Portfolio performance matrices

92. When are portfolio process asset updates done?

    A. As an output to the Develop Portfolio Charter process

    B. As an output to the Define Portfolio Roadmap process

    C. As an input to the Develop Portfolio Charter process

    D. As an output to the Develop Portfolio Strategic Plan process

93. When bottleneck resources or resource downtime are identified, what can be applied?

    A. Resource optimization across the portfolio

    B. Resource allocating and project sequencing techniques

    C. Resource minimizing and project ordering techniques

    D. Resource levelling or project sequencing techniques

94. Joan has just started working on the Manage Portfolio Risks process. She is looking for the portfolio risk register. Where would Joan find this information?

    A. Portfolio management plan

    B. Portfolio process assets

    C. Portfolio reports

    D. Portfolio

95. Evan is currently working on the Manage Portfolio Information process. He is currently creating a graphical representation which will allow him to determine if the resulting impact of a priority change is value-added or adverse. What is Evan creating?

    A. Resource histogram

    B. Dashboard

    C. Communication calendar

    D. None of the answer choices

96. When should the portfolio process assets be updated?

    A. If strategic changes have been made which impact portfolio plans and processes, then the portfolio process assets should be updated

    B. If stakeholder engagement, communication management, performance, and risk sections have changed

    C. If management approach, priorities, or organizational structure have changed

    D. None of the answer choices

97. Grant is in the process of conducting a prioritization analysis to make an assessment of which portfolio components need to be added, removed or changed. What process is Grant conducting and what is the likely outcome of the process?

    A. He is in the Develop Portfolio Charter process which will result in the development of a Portfolio Charter

    B. He is in the Manage Strategic Change process which will result in several updates to the Portfolio process and Portfolio roadmap

    C. He is in the Define Portfolio Roadmap process which will result in the creation of the Portfolio roadmap

    D. He is in the Develop Portfolio Strategic Plan process to develop a Strategic Plan.

98. Josey is currently working on the Develop Portfolio Communication Management Plan process. She is currently performing an analysis to determine stakeholders' concerns, interests, and influence. What type of analysis is Josey performing?

    A. Stakeholder analysis

B. Elicitation techniques

C. Prioritization analysis

D. Communication requirements analysis

99. Jacob is currently working on the Manage Portfolio Value process. He is currently holding meetings with stakeholders to assess criteria and to discern the weight assigned to different benefits and outcomes. What tool and technique is Jacob applying?

   A. Elicitation techniques

   B. Quantitative and qualitative analysis

   C. Value scoring and measurement analysis

   D. Benefits realization analysis

100. Tyson has recently started working on the Manage Portfolio Information process. He is trying to find information on portfolio communication requirements including communication technology available and allowed communication media. Where should Tyson look for this information?

   A. Portfolio component reports

   B. Portfolio charter

   C. Portfolio reports

   D. Portfolio process assets

101. Jason has just started working on the Develop Portfolio Communication Management Plan. He has the portfolio and the portfolio roadmap. What else should Jason have to start this process?

   A. Portfolio reports, portfolio management plan, portfolio process assets

   B. Portfolio charter, portfolio component reports, enterprise environmental factors

   C. Portfolio process assets, enterprise environmental factors, portfolio reports

   D. Portfolio reports, portfolio management plan, portfolio charter

102. A tool and technique for managing strategic change is stakeholder analysis. Why is this important?

   A. Helps to ensure continuity and align key stakeholders expectations with the changing strategy and resulting portfolio alignment

   B. Helps to ensure continuity of portfolio management processes

   C. Helps to ensure continuity and align organization expectations with the changing strategy and resulting portfolio alignment

   D. Helps to ensure continuity and align the project plan with the changing strategy and resulting portfolio alignment

103. Conor is currently working on the Provide Portfolio Oversight process. He is currently in the process of conducting a survey. What tool and technique is Conor utilizing?

   A. Elicitation techniques

   B. Portfolio reports

   C. Portfolio authorization process

   D. Portfolio review meetings

104. Resource capability and capacity management analysis includes all of the following except:

   A. Finite capacity planning and reporting

   B. What-if scenarios

   C. Resource management tools

   D. SWOT

105. Stephanie has been asked by senior executives to determine how much work can be accomplished based on the current resources available. What is she being asked to do?

   A. Interdependency analysis

   B. Scenario analysis

   C. Prioritization analysis

D. Capability and capacity analysis

106. In portfolio structural analysis, the portfolio manager should assign what type of reviews?

    A. Performance review of major resource groups such as employees or contractors

    B. Performance review of major project components

    C. Performance review and reporting roles and responsibilities across each program, project or operational component

    D. Performance review of each program, project or operational component

107. In portfolio component categorization technique, which of the following are examples of "Business imperatives" considerations?

    A. IT compatibility

    B. Internal toolkit

    C. IT upgrades

    D. All of the answer choices

108. In portfolio performance management, what is defined as resource capability?

    A. A competency that enables an organization to execute its operational objectives

    B. A competency that enables an organization to execute its charter

    C. A competency that enables an organization to execute its strategy

    D. A specific competency that enables an organization to execute components and deliver results

109. In portfolio reports, what is a sample representation of progress?

    A. Earned value diagram demonstrating the earned value versus planned value

    B. Burn-down or burn-up chart showing the delivery of a component compared to the portfolio's history

C. Burn-down or burn-up chart showing the delivery of a component compared to the portfolio's budget or time

D. Gantt chart demonstrating program or project progress

110. Currently, analysis is being conducted to compare the current portfolio mix and components with the new strategic direction and the "to be" organizational vision. What type of analysis is being performed?

    A. Readiness assessment

    B. Scenario analysis

    C. Prioritization analysis

    D. Gap analysis

111. PMIS can include all of the following except:

    A. Risk Information

    B. Costs

    C. Performance Metrics

    D. Human Resources Information

112. Russell has nearly finished the Manage Portfolio Value process. During the process, changes were made to the reporting process as it relates to how portfolio components are managed. What does Russell need to update to reflect this change?

    A. Portfolio process assets

    B. Portfolio component inventory

    C. Portfolio management plan

    D. Portfolio reports

113. In stakeholder analysis which of the following should be considered?

    A. Assess levels of interest

    B. Assign levels of influence

C. Assess urgency in communication

D. All of the answer choices

114. What are the tools and techniques used during the Develop Portfolio Performance Management plan process?

    A. Elicitation techniques, portfolio management information system, elicitation techniques

    B. Scenario analysis, Capability and capacity analysis, quantitative and qualitative analysis

    C. Scenario analysis, Capability and capacity analysis, portfolio management information system

    D. Elicitation techniques, portfolio management information system, capability and capacity analysis

115. What are the outputs of the Develop Portfolio Performance Management Plan?

    A. Portfolio process assets updates, portfolio updates

    B. Portfolio reports, portfolio updates

    C. Portfolio updates, portfolio reports, portfolio management plan updates

    D. Portfolio management plan updates, portfolio process assets updates

116. What are the types of risk sources?

    A. Extraneous, Outside

    B. Inside, Outside

    C. Internal, Extraneous

    D. Internal, External

117. What are the four stages of the Manage Portfolio Risk process?

    A. Risks are identified, risks are analyzed, risk responses are developed, risks are mitigated

    B. Risks are defined, risks are evaluated, risks are mitigated

C. Risk impact is established, risks are analyzed, risk responses are developed, risks are monitored and controlled

D. Risks are identified, risks are analyzed, risk responses are developed, risks are monitored and controlled

118. What are the outputs of the Develop Portfolio Risk Management Plan process?

A. Portfolio management plan updates, portfolio process assets updates, portfolio roadmap updates

B. Portfolio roadmap updates, portfolio reports

C. Portfolio process assets updates, portfolio reports, organizational process assets updates

D. Portfolio management plan updates, portfolio process assets updates, organizational process assets updates

119. What can be included in the portfolio charter?

A. It may include communication requirements, high-level scope, benefits, critical success criteria, resources, and a high-level timeline

B. It may include portfolio justification, portfolio roadmap, prioritization analysis, and risk tolerance

C. It may include portfolio objectives, portfolio sponsors, Cost-benefit analysis, and assumptions

D. All of the answer choices

120. What information can be learned from the portfolio strategic plan when developing a portfolio management plan?

A. How to allocate resources to develop component proposals, authorizing components to expend resources and to communicate portfolio decisions

B. A high-level graphical overview of portfolio components

C. How to monitor the portfolio to ensure alignment with the organizational strategy and objectives

D. Portfolio objectives, portfolio management organization structure, benefits, prioritization model, and resource information.

121. What comparison should a portfolio manager make when trying to define a portfolio roadmap?

    A. Cost should be compared against the potential benefits

    B. Strategic objectives, priority objectives, and strategic assessment should be compared against current enterprise portfolios

    C. Organizational strategy should be compared to archived enterprise portfolios

    D. Dependencies the portfolio may have should be compared to other portfolios

122. What does portfolio management ensure? (Select the best answer)

    A. Interrelationships among programs and projects are identified with the emphasis on managing risks

    B. Interrelationships among projects is dysfunctional and therefore resources are unnecessary

    C. That a loose relationship among programs and projects is minimal and that resources are up the manager to decide upon

    D. Interrelationships among programs and projects are identified and that resources are allocated with respect to organizational priorities

123. What does the Portfolio Charter authorize the portfolio manager to do?

    A. To develop a Portfolio strategic plan

    B. To perform a Scenario analysis and Compatibility and capacity analysis

    C. To begin working on a portfolio

    D. To apply portfolio resources to portfolio components and to execute the portfolio management process

124. What information can you expect to find in the portfolio performance management plan?

A. Performance reporting

B. Goals, objectives, strategies, and tactics

C. Resource optimization

D. All of the answer choices

125. What is a Portfolio?

   A. Collection of financial reports related to a specific project or program

   B. Collection of programs, projects, or operations managed as a group to achieve strategic objectives

   C. Collection of programs, projects, or operations managed as a group, but not necessarily to achieve tactical business objectives

   D. Collection of programs and projects aligned with strategic objectives

126. What is the process in both the knowledge area Portfolio Governance Management and the Aligning Process Group?

   A. Optimize portfolio

   B. Authorize portfolio

   C. Optimize project plan

   D. None of the answer choices

127. What is/are the process(es) in both the knowledge area Portfolio Risk Management and the Aligning Process Group:

   A. Manage portfolio risks

   B. Manage financial risk

   C. Manage project risk

   D. None of the answer choices

128. What is the portfolio manager generally responsible for updating and adding to the portfolio process assets?

A. Historical Info

B. Portfolio component files

C. Lessons Learned

D. All of the answer choices

129. What is a key element in producing the Portfolio Strategic Plan?

    A. Portfolio roadmap

    B. Strategic change

    C. Portfolio charter

    D. Organizational strategy and objectives

130. What is the result of the Develop Portfolio Charter process?

    A. Portfolio charter, portfolio strategic plan updates, interdependency analysis

    B. Scenario analysis, capability and capacity analysis

    C. Portfolio strategic plan, portfolio process assets, enterprise environmental factors

    D. Portfolio strategic plan updates, portfolio charter, portfolio process assets updates

131. What is contained in the portfolio roadmap?

    A. Program and project level roadmaps

    B. Program level roadmaps only

    C. Project level roadmaps only

    D. Project level roadmaps outside of the portfolio scope

132. What is one of the key differences between portfolio management and project management as it relates to strategic change?

    A. Change in portfolios follows a similar process as that for change in projects

    B. Frequent change in portfolio management and project management is a common occurrence

C. Changes in project management are a fairly common occurrence where a great deal of elaboration is not required whereas progress elaboration is required with changes in portfolio management

D. Change in portfolios is a normal occurrence and portfolio documents may be reworked where progressive elaboration is required in project management

133. What is required to create the portfolio management plan?

   A. Portfolio assets

   B. Portfolio project plan

   C. Portfolio management plan

   D. Portfolio charter

134. What is generally considered the responsibility of the portfolio manager during the portfolio management processes?

   A. Updating and adding to the portfolio process assets, as necessary

   B. Updating and adding to the prioritization analysis

   C. Updating the Cost-benefit analysis

   D. None of the answer choices

135. What is a typical collaboration technique?

   A. Polling team members by way of anonymous electronic voting

   B. Short memo

   C. Polling the organization

   D. Talking amongst the project team

136. What is the importance of weighted ranking and scoring techniques?

   A. Provide a technique which the stakeholders can rate portfolio components based on their criteria

   B. Provide a subjective technique to rank portfolio components

C. Provide a technique to rank the mandatory components of a portfolio

D. Provide an objective technique to rank portfolio components

137. What is the benefit of a scoring model?

    A. It evaluates portfolio components and makes them comparable

    B. It assigns a financial score to portfolio components

    C. It ranks portfolio components and determines their usefulness

    D. It compares portfolio components and determines their weight

138. What is involved in the Optimize Portfolio process?

    A. Identifying qualified portfolio components to determine whether or not a particular component should be part of the portfolio

    B. Assigning portfolio components to predetermined categories to compare those which address similar organizational needs

    C. Evaluating portfolios based on the organization's business objectives, ranking the portfolio, and creating the ideal portfolio with the greatest potential to support organizational strategy

    D. Evaluating the portfolio based on the organization's selection criteria, ranking the portfolio components, and creating the portfolio component mix with the greatest potential to support organizational strategy

139. What is portfolio performance management?

    A. The systematic planning, measurement, and monitoring of the portfolio's organizational value through achievement against these strategic goals

    B. The integration of subsidiary plans such as performance communication, and risk management plans

    C. The organizational strategy and objectives which provide long-term direction, vision, goals, and objectives

    D. The guiding artifact that establishes portfolio-level dependencies and constraints to allow for effective oversight

140. What is the acronym used for the guideline for measures of portfolio performance management?

A. SWOT

B. SAT

C. SWAT

D. SMART

141. What is the SMART guideline used to help develop?

A. Resource schedules

B. KPIs

C. Resource types

D. Performance measures

142. What is a scenario analysis within the context of the Manage Supply and Demand process?

A. It is an analysis technique used to determine various possibilities of resource allocations and the impact to component schedules

B. It is an analysis technique used to document and assess intangible portfolio benefits

C. It includes various approaches to studying the demand for resources against capacity and constraints to determine how to best allocate resources

D. It studies the capability of resources and matches them against the portfolio's objectives and goals

143. What is done during the Manage Portfolio Information process?

A. Collecting, analyzing, storing, and delivering portfolio information to stakeholders

B. Policies and practices for optimizing portfolio value including revenue growth and increased operating margins are established

C. Stakeholders are identified, different individuals and groups are determined along with their concerns, interests, and influences

D. All of the answer choices

144. What is the main importance of utilizing a histogram?

    A. Portfolio manager needs to determine if the changing organization priorities are value-added or adverse to portfolio assets

    B. Portfolio manager needs to determine if the changing organization priorities are going to result in a scope change request

    C. Portfolio manager needs to determine if the changing organization priorities are beneficial to the project

    D. Portfolio manager needs to determine if the changing organization priorities are value-added or adverse to portfolio performance

145. What is a more likely example of a positive portfolio risk?

    A. Key project cost performance indices (CPI) are less than 1

    B. Major competitor's product launch earlier than expected

    C. Regulatory change tightened requirements for a major project in the portfolio

    D. A major competitor's product launch failed

146. What is the best tool or technique used to assess key risks?

    A. Informal discussions

    B. Phone calls

    C. Emails

    D. Interviews and Meetings

147. What processes are part of portfolio communication management?

    A. Develop Portfolio Communication Management Plan, Provide Communication Oversight

B. Manage Communication, Provide Communication Oversight

C. Develop Portfolio Communication Management Plan, Manage Portfolio Information

D. Manage Communication, Develop Portfolio Communication Management Plan

148. What requires updating when a change takes place?

A. Portfolio management plan

B. Portfolio charter

C. Portfolio Roadmap

D. Portfolio Roadmap and Portfolio Management Plan

149. To define the management of strategic change the following tools and techniques are needed:

A. Gap analysis

B. Stakeholder analysis

C. Readiness Assessment

D. All of the answer choices

150. What tools and techniques are used during the Develop Portfolio Strategic Plan process?

A. Portfolio component inventory, prioritization analysis, organizational strategy and objectives

B. Portfolio charter, portfolio roadmap, organizational strategy and objectives

C. Organizational strategy and objectives, inventory of work, portfolio process assets

D. Portfolio component inventory, Strategic alignment analysis, prioritization analysis

151. What tools and techniques are used during the Manage Strategic Change process?

A. Interdependency analysis, prioritization analysis, gap analysis

B. Scenario analysis, capability and capacity analysis, prioritization analysis

C. Cost-benefit analysis, readiness assessment, stakeholder analysis

D. Stakeholder analysis, gap analysis, readiness assessment

152. What tools and techniques can be applied during the Manage Supply and Demand process?

    A. Capability and capacity analysis, value scoring and measurement analysis

    B. Elicitation techniques, Benefits realization analysis, scenario analysis

    C. Scenario analysis, quantitative and qualitative analysis, elicitation techniques

    D. Scenario analysis, quantitative and qualitative analysis, capability and capacity analysis

153. What tools and techniques are typically applied during the Manage Portfolio Risks process?

    A. Graphical analytical methods, quantitative and qualitative analysis

    B. Elicitation techniques, quantitative and qualitative analysis

    C. Weighted ranking and scoring techniques, graphical analytical methods, quantitative and qualitative analysis

    D. Weighted ranking and scoring techniques, quantitative and qualitative analysis

154. What triggers a portfolio review meeting? All of the following except:

    A. Project scope changes

    B. Financial drivers

    C. Regulatory changes

    D. Completion of significant portfolio components or deliverables

155. What type of process is the development of the portfolio management plan?

    A. Iterative

    B. Recursive

    C. Agile

D. Incremental

156. What type of portfolio reports are consulted during the Authorize Portfolio process?

A. Governance decisions

B. Financials/funding

C. Resources

D. All of the answer choices

157. Portfolio Management processes are started in an organization as a response to all of the following except:

A. constrained resources

B. Issues / conflicts

C. uncertainty

D. strategic objective uncertainty

158. Portfolio process assets provide which of the following:

A. Guidance for defining the portfolio charter

B. Guidance for defining the portfolio budget

C. Guidance for defining portfolio priorities

D. Guidance for defining portfolio components

159. Portfolio value for an organization can be expressed as:

A. Enhancement or protection of reputation and branding

B. Contribution to the community

C. Protection of environmental resources

D. All of the answer choices

160. Portfolio communication management is closely aligned with all of the following management processes except:

A. Risk

B. Strategic

C. Financial

D. Governance

161. Portfolio communication facilitates an effective two-way dialogue between which of the affected internal and external stakeholders, individuals or groups?

A. Governing & regulatory bodies

B. Executive managers

C. Operations managers

D. All of the answer choices

162. At the conclusion of the Manage Portfolio Value process, what type of changes can cause the portfolio management plan to need to be updated?

A. New measurement processes

B. New reporting processes

C. New portfolio component management process

D. All of the answer choices

163. In the development of the Portfolio Risk Management Plan, which technique is most preferable to evaluate risk of multiple portfolios?

A. Capability and capacity analysis

B. Prioritization algorithms

C. Weighted ranking and scoring

D. Elicitation techniques

164. In the Manage Portfolio Risks process which of the following is not an input?

    A. Portfolio Management Plan

    B. Portfolio

    C. Portfolio Financial Plan

    D. Portfolio Reports

165. Is there acceptable risk in portfolio risk management?

    A. Maybe, depending on risk tolerance of the portfolio manager

    B. No, there is no place of uncertainty in a portfolio

    C. Yes, risk is inherent in all investments

    D. Maybe, depending on the risk tolerance of the organization

166. Matthew is working on managing strategic change. He is presently reviewing documentation which highlights the intended approach of managing the portfolio and its components to meet organizational strategy. What is he reviewing?

    A. Portfolio management plan

    B. Project management plan

    C. Portfolio roadmap

    D. Portfolio charter

167. Dustin is currently working on the Manage Portfolio Value process. He is currently running an analysis to compare a portfolio component against a future alternative. What type of analysis is Dustin performing?

    A. Progress measurement techniques

    B. Portfolio efficient frontier

    C. Comparative advantage analysis

    D. Cost-benefit analysis

168. Travis comes to you for advice. He believes he has completed the Develop Portfolio Performance Management Plan process. He tells you that he updated the portfolio process assets. What should Travis have also updated?

    A. Enterprise environmental factors

    B. Portfolio management plan

    C. Portfolio roadmap

    D. Portfolio

169. Troy is about to start working on the Manage Supply and Demand process. He has received some advice from his supervisor that the stakeholders are starting to lose interest in the current initiative. Troy realizes he needs to engage the stakeholders. Where can Troy find the plan for stakeholder engagement?

    A. Portfolio

    B. Portfolio charter

    C. Portfolio management plan

    D. Portfolio reports

170. To define the management of strategic change the following outputs are needed:

    A. Portfolio process assets updates

    B. Portfolio roadmap updates

    C. Portfolio management plan updates

    D. All of the answer choices

9.1.2. Questions and Answers

1. The Aligning Process Group: (Moderate)

    A. How portfolio components will be evaluated in the portfolio

    B. How portfolio components will be categorized in the portfolio

    C. How portfolio components will be selected for inclusion in the portfolio

    D. All of the answer choices

> The correct answer is **D**. Refer to Section 3.1 of the Standard for Portfolio Management - 3rd Edition. Review the descriptions and definition.

2. You are currently engaged in working with focus groups and brainstorming activities to develop the portfolio management plan. What best describes what you are doing? (Difficult)

   A. Facilitation techniques

   B. Portfolio organizational structure analysis

   C. Survey techniques

   D. Collaboration techniques

> The correct answer is **A**. Refer to Section 5.1.2.1 of the Standard for Portfolio Management - 3rd Edition. Review the descriptions and definition.

3. The Authorizing and Controlling Process Group: (Moderate)

   A. Consists of the processes for determining how to authorize the portfolio

   B. Consists of processes for selecting components to the portfolio

   C. Consists of the processes for determining how to authorize the portfolio and providing ongoing oversight of the portfolio

   D. Consists of the processes for providing ongoing portfolio oversight

> The correct answer is **C**. Refer to Section 3.1 of the Standard for Portfolio Management - 3rd Edition. Review the descriptions and definition.

4. Ben comes to you for advice. He understands that there is a strategic management process but is unsure of what stage in the process he is in. He is currently doing a strategic alignment analysis. What phase is he in? (Moderate)

   A. Define Portfolio Roadmap

   B. Develop Portfolio Charter

   C. Manage Strategic Change

   D. Develop Portfolio Strategic Plan

The correct answer is **D**. Refer to Section 4.1 of the Standard for Portfolio Management - 3rd Edition. Review the descriptions and definition.

5. The development of the Portfolio Strategic Plan process includes the following outputs: (Moderate)

   A. Portfolio strategic plan

   B. Portfolio charter

   C. Portfolio Roadmap

   D. None of the answer choices

   The correct answer is **A**. Refer to Section 4.1 of the Standard for Portfolio Management - 3rd Edition. Review the descriptions and definition.

6. How does a portfolio manager address the function of marketing? (Moderate)

   A. Analyzing resources and budget

   B. Not a factor as portfolio managers look at multiple areas

   C. Analyzing Market opportunity

   D. Analyzing Market opportunity and competitive advantage

   The correct answer is **D**. Refer to Section 1.7 of the Standard for Portfolio Management - 3rd Edition. Review the descriptions and definition.

7. The following are all examples of categories that the portfolio component along with its key descriptors can be assigned to except: (Moderate)

   A. Efficiency improvement

   B. Strategic improvement

   C. Process improvement

   D. Continuous improvement

   The correct answer is **B**. Refer to Section 5.2.2.2 of the Standard for Portfolio Management - 3rd Edition. Review the descriptions and definition.

8. Rob has just started working on the Develop Portfolio Risk Management Plan process. He is trying to find information on roles and responsibilities for conducting risk management. Where can Rob find this information? (Moderate)

   A. Portfolio management plan

   B. Enterprise environmental factors

   C. Organizational process assets

   D. Portfolio process assets

   > The correct answer is **A**. Roles and responsibilities are defined in the portfolio management plan.
   > Refer to Section 8.1.1.1 of the Standard for Portfolio Management - 3rd Edition. Review the descriptions and definition.

9. You have been asked to complete a portfolio roadmap. What do you need to start the process? (Moderate)

   A. Portfolio strategic plan, portfolio charter, portfolio management plan

   B. Portfolio process assets, portfolio charter, readiness assessment

   C. Portfolio charter, portfolio, portfolio process assets

   D. Portfolio strategic plan, portfolio charter, portfolio

   > The correct answer is **D**. Refer to Section 4.3 of the Standard for Portfolio Management - 3rd Edition. Review the descriptions and definition.

10. How is success measured for portfolio management? (Easy)

   A. Just generically in terms of how successful the portfolio is

   B. In terms of the aggregate investment performance and benefit realization of the portfolio

   C. Whether it satisfies the needs and benefits for which the portfolio was initially undertaken

   D. As measured by the success of the managers

   > The correct answer is **B**. Refer to Section 1.3 of the Standard for Portfolio Management - 3rd Edition. Review the descriptions and definition.

11. How is the portfolio strategic plan used within the Define Portfolio process? (Moderate)

   A. It is used to describe the approach and intent of management in identifying, approving, and procuring portfolio components

   B. It is not used in this process

   C. It is used to align the portfolio with organizational strategy and objectives including the use of the prioritization model

   D. It is used to identify and categorize qualified portfolio components

   > The correct answer is **C**. Refer to Section 5.2.1.1 of the Standard for Portfolio Management - 3rd Edition. Review the descriptions and definition.

12. How is portfolio value defined? (Moderate)

   A. It is defined as the aggregate value delivered by the portfolio components

   B. It is defined only by quantitative metrics

   C. It is defined by the implementation success of its components

   D. It is defined only in terms of financial value such as revenue growth and increased operating margins

   > The correct answer is **A**. Refer to Section 6.3 of the Standard for Portfolio Management - 3rd Edition. Review the descriptions and definition.

13. How is SWOT analysis used within the Manage Portfolio Value process? (Moderate)

   A. It is used to score and measure organizational value

   B. It is used to measure revenue growth and operating margins

   C. It is used to show the cause and effect relationships between portfolio components

   D. It is used to elicit information to ensure benefits are comprehensively and holistically taken into consideration

   > The correct answer is **D**. Refer to Section 6.3 of the Standard for Portfolio Management - 3rd Edition. Review the descriptions and definition.

14. Lee is working on the Develop Portfolio Communication Management Plan process. He is trying to determine the optimal type of communication for the stakeholders. Which process involved in a stakeholder analysis will help Lee make this assessment? (Difficult)

    A. Assigning stakeholders into groups and classifying them as external or internal

    B. Assigning stakeholders into groups and classifying them as critical or non-critical

    C. Assigning stakeholders into groups and classifying them as influential or non-influential

    D. Assigning stakeholders into groups and classifying them as key or executive

    > The correct answer is **A**. This is identified in the Standard as a key part of a stakeholder analysis.
    > Refer to Section 7.1.2.1 of the Standard for Portfolio Management - 3rd Edition. Review the descriptions and definition.

15. All of the following are key descriptors of portfolio components that a portfolio manager may make use of except: (Moderate)

    A. Portfolio component description

    B. Portfolio component number

    C. Portfolio component code

    D. Portfolio component list

    > The correct answer is **D**. Refer to Section 5.2.2.1 of the Standard for Portfolio Management - 3rd Edition. Review the descriptions and definition.

16. The portfolio of operational projects links a subset of recurring activities managed as projects to the organizations': (Moderate)

    A. Tactics

    B. Finances

    C. Planning

    D. Strategy

    > The correct answer is **D**. Refer to Section 1.7 of the Standard for Portfolio Management - 3rd Edition. Review the descriptions and definition.

17. The portfolio manager must have expertise in ALL of the following application and analysis of quantitative and qualitative techniques except: (Easy)

    A. Opportunity management

    B. Internal risk management

    C. Managing profit and loss

    D. External risk management

    > The correct answer is **C**. Refer to Section 1.8 of the Standard for Portfolio Management - 3rd Edition. Review the descriptions and definition.

18. The portfolio management plan contains which of the following? (Easy)

    A. Managing compliance

    B. Procurement procedures

    C. Portfolio prioritization model

    D. All of the answer choices

    > The correct answer is **D**. Refer to Section 3.2 of the Standard for Portfolio Management - 3rd Edition. Review the descriptions and definition.

19. The portfolio strategic plan key contents are: (Moderate)

    A. High level prioritization

    B. Portfolio prioritization model

    C. Decision making framework

    D. All of the answer choices

    > The correct answer is **D**. Refer to Section 4.1 of the Standard for Portfolio Management - 3rd Edition. Review the descriptions and definition.

20. The portfolio strategic plan: (Moderate)

    A. Is a key source to ensure the organization will meet its objectives

    B. Has nothing to do with the portfolio

C. Is a key source to ensure the organization will meet its project demands

D. Is a key source to ensure the organization will meet its financial obligations

> The correct answer is **A**. Refer to Section 5.2.1 of the Standard for Portfolio Management - 3rd Edition. Review the descriptions and definition.

21. The portfolio performance management plan is a subsidiary plan. What is it a subsidiary plan of? (Easy)

   A. Portfolio process assets

   B. Portfolio roadmap

   C. Portfolio management plan

   D. Enterprise environmental factors

> The correct answer is **C**. Refer to Section 6.1 of the Standard for Portfolio Management - 3rd Edition. Review the descriptions and definition.

22. The portfolio management plan defines all of the following for the risk management plan except: (Moderate)

   A. Process asset risk

   B. Risk categories

   C. Stakeholder risk tolerances

   D. Definition of probability and impact

> The correct answer is **A**. Refer to Section 8.1.1.1 of the Standard for Portfolio Management - 3rd Edition. Review the descriptions and definition.

23. The risk management plan can be a component of which of the following? (Moderate)

   A. Portfolio management plan

   B. Project management plan

   C. Program management plan

   D. All of the answer choices

The correct answer is **D**. Refer to Section 8.1 of the Standard for Portfolio Management - 3rd Edition. Review the descriptions and definition.

24. Tina has recently started working on the Manage Supply and Demand process. She is trying to find the guidelines for reporting delays due to a constraint on resources. Where can Tina find this information? (Moderate)

    A. Portfolio reports

    B. Portfolio roadmap

    C. Portfolio

    D. Portfolio management plan

    The correct answer is **D**. The high level guidelines for these types of situations are found in the portfolio management plan.
    Refer to Section 6.2.1.2 of the Standard for Portfolio Management - 3rd Edition. Review the descriptions and definition.

25. Gina is ready to apply tools and techniques within the Optimize Portfolio process. What tools and techniques are typically applied during this process? (Moderate)

    A. Weighted ranking and scoring techniques, portfolio component inventory, graphical analytical methods

    B. Portfolio component categorization techniques, readiness assessment, enterprise environmental factors

    C. Portfolio component categorization techniques, portfolio component inventory, weighted ranking and scoring techniques

    D. Capability and capacity analysis, weighted ranking and scoring techniques, quantitative and qualitative analysis, graphical analytical methods

    The correct answer is **D**. Tools and techniques defined in The Standard for Optimize Portfolio.
    Refer to Section 5.3 of the Standard for Portfolio Management - 3rd Edition. Review the descriptions and definition.

26. In a simple prioritization model, what can scoring elements be based on? (Moderate)

    A. Strategic alignment, financial costs, risks, and dependencies

B. Enterprise environmental factors, portfolio process assets, portfolio strategic plan

C. Financial costs, risks, scenario analysis

D. All of the answer choices

> The correct answer is **A**. Refer to Section 4.1.2.3 of the Standard for Portfolio Management - 3rd Edition. Review the descriptions and definition.

27. A sample of risk categories in the risk management plan includes all of the following except: (Moderate)

   A. Financial/Budget and Resource risk

   B. Portfolio component risk

   C. Market and Regulatory risk

   D. Risk impact

> The correct answer is **D**. Refer to Section 8.1.3.1 of the Standard for Portfolio Management - 3rd Edition. Review the descriptions and definition.

28. Brianna comes to you for advice and believes she has completed the Manage Portfolio Information process. She shows you that she has completed portfolio reports. What is she missing? (Moderate)

   A. Portfolio management plan updates, portfolio process assets updates

   B. Portfolio charter updates, portfolio process assets updates

   C. Portfolio charter updates, portfolio management plan updates

   D. Portfolio roadmap updates, portfolio process assets updates

> The correct answer is **A**. Outputs of Manage Portfolio Information.
> Refer to Section 7/Figure 7-1 of the Standard for Portfolio Management - 3rd Edition. Review the descriptions and definition.

29. Negative risks not identified and treated become: (Moderate)

   A. Measurable

   B. Worse

C. Impacts

D. Issues

> The correct answer is **D**. Refer to Section 8.2.1.1 of the Standard for Portfolio Management - 3rd Edition. Review the descriptions and definition.

30. Vince comes to you for advice. He recently started working on his portfolio roadmap but he is noticing that not all of his portfolio components are identified. How would you advise Vince? (Difficult)

    A. That roadmaps may not provide details of all identified portfolio components, but can be used to build details later

    B. That roadmaps focus on the detailed aspects of the portfolio components and that all components should be clearly detailed

    C. That roadmaps show components at a high level and very few portfolio components have any detail

    D. None of the answer choices

    > The correct answer is **A**. Refer to Section 4.3 of the Standard for Portfolio Management - 3rd Edition. Review the descriptions and definition.

31. Bryce has been tasked to develop a portfolio strategic plan. Bryce is struggling with where to start. What should Bryce use as a good starting point? (Difficult)

    A. Enterprise environmental factors, portfolio component inventory, organizational process assets

    B. Portfolio charter, portfolio roadmap, organizational strategy and objectives

    C. Prioritization analysis, portfolio process assets, portfolio roadmap

    D. Organizational strategy and objectives, inventory of work, portfolio process assets

    > The correct answer is **D**. Refer to Section 4.1 of the Standard for Portfolio Management - 3rd Edition. Review the descriptions and definition.

32. Process Assets include which of the following: (Easy)

    A. Information on Integrated Schedules

B. Information on component proposals

C. Information on risk and performance data

D. All of the answer choices

> The correct answer is **D**. Refer to Section 3.2 of the Standard for Portfolio Management - 3rd Edition. Review the descriptions and definition.

33. Which best describes risk tolerance? (Moderate)

    A. Organization's willingness to develop comprehensive risk management plan

    B. Organization's willingness to accept risk

    C. Threshold or attitude of the organization towards the positive or negative effects of risk on the portfolio

    D. Threshold or attitude of the organization towards the negative effects of risk on the portfolio

> The correct answer is **C**. Refer to Section 8 of the Standard for Portfolio Management - 3rd Edition. Review the descriptions and definition.

34. Which of the following does not impact strategy relative to a portfolio plan? (Moderate)

    A. Allocating human and financial resources

    B. Maintaining portfolio alignment

    C. Managing risk

    D. Evaluation of a project or program manager

> The correct answer is **D**. Refer to Section 1.5 of the Standard for Portfolio Management - 3rd Edition. Review the descriptions and definition.

35. Which of the following services does a portfolio management office NOT provide to a program or project management office: (Moderate)

    A. Define portfolio management standards

    B. Define portfolio management best practices

    C. Formulating project and program management standards

D. Formulate organizational standards

> The correct answer is **D**. Refer to Section 1.9 of the Standard for Portfolio Management - 3rd Edition. Review the descriptions and definition.

36. Which of the following is an interaction with a portfolio management process group? (Easy)

    A. Organizational strategy and objectives

    B. Organization financial plan

    C. Organization Tactics

    D. None of the answer choices

> The correct answer is **A**. Refer to Section 3.2 of the Standard for Portfolio Management - 3rd Edition. Review the descriptions and definition.

37. Process Assets include which of the following:

    A. Information on techniques, models and tools

    B. Information on techniques

    C. Information on models

    D. None of the answer choices

> The correct answer is **A**. Refer to Section 3.2 of the Standard for Portfolio Management - 3rd Edition. Review the descriptions and definition.

38. Which of the four Portfolio Strategic Management processes enables the portfolio manager to make changes in organizational strategy and to enhance the ability to accept and and act on significant strategic change that impacts portfolio planning and management? (Easy)

    A. Manage Portfolio Change

    B. Manage Strategic Change

    C. Manage Strategic Planning

    D. Manage Portfolio Strategy

> The correct answer is **B**. Refer to Section 4.4 of the Standard for Portfolio Management - 3rd Edition. Review the descriptions and definition.

39. Which of the following is the least important evaluation criterion that a portfolio manager should use? (Moderate)

    A. External risks

    B. Internal risks

    C. Legal/regulatory compliance

    D. Subjective risks

    > The correct answer is **D**. Refer to Section 5.2.2 of the Standard for Portfolio Management - 3rd Edition. Review the descriptions and definition.

40. Which of the following is not an example of a portfolio report? (Moderate)

    A. Project status report

    B. Value or benefits report

    C. Portfolio status report

    D. Capability report

    > The correct answer is **A**. Refer to Section 5.3.1 of the Standard for Portfolio Management - 3rd Edition. Review the descriptions and definition.

41. Which of the following quantitative or qualitative tools and techniques are applicable for optimizing a portfolio? (Moderate)

    A. Business value analysis

    B. Cost-benefit analysis

    C. Market/competitor analysis

    D. All of the answer choices

    > The correct answer is **D**. Refer to Section 5.3.2.3 of the Standard for Portfolio Management - 3rd Edition. Review the descriptions and definition.

42. Which of the following can be a Portfolio Management Information System? (Easy)

    A. Enterprise portfolio systems

    B. Excel-based tools

    C. Resource database

    D. All of the answer choices

    > The correct answer is **D**. Refer to Section 5.4.2.2 of the Standard for Portfolio Management - 3rd Edition. Review the descriptions and definition.

43. Which of the following activities are performed during the Provide Portfolio Oversight process? (Moderate)

    A. Conducting recurring and nonrecurring governance meetings for reviews and decision making

    B. Reporting portfolio changes and information on resources, risks, performance, and financials

    C. Reviewing information on portfolio resources, risks, performance, and financial information

    D. All of the answer choices

    > The correct answer is **D**. Refer to Section 5.5 of the Standard for Portfolio Management - 3rd Edition. Review the descriptions and definition.

44. Which of the following is a Portfolio Performance Management process? (Moderate)

    A. Manage supply and demand

    B. Manage the portfolio progress

    C. Manage portfolio assets

    D. Manage portfolio financials

    > The correct answer is **A**. Refer to Section 6 of the Standard for Portfolio Management - 3rd Edition. Review the descriptions and definition.

45. Which of the following are examples of resource capability and capability management analysis? (Moderate)

A. Finite capacity planning and reporting

B. Resource types

C. Resource schedules

D. All of the answer choices

> The correct answer is **D**. Refer to Section 6.1.2.3 of the Standard for Portfolio Management - 3rd Edition. Review the descriptions and definition.

46. Dashboards are: (Moderate)

A. Effective way to communicate multiple messages on portfolio risk and trending simultaneously

B. Effective way to communicate multiple messages on portfolio communication and trending simultaneously

C. Effective way to communicate multiple messages on portfolio plan and trending simultaneously

D. Effective way to communicate multiple messages on portfolio status and trending simultaneously

> The correct answer is **D**. Refer to Section 7.2.2.4 of the Standard for Portfolio Management - 3rd Edition. Review the descriptions and definition.

47. Which of the following are examples of value scoring and measurement analysis? (Moderate)

A. Value measurement techniques

B. Cost-benefit analysis

C. Scoring models

D. All of the answer choices

> The correct answer is **D**. Refer to Section 6.3.2.2 of the Standard for Portfolio Management - 3rd Edition. Review the descriptions and definition.

48. Which of the following is not a Tool or Technique for the Develop Portfolio Communication Management Plan? (Moderate)

A. SWOT

B. Stakeholder analysis

C. Communication requirements analysis

D. Elicitation techniques

> The correct answer is **A**. Refer to Section 7.1 of the Standard for Portfolio Management - 3rd Edition. Review the descriptions and definition.

49. Which of the following is a classification of stakeholders? (Easy)

    A. Critical, non-critical

    B. Key, non-key

    C. Influential, non-influential

    D. Internal, external

> The correct answer is **D**. Refer to Section 7.1.2.1 of the Standard for Portfolio Management - 3rd Edition. Review the descriptions and definition.

50. Which of the following is not a tool or technique for the Manage Portfolio Information process? (Moderate)

    A. Elicitation techniques

    B. SWOT

    C. Portfolio management information system

    D. Communication methods and requirements analysis

> The correct answer is **B**. Refer to Section 7.2 of the Standard for Portfolio Management - 3rd Edition. Review the descriptions and definition.

51. Which of the following are examples of risk conditions that may exist in an organization's environment that may contribute to portfolio risk? (Moderate)

    A. Integrated management systems

    B. Poor management practices

    C. Excessive number of concurrent projects

D. All of the answer choices

> The correct answer is **D**. Refer to Section 8 of the Standard for Portfolio Management - 3rd Edition. Review the descriptions and definition.

52. Which of the following Enterprise Environmental Factors as inputs to planning for risk management is least relevant? (Moderate)

    A. Market research

    B. Academic studies

    C. Benchmarking

    D. None of the answer choices

> The correct answer is **D**. Refer to Section 8.1.1.4 of the Standard for Portfolio Management - 3rd Edition. Review the descriptions and definition.

53. Which of the following are investment choice tools? (Moderate)

    A. Market-payoff variability

    B. Trade-off analysis

    C. Performance variability analysis

    D. All of the answer choices

> The correct answer is **D**. Refer to Section 8.1.2.3 of the Standard for Portfolio Management - 3rd Edition. Review the descriptions and definition.

54. Which process within portfolio communication management executes the communication plan by collecting data, translating data into meaningful information, and supplying it to identified stakeholders in a timely manner? (Easy)

    A. Manage Communication

    B. Provide Communication Oversight

    C. Develop Portfolio Communication Management Plan

    D. Manage Portfolio Information

55. Mitchell is a portfolio manager and is currently working on the Develop Portfolio
Management Plan. He comes to you for advice. Mitchell knows that he needs to plan to
develop and report on predefined and preapproved metrics. However, Mitchell isn't sure
what these metrics are used to monitor. How would you advise him? (Difficult)

   A. I would tell Mitchell that the metrics are used to monitor strategic goal achievement,
      financial contribution, stakeholder satisfaction, risk profile, and resource utilization

   B. I would tell Mitchell that the metrics are mainly used to monitor profitability

   C. I would advise Mitchell that the metrics are mainly used to determine if portfolio
      components are having a positive or negative influence on the portfolio

   D. I would advise Mitchell that the metrics are used almost exclusively to monitor
      resource utilization

   The correct answer is **A**. Metrics are used to monitor strategic goal
   achievement, financial contribution, stakeholder satisfaction, risk profile, and
   resource utilization.
   Refer to Section 6.1.2.1 of the Standard for Portfolio Management - 3rd
   Edition. Review the descriptions and

56. In creating a Stakeholder Matrix for use in Stakeholder Analysis, which of the following is
not analyzed? (Moderate)

   A. Stakeholder interests

   B. Stakeholder roles

   C. Stakeholder assets

   D. Stakeholder expectations

   The correct answer is **C**. Refer to Section 7.1.2.1 of the Standard for Portfolio
   Management - 3rd Edition. Review the descriptions and definition.

57. To define the management of strategic change the following inputs are needed:
(Moderate)

   A. Portfolio

B. Portfolio strategic plan

C. Portfolio charter

D. All of the answer choices

> The correct answer is **D**. Refer to Section 4.1 of the Standard for Portfolio Management - 3rd Edition. Review the descriptions and definition.

58. What role does the portfolio charter play in the Manage Strategic Change process? (Easy)

   A. The original charter should only be consulted to ensure that the strategic goals are still in alignment with the original charter

   B. The charter does not play a role in this process

   C. The charter does not get updated and is static once it is created

   D. The original or revised charter should be reviewed to ensure that the charter and portfolio remain in alignment are updated as required

> The correct answer is **D**. Refer to Section 4.4.1.2 of the Standard for Portfolio Management - 3rd Edition. Review the descriptions and definition.

59. Dwayne is currently working on the Manage Supply and Demand process. He is currently in the process of studying skill sets and certifications and trying to match them up against the portfolio's objectives and goals to try to meet the portfolio demands as much as possible. What type of analysis is Dwayne performing? (Difficult)

   A. Quantitative and qualitative analysis

   B. Trend analysis

   C. Scenario analysis

   D. Capability and capacity analysis

> The correct answer is **D**. The situation describes a study of capability and capacity.
> Refer to Section 6.2.2.3 of the Standard for Portfolio Management - 3rd Edition. Review the descriptions and definition.

60. In developing the portfolio for the Portfolio Governance Model, which of the following is not a tool or technique? (Moderate)

A. Portfolio process assets

B. Weighted ranking and scoring techniques

C. Portfolio component inventory

D. Component categorization

> The correct answer is **A**. Refer to Section 5.1 of the Standard for Portfolio Management - 3rd Edition. Review the descriptions and definition.

61. In developing the process for Optimize the Portfolio, which of the following is not a tool or technique? (Moderate)

    A. Graphical analytic methods

    B. Capability and capacity analysis

    C. Quantitative and qualitative analysis

    D. Mathematical modeling

> The correct answer is **D**. Refer to Section 5.1 of the Standard for Portfolio Management - 3rd Edition. Review the descriptions and definition.

62. Cindy is working on developing the portfolio charter. As she is working on the charter, she keeps finding different constraints in the form of corporate and government policies. What is Cindy describing? (Moderate)

    A. The impact of portfolio process assets

    B. The impact of a portfolio roadmap

    C. The impact of a scenario analysis

    D. The impact of enterprise environmental factors

> The correct answer is **D**. Refer to Section 4.2.1.3 of the Standard for Portfolio Management - 3rd Edition. Review the descriptions and definition.

63. Some examples of internal risks include all of the following except: (Easy)

    A. Funding reallocation

    B. Natural events

C. Bankruptcy

D. Corporate / organizational realignments

> The correct answer is **B**. Refer to Section 8 of the Standard for Portfolio Management - 3rd Edition. Review the descriptions and definition.

64. Once the Portfolio Strategic Plan is developed, it should contain which of the following key contents? (Difficult)

    A. Key assumptions, resources required, measurable goals, scenario analysis

    B. Resources required by type and quantity, risk tolerance, portfolio strategic plan update, portfolio process assets updates

    C. Portfolio strategic plan, risk tolerance, capability and capacity analysis

    D. Portfolio prioritization model, portfolio benefits, allocation of funds to different types of initiatives, organizational structure and organization areas

> The correct answer is **D**. Refer to Section 4.1.3.1 of the Standard for Portfolio Management - 3rd Edition. Review the descriptions and definition.

65. Jeremy is working on developing a portfolio strategic plan. He is trying to find a tool or technique that will focus on the changing the organizational strategy and objectives and showing where gaps in focus, investment, or alignment exist within the portfolio. What tool and technique should Jeremy use? (Moderate)

    A. Portfolio current inventory

    B. Enterprise environmental factors

    C. Prioritization analysis

    D. Strategic alignment analysis

> The correct answer is **D**. Refer to Section 4.1.2.2 of the Standard for Portfolio Management - 3rd Edition. Review the descriptions and definition.

66. Karen comes to you for advice. She is about to start working on the Manage Portfolio Information process. She has the portfolio and the portfolio management plan. What is Karen missing that she will need to start this process? (Difficult)

    A. Portfolio reports, portfolio component reports, portfolio process assets

B. Portfolio charter, organizational process assets, enterprise environmental factors

C. Portfolio component reports, portfolio roadmap, portfolio process assets

D. Enterprise environmental factors, portfolio reports, portfolio charter

> The correct answer is **A**. Inputs to Manage Portfolio Information.
> Refer to Section 7/Figure 7-1 of the Standard for Portfolio Management - 3rd Edition. Review the descriptions and definition.

67. James has been advised that organization strategy has changed. He understands that he needs to manage this strategic change. What should James ensure that the portfolio remains in alignment with? (Moderate)

A. Portfolio component inventory

B. Stakeholder analysis

C. Readiness assessment

D. Portfolio Strategic Plan

> The correct answer is **D**. Refer to Section 4.4.1.2 of the Standard for Portfolio Management - 3rd Edition. Review the descriptions and definition.

68. Ernest is currently involved in reporting portfolio changes and information on resources, risks, performance, and financials. He is also ensuring compliance with organizational standards. Which portfolio governance process is Ernest involved in? (Difficult)

A. Authorize Portfolio

B. Define Portfolio

C. Optimize Portfolio

D. Provide Portfolio Oversight

> The correct answer is **D**. The two activities described are done during Provide Portfolio Oversight.
> Refer to Section 5.5 of the Standard for Portfolio Management - 3rd Edition. Review the descriptions and definition.

69. Performance metrics are the mechanism used for targeting areas of measurement for assessing how the mix or portfolio components are performing.   Quantitative measures include all of the following except: (Easy)

   A. NPV

   B. CPI

   C. ROI

   D. IRR

   > The correct answer is **B**. Refer to Section 6 of the Standard for Portfolio Management - 3rd Edition. Review the descriptions and definition.

70. Maggie is working on the performance management plan. She knows that there are three key things that she needs to document regarding how the organization plans to measure, monitor, control, and report on them. What are they? (Difficult)

   A. Portfolio performance, resource management, portfolio value

   B. Portfolio management, portfolio value, portfolio status

   C. Portfolio value, portfolio value planning, portfolio management

   D. Resource management, portfolio value, portfolio status

   > The correct answer is **A**. This is defined in the Standard where it states that the performance management plan documents how the organization plans to measures, monitor and control portfolio performance, resource management, and portfolio value.
   > Refer to Section 6.1 of the Standa

71. Michael is developing a portfolio strategic plan. He is having difficulty understanding the objectives, expected benefits, performance, and prioritization criteria. What tool and technique would you recommend to Michael? (Difficult)

   A. Strategic alignment analysis

   B. Enterprise environmental factors

   C. Prioritization analysis

   D. Portfolio component inventory

72. Perhaps the most common tool used to demonstrate progress is a: (Easy)

    A. Portfolio Roadmap

    B. Portfolio charter

    C. Portfolio management plan

    D. Portfolio dashboard

73. Which of the following are examples of resource capability and capacity management analysis? (Moderate)

    A. Resource types

    B. What-if scenarios

    C. Resource management tools

    D. All of the answer choices

74. Within the Manage Portfolio Risks process, which of the following are fallback plans a risk owner would consider should the originally selected risk strategy not be successful? (Difficult)

    A. Risk methodology, risk roles and responsibilities, risk frequency

    B. Response strategy selection, strategies for both threats and opportunities, scenario analysis

    C. Risk methodology, strategies for both threats and opportunities

    D. Response strategy selection, strategies for both threats and opportunities, risk frequency

> The correct answer is **B**. Per the Standard, a risk owner should have a fallback plan for execution if the originally selected strategy is not successful.
> Refer to Section 8.2.2.2 of the Standard for Portfolio Management - 3rd Edition. Review the descriptions and definition.

75. Within the portfolio strategic plan, what is useful as a decision framework to structure the portfolio components? (Moderate)

    A. Portfolio roadmap

    B. Prioritization model

    C. Scenario analysis

    D. Interdependency analysis

    > The correct answer is **B**. Refer to Section 4.2.1.1 of the Standard for Portfolio Management - 3rd Edition. Review the descriptions and definition.

76. Within portfolio performance management, what does portfolio reporting provide? (Difficult)

    A. It enables the portfolio sponsors to quickly understand the status of a portfolio's progress

    B. It provides stakeholders and the governing body with metrics to determine where the portfolio is meeting the organization strategy

    C. It provides those responsible for executing portfolio components with meaningful information on the status of the respective portfolio components in the context of other components and the overall portfolio

    D. All of the answer choices

    > The correct answer is **D**. Refer to Section 6.1 of the Standard for Portfolio Management - 3rd Edition. Review the descriptions and definition.

77. Anthony has come to you for advice. He believes that he has completed the Optimize Portfolio process. However, he doesn't appear to have any of the normal outputs for the process. What should he have? (Difficult)

    A. Portfolio updates, portfolio charter updates, portfolio management plan updates, portfolio reports, portfolio process asset updates

B. Portfolio charter, portfolio roadmap, portfolio management plan

C. Portfolio updates, portfolio roadmap updates, portfolio management plan updates

D. Portfolio updates, portfolio roadmap updates, portfolio management plan updates, portfolio reports, portfolio process asset updates

> The correct answer is **D**. Outputs of the Optimize Portfolio.
> Refer to Section 5.3 of the Standard for Portfolio Management - 3rd Edition.
> Review the descriptions and definition.

78. Business value may be created by: (Easy)

    A. The effective change in present operations

    B. The better costing of projects

    C. The effective management of finances

    D. The effective management of ongoing operations

> The correct answer is **D**. Refer to Section 1.6 of the Standard for Portfolio Management - 3rd Edition. Review the descriptions and definition.

79. During the alignment of the organizational strategy and objectives, the portfolio manager refers to and is guided by the portfolio's plans, policies, procedures, and guidelines. What is the portfolio manager referencing? (Moderate)

    A. Enterprise environmental factors

    B. Portfolio component inventory

    C. Organizational process assets

    D. Portfolio process assets

> The correct answer is **D**. Refer to Section 4.1.1.3 of the Standard for Portfolio Management - 3rd Edition. Review the descriptions and definition.

80. During the Provide Portfolio Oversight process, Keith holds regular meetings to review the current status of the portfolio and determine if any changes are necessary. What tool and technique is Keith utilizing? (Easy)

    A. Portfolio authorization process

B. Business value analysis

C. Portfolio review meetings

D. Elicitation techniques

> The correct answer is **C**. Refer to Section 5.5.2.2 of the Standard for Portfolio Management - 3rd Edition. Review the descriptions and definition.

81. Christy is working on defining a portfolio roadmap. She needs to use a tool which will identify portfolio dependencies as it relates to other portfolios. What tool and technique should be used? (Easy)

A. Prioritization analysis

B. Cost-benefit analysis

C. Scenario analysis

D. Interdependency analysis

> The correct answer is **D**. Refer to Section 4.3.2.1 of the Standard for Portfolio Management - 3rd Edition. Review the descriptions and definition.

82. As it relates to the Authorize Portfolio process, what information does the portfolio management plan provide? (Moderate)

A. It describes the process to authorize the portfolio components to allow and reallocate resources and funding and to define the key communication needs within the portfolio management process

B. It is used to describe the approach and intent of management in identifying, approving, and procuring portfolio components

C. It contains relevant data, tools, and templates regarding the portfolio

D. None of the answer choices

> The correct answer is **A**. Refer to Section 5.4.1.2 of the Standard for Portfolio Management - 3rd Edition. Review the descriptions and definition.

83. Ricardo has all of the inputs for the Develop Portfolio Communication Plan. He comes to you for advice as he is overwhelmed with the information and isn't sure where to start in

terms of analyzing it. How would you advise Ricardo to proceed in terms of applying tools and techniques? (Moderate)

A. Communication methods, communication requirements analysis

B. Gap analysis, communication methods, portfolio component reports

C. Elicitation techniques, portfolio management information system, communication requirements analysis, communication methods

D. Stakeholder analysis, elicitation techniques, communication requirements analysis

> The correct answer is **D**. Tools and techniques of Develop Portfolio Communication Management Plan.
> Refer to Section 7/Figure 7-1 of the Standard for Portfolio Management - 3rd Edition. Review the descriptions and definition.

84. Hank runs the portfolio management office within his organization. He is currently working on the Develop Portfolio Management Plan process. Some stakeholders have identified metrics that they believe no longer support organizational strategy. What should Hank do as director of the PMO? (Difficult)

A. He should eliminate the metrics the stakeholders identified but not add any new ones at this time

B. He should develop new metrics which better match organizational strategy

C. He should develop a very large number of new metrics to show the stakeholders that he is trying to create metrics that are better aligned with organizational strategy

D. He should explain to the stakeholders that the metrics cannot be changed at this point in the process

> The correct answer is **B**. New metrics should be developed which are in better alignment with organization strategy. As part of this process, a large number of new metrics should not be developed as it can overwhelm stakeholders.
> Refer to Section 6.1.2.1 of the Standard for Portfo

85. Becky is working on the process of managing strategic change. She has all of the inputs to the process but is unfamiliar with the tools and techniques typically used. What should she be using? (Moderate)

A. Readiness assessment, stakeholder analysis, prioritization analysis

B. Stakeholder analysis, gap analysis, readiness assessment

C. Portfolio process assets, portfolio charter, gap analysis

D. Stakeholder analysis, gap analysis, capability and capacity analysis

> The correct answer is **D**. Refer to Section 4.4 of the Standard for Portfolio Management - 3rd Edition. Review the descriptions and definition.

86. Bill is working on the Manage Portfolio Information process. He has all of the inputs to the process. What tools and techniques would Bill typically apply during this process? (Moderate)

   A. Elicitation techniques, portfolio management information system, communication requirements analysis, communication methods

   B. Stakeholder analysis, elicitation techniques, communication requirements analysis

   C. Portfolio management information system, elicitation techniques, communication requirements analysis

   D. Portfolio management information system, communication requirements analysis, communication methods, stakeholder analysis

> The correct answer is **A**. Tools and techniques of Manage Portfolio Information.
> Refer to Section 7/Figure 7-1 of the Standard for Portfolio Management - 3rd Edition. Review the descriptions and definition.

87. Stella is nearly finished the Manage Portfolio Information process. She knows that she needs to make note of the announcement of an upcoming stakeholder meeting as well as a portfolio manager meeting. Where would Stella document this information? (Moderate)

   A. Portfolio process assets

   B. Portfolio charter

   C. Portfolio management plan

   D. Portfolio reports

> The correct answer is **D**. Stakeholder meeting and portfolio manager meeting announcements are part of portfolio reports.

88. Kelly is nearly finished the Manage Portfolio Value process. During the process, there were some cost savings forecasted. Kelly knows she needs to document this. Where should she document it? (Moderate)

    A. Portfolio process assets

    B. Portfolio charter

    C. Portfolio management plan

    D. Portfolio reports

    The correct answer is **D**. Forecasts of the portfolio are contained within portfolio reports.
    Refer to Section 6.3.3.2 of the Standard for Portfolio Management - 3rd Edition. Review the descriptions and definition.

89. In Managing Supply and Demand, the term "Demand" refers to: (Moderate)

    A. Resource requirements from the portfolio components and from the component proposals requesting resources

    B. Resource from the component proposals requesting resources

    C. Resource requirements from the portfolio components

    D. Resource requirements from the portfolio components and from the component proposals requesting only financial funding

    The correct answer is **A**. Refer to Section 6.2 of the Standard for Portfolio Management - 3rd Edition. Review the descriptions and definition.

90. Examples of PMS Tools and Processes include: (Easy)

    A. Communication management processes and tools

    B. Earned value management processes and tools

    C. Knowledge management tools and processes

    D. All of the answer choices

91. Examples of Portfolio Process Assets used as inputs to plan for risk management include all of the following except: (Moderate)

    A. Portfolio issue register

    B. Portfolio risk register

    C. Portfolio change management register

    D. Portfolio performance matrices

    The correct answer is **C**. Refer to Section 8.1.1.2 of the Standard for Portfolio Management - 3rd Edition. Review the descriptions and definition.

92. When are portfolio process asset updates done? (Easy)

    A. As an output to the Develop Portfolio Charter process

    B. As an output to the Define Portfolio Roadmap process

    C. As an input to the Develop Portfolio Charter process

    D. As an output to the Develop Portfolio Strategic Plan process

    The correct answer is **A**. Refer to Section 4.2.3.3 of the Standard for Portfolio Management - 3rd Edition. Review the descriptions and definition.

93. When bottleneck resources or resource downtime are identified, what can be applied? (Moderate)

    A. Resource optimization across the portfolio

    B. Resource allocating and project sequencing techniques

    C. Resource minimizing and project ordering techniques

    D. Resource levelling or project sequencing techniques

    The correct answer is **D**. Refer to Section 6.2.2.2 of the Standard for Portfolio Management - 3rd Edition. Review the descriptions and definition.

94. Joan has just started working on the Manage Portfolio Risks process. She is looking for the portfolio risk register. Where would Joan find this information? (Moderate)

    A. Portfolio management plan

    B. Portfolio process assets

    C. Portfolio reports

    D. Portfolio

    > The correct answer is **D**. The portfolio risk register is part of the portfolio. Refer to Section 8.2.1.1 of the Standard for Portfolio Management - 3rd Edition. Review the descriptions and definition.

95. Evan is currently working on the Manage Portfolio Information process. He is currently creating a graphical representation which will allow him to determine if the resulting impact of a priority change is value-added or adverse. What is Evan creating? (Moderate)

    A. Resource histogram

    B. Dashboard

    C. Communication calendar

    D. None of the answer choices

    > The correct answer is **A**. The description provided essentially reflects the definition of resource histogram.
    > Refer to Section 7.2.2.4 of the Standard for Portfolio Management - 3rd Edition. Review the descriptions and definition.

96. When should the portfolio process assets be updated? (Difficult)

    A. If strategic changes have been made which impact portfolio plans and processes, then the portfolio process assets should be updated

    B. If stakeholder engagement, communication management, performance, and risk sections have changed

    C. If management approach, priorities, or organizational structure have changed

    D. None of the answer choices

97. Grant is in the process of conducting a prioritization analysis to make an assessment of which portfolio components need to be added, removed or changed. What process is Grant conducting and what is the likely outcome of the process? (Moderate)

    A. He is in the Develop Portfolio Charter process which will result in the development of a Portfolio Charter

    B. He is in the Manage Strategic Change process which will result in several updates to the Portfolio process and Portfolio roadmap

    C. He is in the Define Portfolio Roadmap process which will result in the creation of the Portfolio roadmap

    D. He is in the Develop Portfolio Strategic Plan process to develop a Strategic Plan.

98. Josey is currently working on the Develop Portfolio Communication Management Plan process. She is currently performing an analysis to determine stakeholders' concerns, interests, and influence. What type of analysis is Josey performing? (Easy)

    A. Stakeholder analysis

    B. Elicitation techniques

    C. Prioritization analysis

    D. Communication requirements analysis

99. Jacob is currently working on the Manage Portfolio Value process. He is currently holding meetings with stakeholders to assess criteria and to discern the weight assigned to different benefits and outcomes. What tool and technique is Jacob applying? (Moderate)

    A. Elicitation techniques

    B. Quantitative and qualitative analysis

C. Value scoring and measurement analysis

D. Benefits realization analysis

> The correct answer is **A**. Holding meetings with stakeholders is an elicitation technique.
> Refer to Section 6.3.2.1 of the Standard for Portfolio Management - 3rd Edition. Review the descriptions and definition.

100. Tyson has recently started working on the Manage Portfolio Information process. He is trying to find information on portfolio communication requirements including communication technology available and allowed communication media. Where should Tyson look for this information? (Moderate)

   A. Portfolio component reports

   B. Portfolio charter

   C. Portfolio reports

   D. Portfolio process assets

> The correct answer is **D**. Communication requirements are found in portfolio process assets.
> Refer to Section 7.2.1.5 of the Standard for Portfolio Management - 3rd Edition. Review the descriptions and definition.

101. Jason has just started working on the Develop Portfolio Communication Management Plan. He has the portfolio and the portfolio roadmap. What else should Jason have to start this process? (Moderate)

   A. Portfolio reports, portfolio management plan, portfolio process assets

   B. Portfolio charter, portfolio component reports, enterprise environmental factors

   C. Portfolio process assets, enterprise environmental factors, portfolio reports

   D. Portfolio reports, portfolio management plan, portfolio charter

> The correct answer is **A**. Inputs to Develop Portfolio Communication Management Plan.
> Refer to Section 7/Figure 7-1 of the Standard for Portfolio Management - 3rd Edition. Review the descriptions and definition.

102. A tool and technique for managing strategic change is stakeholder analysis. Why is this important? (Moderate)

A. Helps to ensure continuity and align key stakeholders expectations with the changing strategy and resulting portfolio alignment

B. Helps to ensure continuity of portfolio management processes

C. Helps to ensure continuity and align organization expectations with the changing strategy and resulting portfolio alignment

D. Helps to ensure continuity and align the project plan with the changing strategy and resulting portfolio alignment

> The correct answer is **A**. Refer to Section 4.4 of the Standard for Portfolio Management - 3rd Edition. Review the descriptions and definition.

103. Conor is currently working on the Provide Portfolio Oversight process. He is currently in the process of conducting a survey. What tool and technique is Conor utilizing? (Moderate)

A. Elicitation techniques

B. Portfolio reports

C. Portfolio authorization process

D. Portfolio review meetings

> The correct answer is **A**. Refer to Section 5.5.2.2 of the Standard for Portfolio Management - 3rd Edition. Review the descriptions and definition.

104. Resource capability and capacity management analysis includes all of the following except: (Moderate)

A. Finite capacity planning and reporting

B. What-if scenarios

C. Resource management tools

D. SWOT

> The correct answer is **D**. Refer to Section 6.1.2.4 of the Standard for Portfolio Management - 3rd Edition. Review the descriptions and definition.

105. Stephanie has been asked by senior executives to determine how much work can be accomplished based on the current resources available. What is she being asked to do? (Moderate)

    A. Interdependency analysis

    B. Scenario analysis

    C. Prioritization analysis

    D. Capability and capacity analysis

    > The correct answer is **D**. Refer to Section 4.2.2.2 of the Standard for Portfolio Management - 3rd Edition. Review the descriptions and definition.

106. In portfolio structural analysis, the portfolio manager should assign what type of reviews? (Moderate)

    A. Performance review of major resource groups such as employees or contractors

    B. Performance review of major project components

    C. Performance review and reporting roles and responsibilities across each program, project or operational component

    D. Performance review of each program, project or operational component

    > The correct answer is **C**. Refer to Section 5.1.2 of the Standard for Portfolio Management - 3rd Edition. Review the descriptions and definition.

107. In portfolio component categorization technique, which of the following are examples of "Business imperatives" considerations? (Moderate)

    A. IT compatibility

    B. Internal toolkit

    C. IT upgrades

    D. All of the answer choices

    > The correct answer is **D**. Refer to Section 5.2.2.2 of the Standard for Portfolio Management - 3rd Edition. Review the descriptions and definition.

108. In portfolio performance management, what is defined as resource capability? (Moderate)

A. A competency that enables an organization to execute its operational objectives

B. A competency that enables an organization to execute its charter

C. A competency that enables an organization to execute its strategy

D. A specific competency that enables an organization to execute components and deliver results

> The correct answer is **D**. Refer to Section 6.1.2.4 of the Standard for Portfolio Management - 3rd Edition. Review the descriptions and definition.

109. In portfolio reports, what is a sample representation of progress? (Moderate)

A. Earned value diagram demonstrating the earned value versus planned value

B. Burn-down or burn-up chart showing the delivery of a component compared to the portfolio's history

C. Burn-down or burn-up chart showing the delivery of a component compared to the portfolio's budget or time

D. Gantt chart demonstrating program or project progress

> The correct answer is **C**. Refer to Section 6.3.1.3 of the Standard for Portfolio Management - 3rd Edition. Review the descriptions and definition.

110. Currently, analysis is being conducted to compare the current portfolio mix and components with the new strategic direction and the "to be" organizational vision. What type of analysis is being performed? (Easy)

A. Readiness assessment

B. Scenario analysis

C. Prioritization analysis

D. Gap analysis

> The correct answer is **D**. Refer to Section 4.4.2.2 of the Standard for Portfolio Management - 3rd Edition. Review the descriptions and definition.

111. PMIS can include all of the following except: (Moderate)

    A. Risk Information

    B. Costs

    C. Performance Metrics

    D. Human Resources Information

    > The correct answer is **D**. Refer to Section 6.1.2.2 of the Standard for Portfolio Management - 3rd Edition. Review the descriptions and definition.

112. Russell has nearly finished the Manage Portfolio Value process. During the process, changes were made to the reporting process as it relates to how portfolio components are managed. What does Russell need to update to reflect this change? (Moderate)

    A. Portfolio process assets

    B. Portfolio component inventory

    C. Portfolio management plan

    D. Portfolio reports

    > The correct answer is **C**. New reporting procedures should be noted in the portfolio management plan.
    > Refer to Section 6.3.3.1 of the Standard for Portfolio Management - 3rd Edition. Review the descriptions and definition.

113. In stakeholder analysis which of the following should be considered? (Moderate)

    A. Assess levels of interest

    B. Assign levels of influence

    C. Assess urgency in communication

    D. All of the answer choices

    > The correct answer is **D**. Refer to Section 7.1.2.1 of the Standard for Portfolio Management - 3rd Edition. Review the descriptions and definition.

114. What are the tools and techniques used during the Develop Portfolio Performance Management plan process? (Moderate)

A. Elicitation techniques, portfolio management information system, elicitation techniques

B. Scenario analysis, Capability and capacity analysis, quantitative and qualitative analysis

C. Scenario analysis, Capability and capacity analysis, portfolio management information system

D. Elicitation techniques, portfolio management information system, capability and capacity analysis

> The correct answer is **D**. Refer to Section 6/Figure 6-1 of the Standard for Portfolio Management - 3rd Edition. Review the descriptions and definition.

115. What are the outputs of the Develop Portfolio Performance Management Plan? (Moderate)

A. Portfolio process assets updates, portfolio updates

B. Portfolio reports, portfolio updates

C. Portfolio updates, portfolio reports, portfolio management plan updates

D. Portfolio management plan updates, portfolio process assets updates

> The correct answer is **D**. Refer to Section 6/Figure 6-1 of the Standard for Portfolio Management - 3rd Edition. Review the descriptions and definition.

116. What are the types of risk sources? (Easy)

A. Extraneous, Outside

B. Inside, Outside

C. Internal, Extraneous

D. Internal, External

> The correct answer is **D**. Refer to Section 8 of the Standard for Portfolio Management - 3rd Edition. Review the descriptions and definition.

117. What are the four stages of the Manage Portfolio Risk process? (Moderate)

A. Risks are identified, risks are analyzed, risk responses are developed, risks are mitigated

B. Risks are defined, risks are evaluated, risks are mitigated

C. Risk impact is established, risks are analyzed, risk responses are developed, risks are monitored and controlled

D. Risks are identified, risks are analyzed, risk responses are developed, risks are monitored and controlled

> The correct answer is **D**. Refer to Section 8.2 of the Standard for Portfolio Management - 3rd Edition. Review the descriptions and definition.

118. What are the outputs of the Develop Portfolio Risk Management Plan process? (Moderate)

   A. Portfolio management plan updates, portfolio process assets updates, portfolio roadmap updates

   B. Portfolio roadmap updates, portfolio reports

   C. Portfolio process assets updates, portfolio reports, organizational process assets updates

   D. Portfolio management plan updates, portfolio process assets updates, organizational process assets updates

> The correct answer is **D**. Refer to Section 8/Figure 8-1 of the Standard for Portfolio Management - 3rd Edition. Review the descriptions and definition.

119. What can be included in the portfolio charter? (Easy)

   A. It may include communication requirements, high-level scope, benefits, critical success criteria, resources, and a high-level timeline

   B. It may include portfolio justification, portfolio roadmap, prioritization analysis, and risk tolerance

   C. It may include portfolio objectives, portfolio sponsors, Cost-benefit analysis, and assumptions

   D. All of the answer choices

> The correct answer is **A**. Refer to Section 4.2.3.2 of the Standard for Portfolio Management - 3rd Edition. Review the descriptions and definition.

120. What information can be learned from the portfolio strategic plan when developing a portfolio management plan? (Difficult)

A. How to allocate resources to develop component proposals, authorizing components to expend resources and to communicate portfolio decisions

B. A high-level graphical overview of portfolio components

C. How to monitor the portfolio to ensure alignment with the organizational strategy and objectives

D. Portfolio objectives, portfolio management organization structure, benefits, prioritization model, and resource information.

> The correct answer is **D**. Refer to Section 5.1 of the Standard for Portfolio Management - 3rd Edition. Review the descriptions and definition.

121. What comparison should a portfolio manager make when trying to define a portfolio roadmap? (Moderate)

A. Cost should be compared against the potential benefits

B. Strategic objectives, priority objectives, and strategic assessment should be compared against current enterprise portfolios

C. Organizational strategy should be compared to archived enterprise portfolios

D. Dependencies the portfolio may have should be compared to other portfolios

> The correct answer is **B**. Refer to Section 4.3.2.3 of the Standard for Portfolio Management - 3rd Edition. Review the descriptions and definition.

122. What does portfolio management ensure? (Select the best answer) (Moderate)

A. Interrelationships among programs and projects are identified with the emphasis on managing risks

B. Interrelationships among projects is dysfunctional and therefore resources are unnecessary

C. That a loose relationship among programs and projects is minimal and that resources are up the manager to decide upon

D. Interrelationships among programs and projects are identified and that resources are allocated with respect to organizational priorities

123. What does the Portfolio Charter authorize the portfolio manager to do? (Easy)

    A. To develop a Portfolio strategic plan

    B. To perform a Scenario analysis and Compatibility and capacity analysis

    C. To begin working on a portfolio

    D. To apply portfolio resources to portfolio components and to execute the portfolio management process

124. What information can you expect to find in the portfolio performance management plan? (Moderate)

    A. Performance reporting

    B. Goals, objectives, strategies, and tactics

    C. Resource optimization

    D. All of the answer choices

125. What is a Portfolio? (Easy)

    A. Collection of financial reports related to a specific project or program

    B. Collection of programs, projects, or operations managed as a group to achieve strategic objectives

    C. Collection of programs, projects, or operations managed as a group, but not necessarily to achieve tactical business objectives

    D. Collection of programs and projects aligned with strategic objectives

The correct answer is **B**. Refer to Section 1.2 of the Standard for Portfolio Management - 3rd Edition. Review the descriptions and definition.

126. What is the process in both the knowledge area Portfolio Governance Management and the Aligning Process Group? (Moderate)

    A. Optimize portfolio

    B. Authorize portfolio

    C. Optimize project plan

    D. None of the answer choices

    The correct answer is **A**. Refer to Section 3.1 of the Standard for Portfolio Management - 3rd Edition. Review the descriptions and definition.

127. What is/are the process(es) in both the knowledge area Portfolio Risk Management and the Aligning Process Group: (Moderate)

    A. Manage portfolio risks

    B. Manage financial risk

    C. Manage project risk

    D. None of the answer choices

    The correct answer is **A**. Refer to Section 3.1 of the Standard for Portfolio Management - 3rd Edition. Review the descriptions and definition.

128. What is the portfolio manager generally responsible for updating and adding to the portfolio process assets? (Easy)

    A. Historical Info

    B. Portfolio component files

    C. Lessons Learned

    D. All of the answer choices

    The correct answer is **D**. Refer to Section 3.2 of the Standard for Portfolio Management - 3rd Edition. Review the descriptions and definition.

129. What is a key element in producing the Portfolio Strategic Plan? (Easy)

    A. Portfolio roadmap

    B. Strategic change

    C. Portfolio charter

    D. Organizational strategy and objectives

    > The correct answer is **D**. Refer to Section 4.1.3.1 of the Standard for Portfolio Management - 3rd Edition. Review the descriptions and definition.

130. What is the result of the Develop Portfolio Charter process? (Easy)

    A. Portfolio charter, portfolio strategic plan updates, interdependency analysis

    B. Scenario analysis, capability and capacity analysis

    C. Portfolio strategic plan, portfolio process assets, enterprise environmental factors

    D. Portfolio strategic plan updates, portfolio charter, portfolio process assets updates

    > The correct answer is **D**. Refer to Section 4.2 of the Standard for Portfolio Management - 3rd Edition. Review the descriptions and definition.

131. What is contained in the portfolio roadmap? (Moderate)

    A. Program and project level roadmaps

    B. Program level roadmaps only

    C. Project level roadmaps only

    D. Project level roadmaps outside of the portfolio scope

    > The correct answer is **A**. Refer to Section 4.3 of the Standard for Portfolio Management - 3rd Edition. Review the descriptions and definition.

132. What is one of the key differences between portfolio management and project management as it relates to strategic change? (Difficult)

    A. Change in portfolios follows a similar process as that for change in projects

B. Frequent change in portfolio management and project management is a common occurrence

C. Changes in project management are a fairly common occurrence where a great deal of elaboration is not required whereas progress elaboration is required with changes in portfolio management

D. Change in portfolios is a normal occurrence and portfolio documents may be reworked where progressive elaboration is required in project management

The correct answer is **D**. Refer to Section 4.4 of the Standard for Portfolio Management - 3rd Edition. Review the descriptions and definition.

133. What is required to create the portfolio management plan? (Moderate)

A. Portfolio assets

B. Portfolio project plan

C. Portfolio management plan

D. Portfolio charter

The correct answer is **D**. Refer to Section 5.1.1 of the Standard for Portfolio Management - 3rd Edition. Review the descriptions and definition.

134. What is generally considered the responsibility of the portfolio manager during the portfolio management processes? (Moderate)

A. Updating and adding to the portfolio process assets, as necessary

B. Updating and adding to the prioritization analysis

C. Updating the Cost-benefit analysis

D. None of the answer choices

The correct answer is **A**. Refer to Section 5.1.1.4 of the Standard for Portfolio Management - 3rd Edition. Review the descriptions and definition.

135. What is a typical collaboration technique? (Moderate)

A. Polling team members by way of anonymous electronic voting

B. Short memo

C. Polling the organization

D. Talking amongst the project team

> The correct answer is **A**. Refer to Section 5.1.2 of the Standard for Portfolio Management - 3rd Edition. Review the descriptions and definition.

136. What is the importance of weighted ranking and scoring techniques? (Moderate)

    A. Provide a technique which the stakeholders can rate portfolio components based on their criteria

    B. Provide a subjective technique to rank portfolio components

    C. Provide a technique to rank the mandatory components of a portfolio

    D. Provide an objective technique to rank portfolio components

> The correct answer is **D**. Refer to Section 5.2.2.3 of the Standard for Portfolio Management - 3rd Edition. Review the descriptions and definition.

137. What is the benefit of a scoring model? (Moderate)

    A. It evaluates portfolio components and makes them comparable

    B. It assigns a financial score to portfolio components

    C. It ranks portfolio components and determines their usefulness

    D. It compares portfolio components and determines their weight

> The correct answer is **A**. Refer to Section 5.2.2.3 of the Standard for Portfolio Management - 3rd Edition. Review the descriptions and definition.

138. What is involved in the Optimize Portfolio process? (Moderate)

    A. Identifying qualified portfolio components to determine whether or not a particular component should be part of the portfolio

    B. Assigning portfolio components to predetermined categories to compare those which address similar organizational needs

    C. Evaluating portfolios based on the organization's business objectives, ranking the portfolio, and creating the ideal portfolio with the greatest potential to support organizational strategy

D. Evaluating the portfolio based on the organization's selection criteria, ranking the portfolio components, and creating the portfolio component mix with the greatest potential to support organizational strategy

> The correct answer is **D**. Refer to Section 5.3 of the Standard for Portfolio Management - 3rd Edition. Review the descriptions and definition.

139. What is portfolio performance management? (Easy)

A. The systematic planning, measurement, and monitoring of the portfolio's organizational value through achievement against these strategic goals

B. The integration of subsidiary plans such as performance communication, and risk management plans

C. The organizational strategy and objectives which provide long-term direction, vision, goals, and objectives

D. The guiding artifact that establishes portfolio-level dependencies and constraints to allow for effective oversight

> The correct answer is **A**. Refer to Section 6 of the Standard for Portfolio Management - 3rd Edition. Review the descriptions and definition.

140. What is the acronym used for the guideline for measures of portfolio performance management? (Easy)

A. SWOT

B. SAT

C. SWAT

D. SMART

> The correct answer is **D**. Refer to Section 6.1.2 of the Standard for Portfolio Management - 3rd Edition. Review the descriptions and definition.

141. What is the SMART guideline used to help develop? (Moderate)

A. Resource schedules

B. KPIs

C. Resource types

D. Performance measures

> The correct answer is **D**. Refer to Section 6.1.2.1 of the Standard for Portfolio Management - 3rd Edition. Review the descriptions and definition.

142. What is a scenario analysis within the context of the Manage Supply and Demand process? (Easy)

    A. It is an analysis technique used to determine various possibilities of resource allocations and the impact to component schedules

    B. It is an analysis technique used to document and assess intangible portfolio benefits

    C. It includes various approaches to studying the demand for resources against capacity and constraints to determine how to best allocate resources

    D. It studies the capability of resources and matches them against the portfolio's objectives and goals

> The correct answer is **A**. Refer to Section 6.2.2.1 of the Standard for Portfolio Management - 3rd Edition. Review the descriptions and definition.

143. What is done during the Manage Portfolio Information process? (Moderate)

    A. Collecting, analyzing, storing, and delivering portfolio information to stakeholders

    B. Policies and practices for optimizing portfolio value including revenue growth and increased operating margins are established

    C. Stakeholders are identified, different individuals and groups are determined along with their concerns, interests, and influences

    D. All of the answer choices

> The correct answer is **A**. Refer to Section 7.2 of the Standard for Portfolio Management - 3rd Edition. Review the descriptions and definition.

144. What is the main importance of utilizing a histogram? (Moderate)

    A. Portfolio manager needs to determine if the changing organization priorities are value-added or adverse to portfolio assets

B. Portfolio manager needs to determine if the changing organization priorities are going to result in a scope change request

C. Portfolio manager needs to determine if the changing organization priorities are beneficial to the project

D. Portfolio manager needs to determine if the changing organization priorities are value-added or adverse to portfolio performance

> The correct answer is **D**. Refer to Section 7.2.2.4 of the Standard for Portfolio Management - 3rd Edition. Review the descriptions and definition.

145. What is a more likely example of a positive portfolio risk? (Difficult)

    A. Key project cost performance indices (CPI) are less than 1

    B. Major competitor's product launch earlier than expected

    C. Regulatory change tightened requirements for a major project in the portfolio

    D. A major competitor's product launch failed

> The correct answer is **D**. Refer to Section 8 of the Standard for Portfolio Management - 3rd Edition. Review the descriptions and definition.

146. What is the best tool or technique used to assess key risks? (Moderate)

    A. Informal discussions

    B. Phone calls

    C. Emails

    D. Interviews and Meetings

> The correct answer is **D**. Refer to Section 8.1.2.2 of the Standard for Portfolio Management - 3rd Edition. Review the descriptions and definition.

147. What processes are part of portfolio communication management? (Moderate)

    A. Develop Portfolio Communication Management Plan, Provide Communication Oversight

    B. Manage Communication, Provide Communication Oversight

C. Develop Portfolio Communication Management Plan, Manage Portfolio Information

D. Manage Communication, Develop Portfolio Communication Management Plan

> The correct answer is **C**. Refer to Section 7 of the Standard for Portfolio Management - 3rd Edition. Review the descriptions and definition.

148. What requires updating when a change takes place? (Moderate)

    A. Portfolio management plan

    B. Portfolio charter

    C. Portfolio Roadmap

    D. Portfolio Roadmap and Portfolio Management Plan

> The correct answer is **D**. Refer to Section 5.2.3 of the Standard for Portfolio Management - 3rd Edition. Review the descriptions and definition.

149. To define the management of strategic change the following tools and techniques are needed: (Moderate)

    A. Gap analysis

    B. Stakeholder analysis

    C. Readiness Assessment

    D. All of the answer choices

> The correct answer is **D**. Refer to Section 4.1 of the Standard for Portfolio Management - 3rd Edition. Review the descriptions and definition.

150. What tools and techniques are used during the Develop Portfolio Strategic Plan process? (Moderate)

    A. Portfolio component inventory, prioritization analysis, organizational strategy and objectives

    B. Portfolio charter, portfolio roadmap, organizational strategy and objectives

    C. Organizational strategy and objectives, inventory of work, portfolio process assets

    D. Portfolio component inventory, Strategic alignment analysis, prioritization analysis

151. What tools and techniques are used during the Manage Strategic Change process? (Difficult)

    A. Interdependency analysis, prioritization analysis, gap analysis

    B. Scenario analysis, capability and capacity analysis, prioritization analysis

    C. Cost-benefit analysis, readiness assessment, stakeholder analysis

    D. Stakeholder analysis, gap analysis, readiness assessment

152. What tools and techniques can be applied during the Manage Supply and Demand process? (Moderate)

    A. Capability and capacity analysis, value scoring and measurement analysis

    B. Elicitation techniques, Benefits realization analysis, scenario analysis

    C. Scenario analysis, quantitative and qualitative analysis, elicitation techniques

    D. Scenario analysis, quantitative and qualitative analysis, capability and capacity analysis

153. What tools and techniques are typically applied during the Manage Portfolio Risks process? (Moderate)

    A. Graphical analytical methods, quantitative and qualitative analysis

    B. Elicitation techniques, quantitative and qualitative analysis

    C. Weighted ranking and scoring techniques, graphical analytical methods, quantitative and qualitative analysis

    D. Weighted ranking and scoring techniques, quantitative and qualitative analysis

154. What triggers a portfolio review meeting? All of the following except: (Moderate)

    A. Project scope changes

    B. Financial drivers

    C. Regulatory changes

    D. Completion of significant portfolio components or deliverables

> The correct answer is **A**. Refer to Section 5.5.2 of the Standard for Portfolio Management - 3rd Edition. Review the descriptions and definition.

155. What type of process is the development of the portfolio management plan? (Easy)

    A. Iterative

    B. Recursive

    C. Agile

    D. Incremental

> The correct answer is **A**. Refer to Section 5.1.2.3 of the Standard for Portfolio Management - 3rd Edition. Review the descriptions and definition.

156. What type of portfolio reports are consulted during the Authorize Portfolio process? (Moderate)

    A. Governance decisions

    B. Financials/funding

    C. Resources

    D. All of the answer choices

> The correct answer is **D**. Refer to Section 5.4.1.3 of the Standard for Portfolio Management - 3rd Edition. Review the descriptions and definition.

157. Portfolio Management processes are started in an organization as a response to all of the following except: (Easy)

A. constrained resources

B. Issues / conflicts

C. uncertainty

D. strategic objective uncertainty

> The correct answer is **D**. Refer to Section 2.2 of the Standard for Portfolio Management - 3rd Edition. Review the descriptions and definition.

158. Portfolio process assets provide which of the following: (Moderate)

A. Guidance for defining the portfolio charter

B. Guidance for defining the portfolio budget

C. Guidance for defining portfolio priorities

D. Guidance for defining portfolio components

> The correct answer is **D**. Refer to Section 5.2.1 of the Standard for Portfolio Management - 3rd Edition. Review the descriptions and definition.

159. Portfolio value for an organization can be expressed as: (Moderate)

A. Enhancement or protection of reputation and branding

B. Contribution to the community

C. Protection of environmental resources

D. All of the answer choices

> The correct answer is **D**. Refer to Section 6.3 of the Standard for Portfolio Management - 3rd Edition. Review the descriptions and definition.

160. Portfolio communication management is closely aligned with all of the following management processes except: (Moderate)

A. Risk

B. Strategic

C. Financial

D. Governance

> The correct answer is **C**. Refer to Section 7 of the Standard for Portfolio Management - 3rd Edition. Review the descriptions and definition.

161. Portfolio communication facilitates an effective two-way dialogue between which of the affected internal and external stakeholders, individuals or groups? (Moderate)

    A. Governing & regulatory bodies

    B. Executive managers

    C. Operations managers

    D. All of the answer choices

> The correct answer is **D**. Refer to Section 7.1 of the Standard for Portfolio Management - 3rd Edition. Review the descriptions and definition.

162. At the conclusion of the Manage Portfolio Value process, what type of changes can cause the portfolio management plan to need to be updated? (Moderate)

    A. New measurement processes

    B. New reporting processes

    C. New portfolio component management process

    D. All of the answer choices

> The correct answer is **D**. Refer to Section 6.3.3.1 of the Standard for Portfolio Management - 3rd Edition. Review the descriptions and definition.

163. In the development of the Portfolio Risk Management Plan, which technique is most preferable to evaluate risk of multiple portfolios? (Moderate)

    A. Capability and capacity analysis

    B. Prioritization algorithms

    C. Weighted ranking and scoring

    D. Elicitation techniques

164. In the Manage Portfolio Risksprocess which of the following is not an input? (Moderate)

    A. Portfolio Management Plan

    B. Portfolio

    C. Portfolio Financial Plan

    D. Portfolio Reports

> The correct answer is **C**. Refer to Section 8.2 of the Standard for Portfolio Management - 3rd Edition. Review the descriptions and definition.

165. Is there acceptable risk in portfolio risk management? (Moderate)

    A. Maybe, depending on risk tolerance of the portfolio manager

    B. No, there is no place of uncertainty in a portfolio

    C. Yes, risk is inherent in all investments

    D. Maybe, depending on the risk tolerance of the organization

> The correct answer is **C**. Refer to Section 8 of the Standard for Portfolio Management - 3rd Edition. Review the descriptions and definition.

166. Matthew is working on managing strategic change. He is presently reviewing documentation which highlights the intended approach of managing the portfolio and its components to meet organizational strategy. What is he reviewing? (Moderate)

    A. Portfolio management plan

    B. Project management plan

    C. Portfolio roadmap

    D. Portfolio charter

> The correct answer is **A**. Refer to Section 4.4.1.5 of the Standard for Portfolio Management - 3rd Edition. Review the descriptions and definition.

167. Dustin is currently working on the Manage Portfolio Value process. He is currently running an analysis to compare a portfolio component against a future alternative. What type of analysis is Dustin performing? (Moderate)

A. Progress measurement techniques

B. Portfolio efficient frontier

C. Comparative advantage analysis

D. Cost-benefit analysis

> The correct answer is **C**. The big key here in the question is that a comparison is being made.
> Refer to Section 6.3.2.2 of the Standard for Portfolio Management - 3rd Edition. Review the descriptions and definition.

168. Travis comes to you for advice. He believes he has completed the Develop Portfolio Performance Management Plan process. He tells you that he updated the portfolio process assets. What should Travis have also updated? (Moderate)

A. Enterprise environmental factors

B. Portfolio management plan

C. Portfolio roadmap

D. Portfolio

> The correct answer is **B**. Outputs of the process.
> Refer to Section 6.1/Figure 6.2 of the Standard for Portfolio Management - 3rd Edition. Review the descriptions and definition.

169. Troy is about to start working on the Manage Supply and Demand process. He has received some advice from his supervisor that the stakeholders are starting to lose interest in the current initiative. Troy realizes he needs to engage the stakeholders. Where can Troy find the plan for stakeholder engagement? (Difficult)

A. Portfolio

B. Portfolio charter

C. Portfolio management plan

D. Portfolio reports

The correct answer is **C**. Portfolio management plan contains the high level plan for engaging stakeholders.
Refer to Section 6.2.1.2 of the Standard for Portfolio Management - 3rd Edition. Review the descriptions and definition.

170. To define the management of strategic change the following outputs are needed: (Moderate)

A. Portfolio process assets updates

B. Portfolio roadmap updates

C. Portfolio management plan updates

D. All of the answer choices

The correct answer is **D**. Refer to Section 4.1 of the Standard for Portfolio Management - 3rd Edition. Review the descriptions and definition.

1. The Manage Portfolio Risksprocess has how many stages?

    A. Four

    B. Three

    C. Two

    D. One

2. The Aligning Process Group is most active when?

    A. After the portfolio organization has defined and developed its plans

    B. After the portfolio organization has defined and developed its strategic goals

    C. After the portfolio organization has defined its near term budget

    D. All of the answer choices

3. Hal approaches you for advice. He is about to start working on the Define Portfolio process and feels as though everything has already been defined and that this process can be skipped. How would you advise Hal?

    A. I would advise Hal that he can skip the process and proceed to do a portfolio component inventory

    B. I would advise Hal that the he is correct and the process can be skipped.

    C. I would advise Hal that the process should not be skipped and is important because it provides a graphical overview of key portfolio elements

    D. I would advise Hal that the process should not be skipped and is important because the portfolio needs to be organized for evaluation, selection, and prioritization.

4. The best tool to develop a stakeholder communication management strategy is:

    A. Mapping of internal and external stakeholders to quadrants

    B. Mapping of communication assets to quadrants

    C. Mapping of influence and interest to quadrants

D. Mapping of organization chart to quadrants based on influence

5. The communication management plan should include all of the following except:

    A. Communication protocols

    B. Planned frequency

    C. Communication constraints

    D. Communication policies

6. How does a manager measure portfolio component performance?

    A. Portfolio component is undertaken to achieve a strategic goal and its contribution is measured within the context of that goal

    B. Portfolio component is undertaken to achieve primarily a financial goal

    C. Portfolio component is undertaken to achieve primarily a human resource goal

    D. Portfolio component is undertaken to achieve one or more strategic goals

7. How does a portfolio manager address the function of quality management?

    A. Ensuring compliance with set standards

    B. Not a factor as portfolio managers look at multiple areas

    C. Ensuring compliance with voluntary standards and OSHA requirements

    D. Ensuring compliance with voluntary standards and mandatory requirements

8. How does the portfolio management plan utilize information from the roadmap?

    A. To define the direction

    B. To define the project plan

    C. To define the assets

    D. To define low level schedules and timelines

9. The following types of diagrams are all useful to show execution of the portfolio against the overall strategic plan and budget except:

    A. Funnel and bubble charts

    B. Burn-down or burn-up charts

    C. Histograms

    D. Pictograms

10. How is "Change" defined for portfolio management?

    A. Depending on organizations, it can be a random process

    B. Occurs in the broader internal and external environment monitored by the manager

    C. Strictly internal controls that are monitored by the manager

    D. Occurs in the broader internal and external environment but not necessarily monitored

11. How is organizational strategy implemented as it relates to the strategic plan?

    A. Through portfolio components and ongoing operations

    B. Through the prioritization analysis process

    C. Through the capability and capacity analysis

    D. All of the answer choices

12. Ron is working on his portfolio charter and is trying to assess the impact of enterprise environmental factors. Which of the follow scenarios could Ron be facing?

    A. The portfolio structure needs to be changed so that it aligns stakeholder relationships, scope, benefits, and portfolio goals

    B. The portfolio charter needs to be changed to account for the results of the capability and capacity analysis

    C. The portfolio charter needs to align with scenarios examined during scenario analysis

    D. The portfolio structure in the charter needs to align with corporate accounting structure

13. How is the portfolio related to the process Define Portfolio Roadmap?

    A. It quantifies the estimated costs and benefits of portfolio components

    B. It is used to perform a portfolio component inventory

    C. It is used to define organization areas only on the portfolio roadmap

    D. The portfolio and components are referenced to define the portfolio roadmap

14. How is the portfolio management plan utilized during the Manage Portfolio Value process?

    A. It provides for the continual identification and assessment of the value of the portfolio benefits and the impact on organizational objectives

    B. It provides a high-level timeline for expected portfolio component delivery

    C. It provides stakeholder expectations and requirements, governance model, strategic change framework, planning, procurement, and oversight processes including direction for performance, communication, and risk management

    D. All of the answer choices

15. The least likely factors that affect portfolio structural risks is:

    A. Alignment of organizations ability to organize its portfolio mission with hierarchal and clustered structures

    B. Quality of organizations portfolio management

    C. Organizational hierarchy

    D. Methods and approaches in which organization operates and performs its tasks

16. How many people may be in the governing body?

    A. Minimum 2

    B. The more the better

    C. Minimum 5 or more

    D. 1 or more

17. In Communication Requirements Analysis, what is evaluated?

    A. Vehicle or tool used to communicate info to the stakeholders and its frequency

    B. Vehicle or tool used to communicate info to the all stakeholders

    C. Vehicle or tool used to communicate info to the stakeholders and the organization level

    D. Vehicle or tool used to communicate info to the internal stakeholders

18. How many portfolio management process groups are there?

    A. Four

    B. Three

    C. One

    D. Two

19. How many Portfolio Communication Management Processes are there?

    A. Five

    B. Three

    C. Two

    D. Four

20. Why might portfolio process assets need to be updated as a result of the Optimize Portfolio process?

    A. Procedures and guidelines have changed during the process

    B. The approach and criteria to maintaining a balanced portfolio may have changed during the process

    C. Organizational areas, portfolio components, and high level timeline have changed during the process

    D. None of the answer choices

21. All of the following are key descriptors of portfolio components that a portfolio manager may make use of except:

   A. Type of portfolio component

   B. Portfolio management plan

   C. Strategic goals supported

   D. Resources required

22. All of the following are valid for scoring and measuring organizational value except:

   A. Portfolio scoring techniques

   B. Progress measurement techniques

   C. Value measurement techniques

   D. Portfolio efficient frontier

23. The performance management process manages the sourcing of:

   A. Finance, assets, information technology

   B. Finance, vendors, human resources

   C. Finance, assets, human resources

   D. Finance, marketing, assets

24. The portfolio manager must have expertise in ALL of the following application and analysis of quantitative and qualitative techniques except:

   A. Program And project management methods and techniques

   B. Organizational management

   C. Portfolio risk management

   D. Software evaluation

25. The portfolio charter is defined as:

A. The document that formally establishes the portfolio change management plan

B. The document that formally authorizes and structures a portfolio

C. The document that provides the scope and schedule of establishing the portfolio management process

D. The process that initiation the formation of a portfolio

26. The portfolio charter contains which of the following?

    A. Financial analysts

    B. Identification of stakeholders

    C. Project Plan

    D. Identification of C-level executives

27. The portfolio roadmap displays information at what type of level and what type of view?

    A. High-level and chronological

    B. Highly detailed level and alphabetical

    C. High-level and alphabetical

    D. Highly detailed level and chronological

28. The portfolio management plan may refer to different methodologies or approaches that the organization applies to manage different types of portfolio components. This is done based on the specifications from what?

    A. Portfolio charter

    B. Portfolio process assets

    C. Portfolio roadmap

    D. Organizational process assets

29. The portfolio management plan can include each of the following sections except:

    A. Performance management planning

B. Change control and management

C. Managing scope change

D. Balancing portfolio and managing dependencies

30. Environmental Factors include which of the following?

A. Government standards

B. Legal constraints

C. Industry standards

D. All of the answer choices

31. The risk register includes all of the following information except:

A. Probability impact assessment

B. Risk matrix

C. Risk triggers

D. Updated risk categories

32. The strategic change process compares:

A. The "as is" state with the "to be" state

B. The current state with the ideal state

C. The present state with the past state

D. None of the answer choices

33. Lisa Fe has just started working on the Develop Portfolio Performance Management Plan process. She is trying to find information on stakeholder expectation and requirements as well as information about planning and procurement. Where should she look for this information?

A. Portfolio management plan

B. Portfolio management information system

C. Portfolio roadmap

D. Portfolio process assets

34. As a result of risk analysis, there may be specific actions. Which one of the following is least likely:

    A. Change in staff allocation

    B. Increase in funding

    C. Portfolio components added, changed or terminated

    D. Change organizational strategy

35. Sarah just came back from getting advice on how to use the portfolio structure as a guide. She asks you if you have heard of doing this before within the Develop Portfolio Charter process. How do you respond?

    A. It can be used a guide to create the Portfolio strategic plan

    B. It can be used as a guide to create a variety of portfolio scenarios

    C. It can be used as a guide to graphically depict portfolio elements to achieve organizational strategy and objectives

    D. It can be used as a guide to identify portfolio and subportfolios based on organization areas, hierarchies, and goals for each portfolio component

36. Melanie has sought advice from Glenn, a senior member of her office, regarding managing strategic change. Glenn indicated to Melanie that a stakeholder analysis is very important. Why?

    A. It is used to understand the portfolio structure, scope, constraints, dependencies, and resources

    B. It compares the current portfolio mix and components with the new strategic direction and the "to-be" organizational vision

    C. It is used to evaluate strategic objectives, prioritize objectives, and perform strategic assessments again current enterprise portfolios

    D. It helps to ensure continuity and aligns key stakeholders' expectations with the changing strategy and resulting portfolio realignment

37. Bruce is currently working on the Optimize Portfolio process and asks for your guidance. Bruce has decided to remove a portfolio component and knows that his reasoning needs to be documented, but isn't sure where he should document it. How would you advise him?

    A. I would advise Bruce to document his reasoning on the portfolio roadmap

    B. I would advise Bruce to document his reasoning in the portfolio charter

    C. I would advise Bruce to document his reasoning in the portfolio management plan

    D. I would advise Bruce to document his reasoning in the portfolio component information

38. Successful communication planning includes an alignment of which of the following:

    A. People, planning, budgets

    B. People, ideas, information

    C. People, technology, information

    D. People, ideas, technology

39. Which factors indicate that there is a need to revise portfolio components?

    A. Change in priorities, regulatory changes, portfolio process assets

    B. Enterprise environmental factors, organizational process assets, portfolio strategic plan

    C. Obsolete goals, opportunities to be pursued, and response to regular changes

    D. None of the answer choices

40. Which is NOT an assessment activity of the portfolio management process?

    A. Evaluate existing portfolio components to determine if supportive of organization strategy and objectives

    B. Identify gaps in knowledge, structure, resources, processes

    C. assess current portfolio component resource availability and allocations against integrated schedule

D. Identify gaps in financial projections

41. Which is NOT included in assessment results of the portfolio management process?

    A. Understanding the organization's vision

    B. Misinformation that needs to be addressed

    C. Project, program, portfolio and operations management practices in place

    D. Understanding the organization's tax return

42. Measures must be meaningful. The guideline dictates that the performance measures must be "Specific". What does this indicate?

    A. The clear target indicates whether or not it is on budget.

    B. The target is variable - depends on the portfolio.

    C. The target indicates whether or not it is on time.

    D. A clear target must be provided as to what is being measured and the value being realized.

43. Which of the following ways does a PMO NOT support Portfolio Management:

    A. Eliminating risk completely

    B. Assisting with risk identification

    C. Communicating risks and issues

    D. Assisting with risk strategy development

44. Which of the following is an interaction with a portfolio management process group?

    A. Organization process plans

    B. Organizational process assets

    C. Organization process analysis

    D. None of the answer choices

45. Which one of the following is NOT an input to developing a portfolio roadmap?

    A. Portfolio

    B. Portfolio strategic plan

    C. Portfolio charter

    D. Organization strategy

46. Which of the four Portfolio Strategic Management processes involves an output of high-level portfolio planning that graphically depicts all portfolio elements needed to achieve organizational strategy and objectives?

    A. Define Portfolio Process Flow Chart

    B. Define Portfolio Processes

    C. Define Portfolio Roadmap

    D. Define Portfolio Tools & Techniques

47. Which of the four Portfolio Strategic Management processes examines the "as-is" state and compares it with the "to-be" state?

    A. Manage Strategic Planning

    B. Manage Portfolio Change

    C. Manage Strategic Change

    D. Manage Portfolio Strategy

48. Which of the following is an example (or examples) of evaluation criteria that a portfolio manager should apply?

    A. Market growth

    B. Market share

    C. New markets

    D. All of the answer choices

49. Which of the following best describes portfolio optimization?

   A. Maximizing portfolio return within the organizations predefined risk profile and tolerances

   B. Balancing the portfolio for value delivery

   C. Planning and allocating resources according to organizational strategy and objectives

   D. All of the answer choices

50. Which of the following are key activities with the Authorize Portfolio process?

   A. Allocating resources to authorized portfolio components

   B. Authorizing portfolio component proposal development or portfolio component execution

   C. Communicating changes and decisions for the authorized portfolio components

   D. All of the answer choices

51. Which of the following are examples of quantitative measures used in portfolio performance management?

   A. Internal rate of return (IRR) of the portfolio

   B. Increases in revenue attributable to the portfolio

   C. Percentage by which cycle times are reduced due to the portfolio

   D. All of the answer choices

52. Which of the following does not define the Portfolio Performance Management Plan process?

   A. Details how portfolio components are allocated for financial and equipment resources

   B. Explains how portfolio value is defined

   C. Details how portfolio components are allocated for human and material resources

   D. Explains how portfolio assets are defined

53. Which of the following are examples of performance reporting?

    A. Dashboards

    B. Scorecards

    C. Portfolio reports

    D. All of the answer choices

54. Which of the following is not an Input to the Develop Portfolio Communication Management Plan?

    A. Portfolio roadmap

    B. Portfolio process assets

    C. Scope

    D. Management Plan

55. Which of the following is a tool used to capture and record the results of a communication requirements analysis?

    A. Stakeholder matrix

    B. Elicitation techniques

    C. Communication matrix

    D. Data flow diagram

56. Which of the following is not an output for the Manage Portfolio Information process?

    A. Portfolio process assets updates

    B. Portfolio reports

    C. Project charter updates

    D. Portfolio management plan updates

57. Which of the following risk concerns are common to all organizational levels?

    A. Corruption

B. Transparency

C. Organizational integrity

D. All of the answer choices

58. Which of the following areas around risk management are identified by risk planning?

A. Risk processes, Portfolio risks important to the organization

B. Risk owners

C. Risk tolerance

D. All of the answer choices

59. How many portfolio management processes are there?

A. Sixteen

B. Eighteen

C. Twelve

D. Fourteen

60. Nancy attended a meeting with senior leadership who are concerned about the current gap in the alignment between the portfolio and organization's strategy. What should Nancy do first to address their concerns?

A. Nancy should perform a scenario analysis

B. Nancy should encourage leadership to change organization strategy to better fit the portfolio

C. Nancy should make changes to the portfolio so that they fit better with the organization strategy

D. Nancy should develop a strategic plan to evaluate the portfolio as it relates to high-level organization strategy

61. Linda recently started working on the Develop Portfolio Performance Management Plan process. She is trying to find information on the resource schedule, funding schedule, and resource work calendar. Where would she find this information?

    A. Portfolio process assets

    B. Portfolio charter

    C. Portfolio management plan

    D. Enterprise environmental factors

62. To define the management of strategic change the following outputs are needed:

    A. Portfolio updates

    B. Portfolio strategic plan updates

    C. Portfolio charter updates

    D. All of the answer choices

63. To develop a portfolio charter, the following inputs are needed:

    A. Enterprise environmental factors

    B. Portfolio strategic plan

    C. Portfolio process assets

    D. All of the answer choices

64. In developing the portfolio for the Portfolio Governance Model, which of the following is not an output for the model?

    A. Plan metrics

    B. Portfolio updates

    C. Roadmap updates

    D. Management plan updates

65. In developing the process for Authorize the Portfolio, which of the following is not an input?

    A. Portfolio management plan

    B. Portfolio

    C. Portfolio updates

    D. Portfolio reports

66. If during the Provide Portfolio Oversight, portfolio policies, processes, and/or procedures change, what should be updated to reflect the changes?

    A. Portfolio process assets

    B. Enterprise environmental factors

    C. Portfolio roadmap

    D. Portfolio

67. Some examples of external risks include all of the following except:

    A. Technological advances

    B. Competitive market

    C. Political events

    D. Project progress

68. Luke has recently started working on the Manage Supply and Demand process. He is currently reviewing resource utilization reports. Where are resource utilization reports typically found?

    A. Portfolio performance management plan

    B. Portfolio reports

    C. Portfolio charter

    D. Portfolio management plan

69. Kyle has a portfolio management plan which has been produced and approved. He understands the organization is in a specific environment. The decision-making rights and authorities are presented in a particular document. What is this document that he is looking for?

    A. Managing compliance

    B. Performance management planning

    C. Portfolio oversight

    D. Governance model

70. Mike is starting to develop a portfolio. What should Mike have as a good starting point for developing his portfolio?

    A. Strategic alignment analysis

    B. Portfolio component inventory

    C. Prioritization analysis

    D. Inventory of work

71. Pete is working on the Manage Portfolio Risks process. He is currently applying an analysis to identify gaps in investment within the portfolio as a whole. What type of analysis is Pete performing?

    A. Investment choice analysis

    B. Facilitation techniques

    C. Sensitivity analysis

    D. Modeling and simulation

72. Allen wants to able to graphically communicate the link between the organization strategy and portfolio management. What will allow Allen to do this?

    A. Portfolio roadmap

    B. Portfolio charter

    C. Portfolio strategic plan

D. Interdependency analysis

73. A Benefits Realization Analysis can comprise any of the following except:

    A. Graphical methods illustrating realized benefits

    B. Results chain

    C. Outcome probability analysis

    D. Value chain

74. Tyler is working on a portfolio strategic plan. He has been informed that there is a new governmental regulation that may impact the organization's strategy. What type of situation is being described?

    A. Portfolio component inventory

    B. Gap analysis

    C. Enterprise environmental factors

    D. Portfolio process assets

75. Agnes is currently working on the Develop Portfolio Management Plan process. She is currently working on a plan which will help her determine how resource capacity should be managed against resource utilization and changing demand to ensure the portfolio component mix generates maximum value. What is Agnes doing?

    A. Portfolio resource management planning

    B. Portfolio value planning

    C. Portfolio reporting

    D. All of the answer choices

76. Marge just started working on the Develop Portfolio Communication Management Plan process. She is trying to gain an understanding of the structure of the portfolio and any interdependencies that exist between portfolio components. Where can she find this information?

    A. Portfolio management plan

B. Portfolio

C. Portfolio reports

D. Portfolio roadmap

77. Michael comes to you for advice. He has been working on portfolio risk management and is having trouble understanding the difference between risks and opportunities. How would you explain it to him?

   A. All negative risks which are not treated are missed opportunities

   B. If positive risks are not identified and treated, they become missed opportunities

   C. If negative risks are not identified and treated, they become missed opportunities

   D. All risks identified and not treated are missed opportunities

78. Raphael has just started working on the Develop Portfolio Risk Management Plan process. He is trying to find the portfolio risk register and the portfolio issue register. Where can Raphael find this information?

   A. Enterprise environmental factors

   B. Organizational process assets

   C. Portfolio management plan

   D. Portfolio process assets

79. Bethany believes she has completed the Manage Portfolio Risks process. She shows you that she has filed portfolio reports and updated the portfolio management plan. What else does Bethany need to update?

   A. Portfolio charter, enterprise environmental factors

   B. Portfolio process assets, organizational process assets

   C. Portfolio roadmap, portfolio charter

   D. Portfolio process assets, portfolio roadmap

80. Bethany believes she has completed the Manage Supply and Demand process. She shows you the completed portfolio reports. You point out to her that she is not completely finished. What is she missing?

    A. Portfolio roadmap updates, portfolio component inventory

    B. Portfolio roadmap updates, portfolio component inventory

    C. Portfolio roadmap updates, portfolio component inventory

    D. Portfolio updates, portfolio management plan updates

81. As her supervisor, Jackie comes to you and indicates that she has finished the Manage Strategic Change process. What should you be asking her for that would indicate or demonstrate she has completed the process?

    A. Portfolio charter updates, prioritization analysis, scenario analysis

    B. Stakeholder analysis, gap analysis, readiness assessment

    C. Portfolio strategic plan updates, portfolio charter updates, portfolio roadmap updates, portfolio updates, portfolio process assets updates

    D. Portfolio strategic plan updates, portfolio process assets updates, portfolio updates, stakeholder analysis

82. Within portfolio performance management, during which processes would elicitation techniques be used?

    A. Develop Portfolio Performance Management Plan, Manage Supply and Demand

    B. Manage Supply and Demand, Develop Portfolio Management Plan

    C. Develop Portfolio Performance Management Plan, Manage Portfolio Value

    D. Authorize Portfolio, Manage Portfolio Value

83. Within the context of the Manage Portfolio Value process, which of the following is a significant attribute of the weighting and scoring model which leads to portfolio component authorization?

    A. Revenue Growth

    B. Intrinsic Value

C. Operating Margins

D. Expected value

84. Within with Manage Portfolio Value process, the scoring of a component against established criteria is an example of what type of analysis?

    A. Benefits realization analysis

    B. Elicitation techniques

    C. Progress measurement techniques

    D. Value scoring and measurement analysis

85. Nicholas tells you that he is about to start the Authorize Portfolio process, but he doesn't know where to begin. What would you tell him?

    A. I would tell him that he needs to have enterprise environmental factors, prioritization analysis, and the portfolio management plan to start this process

    B. I would tell him that he needs to have a capability and capacity analysis, portfolio component inventory, and cost-benefit analysis to start this process

    C. I would tell him that he needs to have a portfolio charter, portfolio roadmap, and portfolio reports to start this process

    D. I would tell him that he needs to have the portfolio, portfolio management plan, and portfolio reports to start this process

86. Kathryn is working on the Manage Portfolio Risks process. She is currently running a simulation where the model is iterated. What type of tool is Kathryn using?

    A. Sensitivity analysis

    B. Performance variability analysis

    C. Monte Carlo technique

    D. Investment choice analysis

87. Lydia is nearly finished working on the Develop Portfolio Performance Management Plan process. During the process, there were several changes made to the benefits schedule and resource schedule. Where does Lydia need to document these updates?

    A. Portfolio roadmap

    B. Portfolio process assets

    C. Portfolio

    D. Organizational process assets

88. Annie has come to you for advice on the Manage Strategic Change process. She originally asked Bob who said that he thought Annie needed to understand the strategic plan better before going any further. Annie wants to know why it is so important to understand that first?

    A. Bob is incorrect. Understanding the strategic plan won't benefit Annie.

    B. It is important to ensure that all of the correct components within those organization areas with the highest strategic value are included

    C. It is important to go back and review the strategic plan and pay special attention to the Cost-benefit analysis

    D. Bob is correct that it is important, but it is more important for Annie to go back and re-run the prioritization analysis

89. Daniel comes to you for help. He has started working on the Optimize Portfolio process and has the existing portfolio reports, but is unsure how he is supposed to use them as it relates to this process. How would you advise him?

    A. He should look in the portfolio reports to find the approach for defining, optimizing, and authorizing portfolio components

    B. Portfolio reports are not used as part of the Optimize Portfolio process

    C. He should look in the portfolio reports to find portfolio risks associated with portfolio components as well as resource pool report data which is used to understand resource allocation

    D. He should refer to the portfolio reports for information on relevant data, tools, and templates regarding optimizing the portfolio

90. Craig has all of the inputs for the Manage Portfolio Risks process, but is struggling with where to begin in terms of analyzing them. What tools and techniques can Craig apply during this process?

    A. Weighted ranking and scoring techniques, graphical analytical methods

    B. Graphical analytical methods, prioritization analysis

    C. Prioritization analysis, weighted ranking and scoring techniques

    D. Weighted ranking and scoring techniques, quantitative and qualitative analysis

91. Craig is currently working on the Manage Portfolio Value process. He is running an analysis to determine alliance partner value, managerial value, and societal value to the organization. What type of analysis is Craig running?

    A. Comparative advantage analysis

    B. Cost-benefit analysis

    C. Value scoring and measurement analysis

    D. Benefits realization analysis

92. Devin is currently working on the Manage Portfolio Value process. He is currently using a SWOT analysis to gather information to ensure that benefits are comprehensively and holistically taken into consideration. What tool and technique is Devin applying?

    A. Elicitation techniques

    B. Value scoring and measurement analysis

    C. Value measurement techniques

    D. Progress measurement techniques

93. During the Develop Portfolio Management plan process, portfolio process assets should be reviewed to look for what kind of information?

    A. Information about ongoing and planned portfolio management tasks

    B. Performance information from a portfolio's past performance or history (for benchmarking purposes)

    C. Portfolio management decisions and open issues

D. All of the answer choices

94. Claire has nearly finished the Authorize Portfolio process. While she was working on this process, she needed to update the portfolio funding to reflect the funding allocated to authorize portfolio elements. Where would this information be reflected?

    A. Portfolio process assets

    B. Portfolio charter

    C. Portfolio management plan

    D. Portfolio reports

95. Rod recently started working on the Develop Portfolio Communication Management Plan process. He is trying to locate information on portfolio value assessments and portfolio manager roles and responsibilities. Where can he find this information?

    A. Portfolio

    B. Portfolio process assets

    C. Portfolio reports

    D. Portfolio management plan

96. Environmental Factors include which of the following?

    A. Existing human resources

    B. Infrastructure

    C. Personnel administration

    D. All of the answer choices

97. Christy is working on portfolio performance management. She is currently conducting a scenario analysis and quantitative and qualitative analysis. Which process is Christy engaged in?

    A. Manage Portfolio Value

    B. Develop Portfolio Management Plan

C. Manage Supply and Demand

D. Develop Portfolio Performance Management Plan

98. Benjamin is currently working on the Develop Portfolio Communication Management Plan process. He is presently conducting interviews on the effectiveness of communication. What tool and technique is Benjamin applying?

   A. Elicitation techniques

   B. Prioritization analysis

   C. Stakeholder analysis

   D. Communication requirements analysis

99. Blake approaches you for advice. He has recently been working on portfolio risk management. He is trying to understand the difference between risks and issues. How would you explain the difference to him?

   A. If negative risks are not identified and treated, they become issues

   B. All negative risks are issues

   C. If positive risks are not identified and treated, they become issues

   D. All positive risks which are not treated are issues

100. Blake is working on the Optimize Portfolio process. He is currently working on developing histograms, pie charts, and risk vs. return charts. What stage of the process is he in and what he is doing?

   A. Blake is applying tools and techniques with a graphical analytical method

   B. Blake is gathering inputs including the portfolio roadmap

   C. Blake is applying tools and techniques with a qualitative analysis

   D. Blake is applying tools and techniques with a SWOT analysis

101. Stakeholder analysis is performed to assess which of the following?

   A. Level of influence

B. Level of interest

C. Level of urgency

D. All of the answer choices

102. Carl is about to start working on the Manage Portfolio Value process. What should he have to start working on this process?

    A. Portfolio, portfolio management plan, portfolio reports

    B. Portfolio charter, portfolio roadmap, portfolio

    C. Portfolio reports, portfolio charter, portfolio management plan

    D. Portfolio roadmap, portfolio management plan, portfolio reports

103. Kayla is currently conducting portfolio review meetings and just recently completed utilizing elicitation techniques. Which portfolio governance process is Kayla working on?

    A. Provide Portfolio Oversight

    B. Develop Portfolio Management Plan

    C. Authorize Portfolio

    D. Define Portfolio

104. While implementing a particular technique during the Develop Portfolio Performance Management Plan process, Steve is regularly consulting with stakeholders and key subject matter experts through planning meetings and brainstorming sessions to develop measures and ensure that the correct items are being measured to ensure optimal resource performance. What technique is Steve using?

    A. Capability and capacity analysis

    B. Portfolio management information system

    C. Facilitation techniques

    D. Elicitation techniques

105. Examples of Organizational Process Assets used as inputs to planning for risk management include all of the following except:

A. Organizational chart

B. Vision and mission statements

C. Organizational strategy and objectives

D. Organizational risk tolerance and lessons learned

106. When developing the portfolio management plan it is important to be guided by the:

A. Management Plan

B. Financial Plan

C. Project Plan

D. Strategic Plan

107. When new strategic direction is given during the Manage Strategic Change process, what needs to be considered before and during portfolio changes?

A. Executives and key stakeholders' expectations and communication requirements

B. Cost-benefit analysis, prioritization analysis

C. Previous strategic direction provided by Executives, Readiness assessment

D. None of the answer choices

108. Funnel charts, bubble charts, histograms, burn-down charts, burn-up charts, and other types of diagrams are all stored where?

A. Portfolio reports

B. Portfolio management plan

C. Portfolio

D. Portfolio roadmap

109. Glenn is currently involved in the Authorize Portfolio process. He is describing to you a tool and technique he is currently applying which identifies which portfolio components have been assigned resources. What is Glenn describing?

A. Portfolio management information system

B. Portfolio component inventory

C. Portfolio component categorization techniques

D. Portfolio authorization technique

110. Jenny has been asked to make a determination as to how prepared the organization is to perform the steps needed to bridge the gap between the "as-is" portfolio state and the "to-be" state. What is she being asked to perform?

A. Readiness assessment

B. Cost-benefit analysis

C. Stakeholder analysis

D. Gap analysis

111. A tool and technique for managing strategic change is a readiness assessment. Why is this important?

A. Determines the if, when, what and how of implementing change

B. Determines the if, when, what and how of implementing a plan

C. Determines the if, when, what and how of implementing strategy

D. None of the answer choices

112. In order to assess stakeholder influence, which of the following questions may be asked?

A. Which of the stakeholders are considered leaders, influencers, or early adopters?

B. Is their role as a stakeholder recognized by the organization?

C. What are the interrelationships among the stakeholders?

D. All of the answer choices

113. In order to assess stakeholder influence, which of the following questions may be asked?

   A. Which stakeholders are known to resist change?

   B. Who are the members of the governing body?

   C. What level of authority does each stakeholder have affecting the portfolio and the organization?

   D. All of the answer choices

114. Resource capability and capacity management analyze which of the following:

   A. Resource types and schedules

   B. Strategic objectives

   C. Portfolio value assessments

   D. All of the Answer Choices

115. Stephanie is working on the Develop Portfolio Performance Management Plan process. She has setup an automated tool to collect information in order to support the portfolio management process. What type of tool and techniques has Stephanie setup?

   A. Portfolio management information system

   B. Portfolio component inventory

   C. Elicitation techniques

   D. Capability and capacity analysis

116. Stephen has received a list of risks. This list of risks includes concerns regarding portfolio components' cost, time and, scope. What organizational level likely provided these risks to Stephen?

   A. Executive Management

   B. Operations Management

   C. Portfolio Manager

D. Program or Project Teams

117. In portfolio component categorization technique, which of the following are examples of "increased profitability" considerations?

A. Cost reduction and avoidance

B. Revenue increase

C. Revenue generation

D. All of the answer choices

118. Laura Ann is approached by a senior manager during the Provide Portfolio Oversight process who is inquiring about a proposal they made concerning a change in funding allocation. Where can Laura Ann find this information?

A. Portfolio

B. Portfolio process assets

C. Portfolio management plan

D. Portfolio reports

119. Andre is currently working on the Manage Portfolio Value process. He is currently using earned value as part of value scoring and measurement analysis to evaluate the portfolio. What type of technique is Andre using?

A. Progress measurement technique

B. Cost-benefit analysis

C. Portfolio efficient frontier

D. Comparative advantage analysis

120. George is approached by a key stakeholder who wants George to be able to drill down on the expected benefits for a particular portfolio while also detailing how they will be measured. Where can George tell the stakeholder his concerns are typically addressed?

A. Portfolio management plan

B. Portfolio charter

C. Portfolio reports

D. Portfolio performance management plan

121. In risk management, which is the most difficult to quantitatively or qualitatively evaluate?

   A. Risk probability

   B. Risk impact

   C. Risk importance

   D. Risk interdependencies

122. Courtney comes to you for advice. She understands that there is a strategic management process but is unsure of what stage in the process she is in. She is currently doing a scenario analysis and analyzing capacity. What phase is she in?

   A. Develop Portfolio Strategic Plan

   B. Manage Strategic Change

   C. Define Portfolio Roadmap

   D. Develop Portfolio Charter

123. Which of the following is NOT considered a primary activity for portfolio management? (Select the best answer)

   A. Identifying and aligning organizational priorities

   B. Managing the details of programs and projects

   C. Managing risk, communication and resources

   D. Determining a governance and performance management framework

124. Measures must be meaningful. The guideline dictates that the performance measures must be "Realistic". What does this indicate?

A. Target is achievable given the organization's human resource capacity and it can be challenging but is achievable.

B. Target is achievable given who the portfolio manager is assigned to it.

C. Target is achievable given the organization's financial resources and it can be challenging but is achievable.

D. Target is achievable given the organization's capabilities and capacity - can be challenging but achievable.

125. Betsy has nearly finished the Develop Portfolio Communication Management Plan process. During the process, there were several changes made to portfolio risks and issues. What should Betsy update to reflect this change?

    A. Portfolio management plan

    B. Portfolio roadmap

    C. Portfolio charter

    D. Portfolio process assets

126. What are enterprise environmental factors?

    A. The portfolio's plans, policies, procedures, and guidelines

    B. Factors within the organization which do not have an impact on the portfolio strategy and plan

    C. Factors which may consist of corporate, environmental, and governmental variables that contribute to the Develop Portfolio Strategic Plan process

    D. None of the answer choices

127. What are the tools and techniques used to develop a portfolio charter?

    A. Interdependency analysis, capability and capacity analysis

    B. Prioritization analysis, gap analysis

    C. Scenario analysis, cost-benefit analysis

    D. Scenario analysis, capability and capacity analysis

128. What are the inputs to the Develop Portfolio Charter process?

   A. Cost-benefit analysis, portfolio strategic plan, scenario analysis

   B. Portfolio process assets updates, capability and capacity analysis, enterprise environmental factors

   C. Portfolio strategic plan, scenario analysis, portfolio process assets

   D. Portfolio strategic plan, portfolio process assets, enterprise environmental factors

129. What are the inputs to the Develop Portfolio Performance Management Plan process?

   A. Portfolio roadmap, portfolio reports, portfolio charter

   B. Portfolio management plan, portfolio process assets, organizational process assets, enterprise environmental factors

   C. Portfolio roadmap, portfolio charter, organizational process assets, enterprise environmental factors

   D. Portfolio management plan, portfolio process assets, organizational process assets, portfolio reports

130. What are the purposes of the Portfolio Communication Management processes?

   A. To further develop the portfolio management plan and align it with organizational strategy

   B. To implement communication policy into the portfolio charter

   C. To develop the portfolio communication management plan and to manage portfolio information

   D. None of the answer choices

131. What are the inputs to the Develop Portfolio Communication Management Plan process?

   A. Enterprise environmental factors, portfolio process assets, portfolio reports

   B. Portfolio charter, portfolio, portfolio reports

C. Portfolio charter, portfolio management plan, portfolio reports, portfolio process assets

D. Portfolio, portfolio roadmap, portfolio management plan, portfolio reports, portfolio process assets

132. What does the strategic alignment analysis focus on?

    A. Gaps and changes to the organization strategy and objectives

    B. Portfolio roadmap

    C. Where there are gaps in focus , investment or alignment with the portfolio

    D. New or changing organization strategy and objectives

133. What does the portfolio structure identify?

    A. It identifies the portfolio, subportfolios, programs, and projects based on organization areas

    B. It identifies the Portfolio strategic plan and Portfolio charter

    C. It identifies strategies and priorities, and portfolio components are grouped to facilitate effective management

    D. All of the answer choices

134. What does the score measure in a scoring model?

    A. Whether or not each percentage was calculated correctly

    B. Whether or not each criterion is met

    C. Whether or not each weight is correct

    D. Whether or not each category is similar

135. What does the portfolio communication management plan define?

    A. All communications needs, establishes communication requirements, specifies frequency, and identifies recipients for information associated with the portfolio management process

B. It defines policies and practices for optimizing portfolio value including revenue growth and increased operating margins

C. It identifies the stakeholders, determines the different individuals and groups, and determines their concerns, interests, and influence

D. None of the answer choices

136. What information does the portfolio management plan provide as it relates to the Develop Portfolio Management Plan process?

A. It provides stakeholder expectations and requirements, governance model, strategic change framework, planning, procurement, and oversight processes including direction for performance, communication, and risk management

B. It contains portfolio-related documents such as the portfolio charter and portfolio strategic plan

C. It provides stakeholder expectations and requirements, governance model, strategic change framework, planning, procurement, and oversight processes with the primary objective to maximize profit

D. All of the answer choices

137. What is the purpose of the Authorize Portfolio process?

A. To provide critical information of portfolio components that is required by portfolio oversight

B. To optimize and balance the portfolio for performance and value delivery

C. To evaluate portfolio components based on ranking criteria, dependencies, and goals

D. To activate selected portfolio components by allocating resources to develop component proposals or execute portfolio components

138. What is/are the process(es) in both the knowledge area Portfolio Governance Management and the Authorizing and Controlling Process Group?

A. Authorize portfolio

B. Optimize portfolio

C. Provide portfolio oversight

D. Provide portfolio oversight AND authorize portfolio

139. What is the portfolio manager generally responsible for updating and adding to the portfolio process assets?

    A. Performance measurement criteria

    B. Specifications and work instructions

    C. Proposal evaluation criteria

    D. All of the answer choices

140. What is contained in Portfolio Reports?

    A. Project dashboard

    B. Project management plan

    C. Program status report

    D. None of the answer choices

141. What is capability and capacity analysis?

    A. Performed to understand how much work is able to be performed based on the resources available

    B. Performed to understand the ability to finance the work to be performed

    C. Performed to understand how much work is able to be performed

    D. Performed to understand how much work is able to be performed based on the resources available as well as the ability of the organization to source and execute the selected portfolio

142. What is the purpose of a cost-benefit analysis as it relates to defining the portfolio roadmap?

    A. It quantifies estimated costs and benefits and lists qualitative considerations of alternative portfolio components for evaluation

B. It helps to identify dependencies the portfolio has in relationship to the portfolio environment

C. It allows the portfolio manager to compare strategic objectives and prioritize objectives

D. None of the answer choices

143. What is the purpose of conducting gap analysis?

A. To ensure continuity and aligns key stakeholders' expectations with the changing strategy and resulting portfolio realignment

B. To enable management of the portfolio and demonstrates a clear path from the "as-is" to the "to-be" state

C. To compare the current portfolio mix and components with the new strategic direction and the "to-be" organizational vision

D. None of the answer choices

144. What is involved in the integration of portfolio management plans during the process of developing the portfolio management plan?

A. In involves eliciting requirements from a variety of sources utilizing different methods

B. It involves assigning performance review roles and responsibilities across each program, projects, or operational component

C. It involves referencing subsidiary plans which are always developed prior to starting the integration of portfolio management plans

D. It involves the development of subsidiary plans and the analysis of those plans to ensure they are aligned for consistency

145. What is the purpose of using a scoring model to evaluate portfolio components?

A. It makes the portfolio components comparable for evaluation purposes.

B. It is used to satisfy regulatory and compliance requirements

C. It is used to as part of process improvement

D. None of the answer choices

146. What is the purpose of the Provide Portfolio Oversight process?

   A. To activate selected portfolio components by allocating resources to develop component proposals or execute portfolio components

   B. To optimize and balance the portfolio for performance and value delivery

   C. To evaluate portfolio components based on ranking criteria, dependencies, and goals

   D. To monitor the portfolio to ensure alignment with organizational strategy and objectives

147. What is the purpose of the portfolio performance management plan?

   A. To explain how portfolio value is defined and to detail how portfolio components are allocated for resources

   B. To optimize and balance the portfolio for performance and value delivery

   C. To activate selected portfolio components by allocating resources to develop component proposals or execute portfolio components

   D. None of the answer choices

148. What is a potential goal in managing supply and demand?

   A. Ensure resource capacity is optimally allocated against resource requirements

   B. Ensure resource capacity is optimally allocated against demand based on known organizational priorities and potential value

   C. Minimize both unused resources and unmet demands

   D. All of the answer choices

149. What is resource leveling?

   A. A technique used to assess criteria and to discern the weight assigned to different benefits and outcomes

   B. A technique used to analyze the various inputs to determine how portfolio value is impacted by change

C. A technique used to indicate whether resource capacity has been optimally matched against resource demands and highlights areas that need adjustment

D. A technique which strives to smooth performance levels by managing bottleneck areas and communicating delayed schedules

150. What is the goal in defining portfolio value?

A. To deliver the maximum value possible aligned with strategic objectives and with limited consideration on risk

B. To deliver the maximum value possible aligned with strategic objectives and with an acceptable level of risk based on the level of risk tolerance

C. To deliver the maximum value possible aligned with financial objectives and with an acceptable level of risk based on the level of risk tolerance

D. To deliver the acceptable value at acceptable risk

151. What is the best rationale to institute portfolio risk management?

A. Manage interdependencies of risks among the portfolio components

B. It is the right thing to do

C. Manage the financial impact of portfolio components

D. Manage the execution details of portfolio components

152. What is portfolio risk?

A. It is the process of identifying risk while trying to maximize financial profit

B. It is an uncertain event or condition that, if it occurs, has a positive or negative effective on one or more project objectives

C. It is an uncertain event or condition that, if it occurs, has only a negative effective on one or more project objectives

D. None of the answer choices

153. Matt is working on the Develop Portfolio Risk Management Plan process. He is currently in the process of trying to better balance risk by reallocating the portfolio in instances where it has deviated away from organization strategy. What is Matt doing?

   A. Outcome probability analysis

   B. Portfolio risk exposure chart

   C. Rebalancing methods

   D. Investment choice

154. What role do portfolio process assets play in the Develop Portfolio Charter process?

   A. They allow the portfolio manager to identify corporate, environmental, and governmental variables that may contribute to and constrain the process

   B. They allow the portfolio manager to understand the ability of the organization to source and execute the selected portfolio

   C. They allow the portfolio manager to leverage the portfolio's plans, policies, procedures, guidelines and any other documentation of stakeholder relationships, scope, benefits, and portfolio goals

   D. None of the answer choices

155. What role does the portfolio play in the Manage Strategic Change process?

   A. It is used to evaluate strategic objectives, prioritize objectives, and perform strategic assessments again current enterprise portfolios

   B. It does not play a role in the process

   C. It is used to understand the portfolio structure, scope, constraints, dependencies, and resources

   D. It is the means to the "to be" vision

156. What should be the primary focus when selecting a communication strategy?

   A. The primary focus should be on satisfying the most important information needs of stakeholders so that effective decisions are made and organizational objectives are met

B. The primary focus should be on communicating as frequently as possible with all stakeholders

C. The primary focus should be on communicating only the essential information to senior and executive level stakeholders

D. None of the answer choices

157. What tends to happen during the early stages of developing a portfolio?

A. The portfolio may evolve as more details are obtained such as dependencies, timelines, and strategic changes

B. The portfolio tends to have a limited amount of change

C. The portfolio may evolve due to internal factors only

D. None of the answer choices

158. What type of stakeholder information is collected in a stakeholder matrix?

A. Stakeholder expectations

B. Stakeholder roles

C. Stakeholder interests

D. All of the answer choices

159. Portfolio Review Meetings are:

A. Recurring, formal, scheduled around significant milestones

B. Random, informal, scheduled around significant milestones

C. Random, formal, scheduled around significant milestones

D. Recurring, informal, scheduled around significant milestones

160. Portfolio process assets that refer to portfolio communication requirements include all of the following except:

A. Allowable communication media

B. Communication technology available

C. Record retention policies and security requirements

D. Information technology policy

161. In the Manage Strategic Change process, what vehicles are used to plan and execute the strategic change?

   A. Portfolio strategic plan, portfolio management plan

   B. Portfolio charter, portfolio roadmap

   C. Portfolio management plan, portfolio roadmap

   D. Portfolio strategic plan, portfolio charter

162. In the Authorize Portfolio process, which of the following does not get updated?

   A. Portfolio Process Assets

   B. Portfolio Management Plan

   C. Portfolio Reports

   D. Portfolio Charter

163. In the process Develop Portfolio Risk Management Plan which of the following is not an input?

   A. Enterprise environmental factors

   B. Portfolio management plan

   C. Portfolio and Organizational Process Assets

   D. Project Charter

164. Patti is currently working on the Manage Portfolio Value process. She is currently performing analysis to determine earned value, assessed value, and measuring portfolio performance. What tool and technique is Patti applying?

   A. Elicitation techniques

B. Benefits realization analysis

C. Benefits realization analysis

D. Value scoring and measurement analysis

165. Scott comes to you as his supervisor and indicates that he has finished the Develop Portfolio Management Plan process. He hands you a copy of the changes he made to the portfolio strategic plan. What is Scott missing?

    A. Portfolio roadmap, portfolio process assets updated, portfolio management plan

    B. Elicitation techniques, portfolio organizational structure analysis, integration of portfolio management plans

    C. Portfolio management plan, portfolio process assets update

    D. Portfolio charter, portfolio management plan

166. Gary is performing analysis to understand how much work can be performed based on the resources available as well as the ability of the organization to source and execute the selected portfolio and to determine the constraints generated by skill set limitations. What analysis is Gary performing?

    A. Resource analysis

    B. Interdependency analysis

    C. Prioritization analysis

    D. Capability and capacity analysis

167. Tony is working on defining the portfolio roadmap. He has been approached by an executive level stakeholder who has expressed concern about cost as it relates to certain portfolio elements. How should Tony proceed?

    A. Tony should run an interdependency analysis

    B. Tony should refer to the portfolio charter

    C. Tony should run a prioritization analysis

    D. Tony should run a cost-benefit analysis

168. Dwayne is the portfolio manager. During the Develop Portfolio Risk Management Plan process, Dwayne developed new risk checklists and new risk categories. What needs to be updated as a result of the change?

    A. Organizational process assets

    B. Portfolio management plan

    C. Portfolio reports

    D. Portfolio process assets

169. A typical "what-if scenario":

    A. Tracks impacts of portfolio management decisions on resource capacity

    B. Tracks impacts of portfolio management decisions on portfolio assets

    C. Tracks impacts of portfolio optimization decisions on resource capacity

    D. Tracks impacts of portfolio optimization decisions on portfolio assets

170. A typical tool for communication is:

    A. Email

    B. Meeting

    C. Dashboard

    D. All of the answer choices

9.2.2. Questions and Answers

1. The Manage Portfolio Risksprocess has how many stages? (Moderate)

    A. Four

    B. Three

    C. Two

    D. One

> The correct answer is **A**. Refer to Section 8.2 of the Standard for Portfolio Management - 3rd Edition. Review the descriptions and definition.

2. The Aligning Process Group is most active when? (Moderate)

   A. After the portfolio organization has defined and developed its plans

   B. After the portfolio organization has defined and developed its strategic goals

   C. After the portfolio organization has defined its near term budget

   D. All of the answer choices

   > The correct answer is **D**. Refer to Section 3.1 of the Standard for Portfolio Management - 3rd Edition. Review the descriptions and definition.

3. Hal approaches you for advice. He is about to start working on the Define Portfolio process and feels as though everything has already been defined and that this process can be skipped. How would you advise Hal? (Difficult)

   A. I would advise Hal that he can skip the process and proceed to do a portfolio component inventory

   B. I would advise Hal that the he is correct and the process can be skipped.

   C. I would advise Hal that the process should not be skipped and is important because it provides a graphical overview of key portfolio elements

   D. I would advise Hal that the process should not be skipped and is important because the portfolio needs to be organized for evaluation, selection, and prioritization.

   > The correct answer is **D**. This is a very important process involving organizing the portfolio.
   > Refer to Section 5.2 of the Standard for Portfolio Management - 3rd Edition. Review the descriptions and definition.

4. The best tool to develop a stakeholder communication management strategy is: (Moderate)

   A. Mapping of internal and external stakeholders to quadrants

   B. Mapping of communication assets to quadrants

   C. Mapping of influence and interest to quadrants

   D. Mapping of organization chart to quadrants based on influence

5. The communication management plan should include all of the following except: (Moderate)

    A. Communication protocols

    B. Planned frequency

    C. Communication constraints

    D. Communication policies

    The correct answer is **A**. Refer to Section 7.1.3.1 of the Standard for Portfolio Management - 3rd Edition. Review the descriptions and definition.

6. How does a manager measure portfolio component performance? (Moderate)

    A. Portfolio component is undertaken to achieve a strategic goal and its contribution is measured within the context of that goal

    B. Portfolio component is undertaken to achieve primarily a financial goal

    C. Portfolio component is undertaken to achieve primarily a human resource goal

    D. Portfolio component is undertaken to achieve one or more strategic goals

    The correct answer is **A**. Refer to Section 1.5 of the Standard for Portfolio Management - 3rd Edition. Review the descriptions and definition.

7. How does a portfolio manager address the function of quality management? (Moderate)

    A. Ensuring compliance with set standards

    B. Not a factor as portfolio managers look at multiple areas

    C. Ensuring compliance with voluntary standards and OSHA requirements

    D. Ensuring compliance with voluntary standards and mandatory requirements

    The correct answer is **D**. Refer to Section 1.7 of the Standard for Portfolio Management - 3rd Edition. Review the descriptions and definition.

8. How does the portfolio management plan utilize information from the roadmap? (Moderate)

   A. To define the direction

   B. To define the project plan

   C. To define the assets

   D. To define low level schedules and timelines

   > The correct answer is **D**. Refer to Section 5.1.1 of the Standard for Portfolio Management - 3rd Edition. Review the descriptions and definition.

9. The following types of diagrams are all useful to show execution of the portfolio against the overall strategic plan and budget except: (Moderate)

   A. Funnel and bubble charts

   B. Burn-down or burn-up charts

   C. Histograms

   D. Pictograms

   > The correct answer is **D**. Refer to Section 6.2.3.3 of the Standard for Portfolio Management - 3rd Edition. Review the descriptions and definition.

10. How is "Change" defined for portfolio management? (Easy)

   A. Depending on organizations, it can be a random process

   B. Occurs in the broader internal and external environment monitored by the manager

   C. Strictly internal controls that are monitored by the manager

   D. Occurs in the broader internal and external environment but not necessarily monitored

   > The correct answer is **B**. Refer to Section 1.3 of the Standard for Portfolio Management - 3rd Edition. Review the descriptions and definition.

11. How is organizational strategy implemented as it relates to the strategic plan? (Easy)

   A. Through portfolio components and ongoing operations

B. Through the prioritization analysis process

C. Through the capability and capacity analysis

D. All of the answer choices

> The correct answer is **A**. Refer to Section 4.1.3.1 of the Standard for Portfolio Management - 3rd Edition. Review the descriptions and definition.

12. Ron is working on his portfolio charter and is trying to assess the impact of enterprise environmental factors. Which of the follow scenarios could Ron be facing? (Difficult)

   A. The portfolio structure needs to be changed so that it aligns stakeholder relationships, scope, benefits, and portfolio goals

   B. The portfolio charter needs to be changed to account for the results of the capability and capacity analysis

   C. The portfolio charter needs to align with scenarios examined during scenario analysis

   D. The portfolio structure in the charter needs to align with corporate accounting structure

> The correct answer is **D**. Refer to Section 4.2.1.3 of the Standard for Portfolio Management - 3rd Edition. Review the descriptions and definition.

13. How is the portfolio related to the process Define Portfolio Roadmap? (Easy)

   A. It quantifies the estimated costs and benefits of portfolio components

   B. It is used to perform a portfolio component inventory

   C. It is used to define organization areas only on the portfolio roadmap

   D. The portfolio and components are referenced to define the portfolio roadmap

> The correct answer is **D**. Refer to Section 4.3.1.3 of the Standard for Portfolio Management - 3rd Edition. Review the descriptions and definition.

14. How is the portfolio management plan utilized during the Manage Portfolio Value process? (Moderate)

   A. It provides for the continual identification and assessment of the value of the portfolio benefits and the impact on organizational objectives

B. It provides a high-level timeline for expected portfolio component delivery

C. It provides stakeholder expectations and requirements, governance model, strategic change framework, planning, procurement, and oversight processes including direction for performance, communication, and risk management

D. All of the answer choices

> The correct answer is **A**. Refer to Section 6.3.1.2 of the Standard for Portfolio Management - 3rd Edition. Review the descriptions and definition.

15. The least likely factors that affect portfolio structural risks is: (Moderate)

A. Alignment of organizations ability to organize its portfolio mission with hierarchal and clustered structures

B. Quality of organizations portfolio management

C. Organizational hierarchy

D. Methods and approaches in which organization operates and performs its tasks

> The correct answer is **C**. Refer to Section 8 of the Standard for Portfolio Management - 3rd Edition. Review the descriptions and definition.

16. How many people may be in the governing body? (Easy)

A. Minimum 2

B. The more the better

C. Minimum 5 or more

D. 1 or more

> The correct answer is **D**. Refer to Section 1.9 of the Standard for Portfolio Management - 3rd Edition. Review the descriptions and definition.

17. How many portfolio management processes are there? (Easy)

A. Sixteen

B. Eighteen

C. Twelve

D. Fourteen

> The correct answer is **A**. Refer to Section 3.1 of the Standard for Portfolio Management - 3rd Edition. Review the descriptions and definition.

18. How many portfolio management process groups are there? (Easy)

   A. Four

   B. Three

   C. One

   D. Two

> The correct answer is **B**. Refer to Section 3.1 of the Standard for Portfolio Management - 3rd Edition. Review the descriptions and definition.

19. How many Portfolio Communication Management Processes are there? (Moderate)

   A. Five

   B. Three

   C. Two

   D. Four

> The correct answer is **C**. Refer to Section 7 of the Standard for Portfolio Management - 3rd Edition. Review the descriptions and definition.

20. Why might portfolio process assets need to be updated as a result of the Optimize Portfolio process? (Moderate)

   A. Procedures and guidelines have changed during the process

   B. The approach and criteria to maintaining a balanced portfolio may have changed during the process

   C. Organizational areas, portfolio components, and high level timeline have changed during the process

   D. None of the answer choices

The correct answer is **A**. Refer to Section 5.3.3.5 of the Standard for Portfolio Management - 3rd Edition. Review the descriptions and definition.

21. All of the following are key descriptors of portfolio components that a portfolio manager may make use of except: (Moderate)

    A. Type of portfolio component

    B. Portfolio management plan

    C. Strategic goals supported

    D. Resources required

    The correct answer is **B**. Refer to Section 5.2.2.1 of the Standard for Portfolio Management - 3rd Edition. Review the descriptions and definition.

22. All of the following are valid for scoring and measuring organizational value except: (Moderate)

    A. Portfolio scoring techniques

    B. Progress measurement techniques

    C. Value measurement techniques

    D. Portfolio efficient frontier

    The correct answer is **A**. Refer to Section 6.3.2.2 of the Standard for Portfolio Management - 3rd Edition. Review the descriptions and definition.

23. The performance management process manages the sourcing of: (Moderate)

    A. Finance, assets, information technology

    B. Finance, vendors, human resources

    C. Finance, assets, human resources

    D. Finance, marketing, assets

    The correct answer is **C**. Refer to Section 6 of the Standard for Portfolio Management - 3rd Edition. Review the descriptions and definition.

24. The portfolio manager must have expertise in ALL of the following application and analysis of quantitative and qualitative techniques except: (Easy)

    A. Program And project management methods and techniques

    B. Organizational management

    C. Portfolio risk management

    D. Software evaluation

    > The correct answer is **D**. Refer to Section 1.8 of the Standard for Portfolio Management - 3rd Edition. Review the descriptions and definition.

25. The portfolio charter is defined as: (Difficult)

    A. The document that formally establishes the portfolio change management plan

    B. The document that formally authorizes and structures a portfolio

    C. The document that provides the scope and schedule of establishing the portfolio management process

    D. The process that initiation the formation of a portfolio

    > The correct answer is **B**. Refer to Section 3.2 of the Standard for Portfolio Management - 3rd Edition. Review the descriptions and definition.

26. The portfolio charter contains which of the following? (Easy)

    A. Financial analysts

    B. Identification of stakeholders

    C. Project Plan

    D. Identification of C-level executives

    > The correct answer is **B**. Refer to Section 3.2 of the Standard for Portfolio Management - 3rd Edition. Review the descriptions and definition.

27. The portfolio roadmap displays information at what type of level and what type of view? (Moderate)

    A. High-level and chronological

B. Highly detailed level and alphabetical

C. High-level and alphabetical

D. Highly detailed level and chronological

> The correct answer is **A**. Refer to Section 4.3.3.1 of the Standard for Portfolio Management - 3rd Edition. Review the descriptions and definition.

28. The portfolio management plan may refer to different methodologies or approaches that the organization applies to manage different types of portfolio components. This is done based on the specifications from what? (Difficult)

    A. Portfolio charter

    B. Portfolio process assets

    C. Portfolio roadmap

    D. Organizational process assets

> The correct answer is **C**. Refer to Section 5.1.1.3 of the Standard for Portfolio Management - 3rd Edition. Review the descriptions and definition.

29. The portfolio management plan can include each of the following sections except: (Moderate)

    A. Performance management planning

    B. Change control and management

    C. Managing scope change

    D. Balancing portfolio and managing dependencies

> The correct answer is **C**. Refer to Section 5.1.2 of the Standard for Portfolio Management - 3rd Edition. Review the descriptions and definition.

30. Rod recently started working on the Develop Portfolio Communication Management Plan process. He is trying to locate information on portfolio value assessments and portfolio manager roles and responsibilities. Where can he find this information? (Difficult)

    A. Portfolio

    B. Portfolio process assets

C. Portfolio reports

D. Portfolio management plan

> The correct answer is **B**. Information on portfolio value assessments and portfolio manager roles and responsibilities are part of portfolio process assets.
> Refer to Section 7.1.1.5 of the Standard for Portfolio Management - 3rd Edition. Review the descriptions and definition.

31. The risk register includes all of the following information except: (Moderate)

    A. Probability impact assessment

    B. Risk matrix

    C. Risk triggers

    D. Updated risk categories

> The correct answer is **B**. Refer to Section 8.2.1.1 of the Standard for Portfolio Management - 3rd Edition. Review the descriptions and definition.

32. The strategic change process compares: (Moderate)

    A. The "as is" state with the "to be" state

    B. The current state with the ideal state

    C. The present state with the past state

    D. None of the answer choices

> The correct answer is **A**. Refer to Section 4.4 of the Standard for Portfolio Management - 3rd Edition. Review the descriptions and definition.

33. Lisa Fe has just started working on the Develop Portfolio Performance Management Plan process. She is trying to find information on stakeholder expectation and requirements as well as information about planning and procurement. Where should she look for this information? (Moderate)

    A. Portfolio management plan

    B. Portfolio management information system

C. Portfolio roadmap

D. Portfolio process assets

> The correct answer is **A**. The portfolio management plan contains information on stakeholder expectations, planning, and procurement.
> Refer to Section 6.1.1.1 of the Standard for Portfolio Management - 3rd Edition. Review the descriptions and definition.

34. As a result of risk analysis, there may be specific actions. Which one of the following is least likely: (Easy)

    A. Change in staff allocation

    B. Increase in funding

    C. Portfolio components added, changed or terminated

    D. Change organizational strategy

    > The correct answer is **D**. Refer to Section 8.2.3.2 of the Standard for Portfolio Management - 3rd Edition. Review the descriptions and definition.

35. Sarah just came back from getting advice on how to use the portfolio structure as a guide. She asks you if you have heard of doing this before within the Develop Portfolio Charter process. How do you respond? (Moderate)

    A. It can be used a guide to create the Portfolio strategic plan

    B. It can be used as a guide to create a variety of portfolio scenarios

    C. It can be used as a guide to graphically depict portfolio elements to achieve organizational strategy and objectives

    D. It can be used as a guide to identify portfolio and subportfolios based on organization areas, hierarchies, and goals for each portfolio component

    > The correct answer is **D**. Refer to Section 4.2.3.3 of the Standard for Portfolio Management - 3rd Edition. Review the descriptions and definition.

36. Melanie has sought advice from Glenn, a senior member of her office, regarding managing strategic change. Glenn indicated to Melanie that a stakeholder analysis is very important. Why? (Difficult)

A. It is used to understand the portfolio structure, scope, constraints, dependencies, and resources

B. It compares the current portfolio mix and components with the new strategic direction and the "to-be" organizational vision

C. It is used to evaluate strategic objectives, prioritize objectives, and perform strategic assessments again current enterprise portfolios

D. It helps to ensure continuity and aligns key stakeholders' expectations with the changing strategy and resulting portfolio realignment

> The correct answer is **D**. Refer to Section 4.4.2.1 of the Standard for Portfolio Management - 3rd Edition. Review the descriptions and definition.

37. Bruce is currently working on the Optimize Portfolio process and asks for your guidance. Bruce has decided to remove a portfolio component and knows that his reasoning needs to be documented, but isn't sure where he should document it. How would you advise him (Difficult)

A. I would advise Bruce to document his reasoning on the portfolio roadmap

B. I would advise Bruce to document his reasoning in the portfolio charter

C. I would advise Bruce to document his reasoning in the portfolio management plan

D. I would advise Bruce to document his reasoning in the portfolio component information

> The correct answer is **D**. Refer to Section 5.3.3.1 of the Standard for Portfolio Management - 3rd Edition. Review the descriptions and definition.

38. Successful communication planning includes an alignment of which of the following: (Moderate)

A. People, planning, budgets

B. People, ideas, information

C. People, technology, information

D. People, ideas, technology

39. Which factors indicate that there is a need to revise portfolio components? (Difficult)

    A. Change in priorities, regulatory changes, portfolio process assets

    B. Enterprise environmental factors, organizational process assets, portfolio strategic plan

    C. Obsolete goals, opportunities to be pursued, and response to regular changes

    D. None of the answer choices

    The correct answer is **C**. Results of the analysis become part of the portfolio process assets but they are not a factor in revising portfolio components. Refer to Section 4.1.2.2 of the Standard for Portfolio Management - 3rd Edition. Review the descriptions and definition.

40. Which is NOT an assessment activity of the portfolio management process? (Moderate)

    A. Evaluate existing portfolio components to determine if supportive of organization strategy and objectives

    B. Identify gaps in knowledge, structure, resources, processes

    C. assess current portfolio component resource availability and allocations against integrated schedule

    D. Identify gaps in financial projections

    The correct answer is **D**. Refer to Section 2.2 of the Standard for Portfolio Management - 3rd Edition. Review the descriptions and definition.

41. Which is NOT included in assessment results of the portfolio management process? (Moderate)

    A. Understanding the organization's vision

    B. Misinformation that needs to be addressed

    C. Project, program, portfolio and operations management practices in place

    D. Understanding the organization's tax return

> The correct answer is **D**. Refer to Section 2.2 of the Standard for Portfolio Management - 3rd Edition. Review the descriptions and definition.

42. Which of the following is NOT considered a primary activity for portfolio management? (Select the best answer) (Difficult)

    A. Identifying and aligning organizational priorities

    B. Managing the details of programs and projects

    C. Managing risk, communication and resources

    D. Determining a governance and performance management framework

    > The correct answer is **B**. Refer to Section 1.2 of the Standard for Portfolio Management - 3rd Edition. Review the descriptions and definition.

43. Which of the following ways does a PMO NOT support Portfolio Management: (Moderate)

    A. Eliminating risk completely

    B. Assisting with risk identification

    C. Communicating risks and issues

    D. Assisting with risk strategy development

    > The correct answer is **A**. Refer to Section 1.9 of the Standard for Portfolio Management - 3rd Edition. Review the descriptions and definition.

44. Which of the following is an interaction with a portfolio management process group? (Moderate)

    A. Organization process plans

    B. Organizational process assets

    C. Organization process analysis

    D. None of the answer choices

    > The correct answer is **B**. Refer to Section 3.2 of the Standard for Portfolio Management - 3rd Edition. Review the descriptions and definition.

45. Which one of the following is NOT an input to developing a portfolio roadmap? (Moderate)

    A. Portfolio

    B. Portfolio strategic plan

    C. Portfolio charter

    D. Organization strategy

    > The correct answer is **D**. Refer to Section 4.1 of the Standard for Portfolio Management - 3rd Edition. Review the descriptions and definition.

46. Which of the four Portfolio Strategic Management processes involves an output of high-level portfolio planning that graphically depicts all portfolio elements need to achieve organizational strategy and objectives? (Easy)

    A. Define Portfolio Process Flow Chart

    B. Define Portfolio Processes

    C. Define Portfolio Roadmap

    D. Define Portfolio Tools & Techniques

    > The correct answer is **C**. Refer to Section 4.3 of the Standard for Portfolio Management - 3rd Edition. Review the descriptions and definition.

47. Which of the four Portfolio Strategic Management processes examines the "as-is" state and compares it with the "to-be" state? (Easy)

    A. Manage Strategic Planning

    B. Manage Portfolio Change

    C. Manage Strategic Change

    D. Manage Portfolio Strategy

    > The correct answer is **C**. Refer to Section 4.4 of the Standard for Portfolio Management - 3rd Edition. Review the descriptions and definition.

48. Which of the following is an example (or examples) of evaluation criteria that a portfolio manager should apply? (Moderate)

    A. Market growth

    B. Market share

    C. New markets

    D. All of the answer choices

    > The correct answer is **D**. Refer to Section 5.2.2 of the Standard for Portfolio Management - 3rd Edition. Review the descriptions and definition.

49. Which of the following best describes portfolio optimization? (Moderate)

    A. Maximizing portfolio return within the organizations predefined risk profile and tolerances

    B. Balancing the portfolio for value delivery

    C. Planning and allocating resources according to organizational strategy and objectives

    D. All of the answer choices

    > The correct answer is **D**. Refer to Section 5.3 of the Standard for Portfolio Management - 3rd Edition. Review the descriptions and definition.

50. Which of the following are key activities with the Authorize Portfolio process? (Moderate)

    A. Allocating resources to authorized portfolio components

    B. Authorizing portfolio component proposal development or portfolio component execution

    C. Communicating changes and decisions for the authorized portfolio components

    D. All of the answer choices

    > The correct answer is **D**. Refer to Section 5.4 of the Standard for Portfolio Management - 3rd Edition. Review the descriptions and definition.

51. Which of the following are examples of quantitative measures used in portfolio performance management? (Moderate)

A. Internal rate of return (IRR) of the portfolio

B. Increases in revenue attributable to the portfolio

C. Percentage by which cycle times are reduced due to the portfolio

D. All of the answer choices

> The correct answer is **D**. Refer to Section 6 of the Standard for Portfolio Management - 3rd Edition. Review the descriptions and definition.

52. Which of the following does not define the Portfolio Performance Management Plan process? (Moderate)

A. Details how portfolio components are allocated for financial and equipment resources

B. Explains how portfolio value is defined

C. Details how portfolio components are allocated for human and material resources

D. Explains how portfolio assets are defined

> The correct answer is **D**. Refer to Section 6.1 of the Standard for Portfolio Management - 3rd Edition. Review the descriptions and definition.

53. Which of the following are examples of performance reporting? (Moderate)

A. Dashboards

B. Scorecards

C. Portfolio reports

D. All of the answer choices

> The correct answer is **D**. Refer to Section 6.1.3.1 of the Standard for Portfolio Management - 3rd Edition. Review the descriptions and definition.

54. Which of the following is not an Input to the Develop Portfolio Communication Management Plan? (Moderate)

A. Portfolio roadmap

B. Portfolio process assets

C. Scope

D. Management Plan

> The correct answer is **C**. Refer to Section 7.1 of the Standard for Portfolio Management - 3rd Edition. Review the descriptions and definition.

55. Which of the following is a tool used to capture and record the results of a communication requirements analysis? (Moderate)

    A. Stakeholder matrix

    B. Elicitation techniques

    C. Communication matrix

    D. Data flow diagram

> The correct answer is **C**. Refer to Section 7.1.2.3 of the Standard for Portfolio Management - 3rd Edition. Review the descriptions and definition.

56. Which of the following is not an output for the Manage Portfolio Information process? (Moderate)

    A. Portfolio process assets updates

    B. Portfolio reports

    C. Project charter updates

    D. Portfolio management plan updates

> The correct answer is **C**. Refer to Section 7.2 of the Standard for Portfolio Management - 3rd Edition. Review the descriptions and definition.

57. Which of the following risk concerns are common to all organizational levels? (Moderate)

    A. Corruption

    B. Transparency

    C. Organizational integrity

    D. All of the answer choices

58. Which of the following areas around risk management are identified by risk planning? (Difficult)

    A. Risk processes, Portfolio risks important to the organization

    B. Risk owners

    C. Risk tolerance

    D. All of the answer choices

59. In Communication Requirements Analysis, what is evaluated? (Moderate)

    A. Vehicle or tool used to communicate info to the stakeholders and its frequency

    B. Vehicle or tool used to communicate info to the all stakeholders

    C. Vehicle or tool used to communicate info to the stakeholders and the organization level

    D. Vehicle or tool used to communicate info to the internal stakeholders

60. Nancy attended a meeting with senior leadership who are concerned about the current gap in the alignment between the portfolio and organization's strategy. What should Nancy do first to address their concerns? (Difficult)

    A. Nancy should perform a scenario analysis

    B. Nancy should encourage leadership to change organization strategy to better fit the portfolio

    C. Nancy should make changes to the portfolio so that they fit better with the organization strategy

D. Nancy should develop a strategic plan to evaluate the portfolio as it relates to high-level organization strategy

> The correct answer is **D**. "Nancy should make changes to the portfolio so that they fit better with the organization strategy" is a true statement but not correct for this question because the strategic plan should be done first.
> Refer to Section 4 of the Standard for Portfolio Ma

61. Linda recently started working on the Develop Portfolio Performance Management Plan process. She is trying to find information on the resource schedule, funding schedule, and resource work calendar. Where would she find this information? (Difficult)

   A. Portfolio process assets

   B. Portfolio charter

   C. Portfolio management plan

   D. Enterprise environmental factors

> The correct answer is **A**. Portfolio process assets contains the information described.
> Refer to Section 6.1.1.2 of the Standard for Portfolio Management - 3rd Edition. Review the descriptions and definition.

62. To define the management of strategic change the following outputs are needed: (Moderate)

   A. Portfolio updates

   B. Portfolio strategic plan updates

   C. Portfolio charter updates

   D. All of the answer choices

> The correct answer is **D**. Refer to Section 4.1 of the Standard for Portfolio Management - 3rd Edition. Review the descriptions and definition.

63. To develop a portfolio charter, the following inputs are needed: (Moderate)

   A. Enterprise environmental factors

   B. Portfolio strategic plan

C. Portfolio process assets

D. All of the answer choices

> The correct answer is **D**. Refer to Section 4.1 of the Standard for Portfolio Management - 3rd Edition. Review the descriptions and definition.

64. In developing the portfolio for the Portfolio Governance Model, which of the following is not an output for the model? (Moderate)

    A. Plan metrics

    B. Portfolio updates

    C. Roadmap updates

    D. Management plan updates

> The correct answer is **A**. Refer to Section 5.1 of the Standard for Portfolio Management - 3rd Edition. Review the descriptions and definition.

65. In developing the process for Authorize the Portfolio, which of the following is not an input? (Moderate)

    A. Portfolio management plan

    B. Portfolio

    C. Portfolio updates

    D. Portfolio reports

> The correct answer is **C**. Refer to Section 5.1 of the Standard for Portfolio Management - 3rd Edition. Review the descriptions and definition.

66. If during the Provide Portfolio Oversight, portfolio policies, processes, and/or procedures change, what should be updated to reflect the changes? (Moderate)

    A. Portfolio process assets

    B. Enterprise environmental factors

    C. Portfolio roadmap

    D. Portfolio

67. Some examples of external risks include all of the following except: (Easy)

    A. Technological advances

    B. Competitive market

    C. Political events

    D. Project progress

    The correct answer is **D**. Refer to Section 8 of the Standard for Portfolio Management - 3rd Edition. Review the descriptions and definition.

68. Luke has recently started working on the Manage Supply and Demand process. He is currently reviewing resource utilization reports. Where are resource utilization reports typically found? (Moderate)

    A. Portfolio performance management plan

    B. Portfolio reports

    C. Portfolio charter

    D. Portfolio management plan

    The correct answer is **B**. Resource utilization reports are located within portfolio reports.
    Refer to Section 6.2.1.3 of the Standard for Portfolio Management - 3rd Edition. Review the descriptions and definition.

69. Kyle has a portfolio management plan which has been produced and approved. He understands the organization is in a specific environment. The decision-making rights and authorities are presented in a particular document. What is this document that he is looking for? (Moderate)

    A. Managing compliance

    B. Performance management planning

    C. Portfolio oversight

D. Governance model

> The correct answer is **D**. The key words here are specific environment, decision-making rights, and authorities. They all describe governance model. Refer to Section 5.1.3.2 of the Standard for Portfolio Management - 3rd Edition. Review the descriptions and definition.

70. Mike is starting to develop a portfolio. What should Mike have as a good starting point for developing his portfolio? (Moderate)

    A. Strategic alignment analysis

    B. Portfolio component inventory

    C. Prioritization analysis

    D. Inventory of work

> The correct answer is **D**. Refer to Section 4.1.1.2 of the Standard for Portfolio Management - 3rd Edition. Review the descriptions and definition.

71. Pete is working on the Manage Portfolio Risks process. He is currently applying an analysis to identify gaps in investment within the portfolio as a whole. What type of analysis is Pete performing? (Easy)

    A. Investment choice analysis

    B. Facilitation techniques

    C. Sensitivity analysis

    D. Modeling and simulation

> The correct answer is **A**. Refer to Section 8.2.2.2 of the Standard for Portfolio Management - 3rd Edition. Review the descriptions and definition.

72. Allen wants to able to graphically communicate the link between the organization strategy and portfolio management. What will allow Allen to do this? (Easy)

    A. Portfolio roadmap

    B. Portfolio charter

    C. Portfolio strategic plan

D. Interdependency analysis

> The correct answer is **A**. Refer to Section 4.3 of the Standard for Portfolio Management - 3rd Edition. Review the descriptions and definition.

73. A Benefits Realization Analysis can comprise any of the following except: (Moderate)

    A. Graphical methods illustrating realized benefits

    B. Results chain

    C. Outcome probability analysis

    D. Value chain

    > The correct answer is **D**. Refer to Section 6.3.2.3 of the Standard for Portfolio Management - 3rd Edition. Review the descriptions and definition.

74. Tyler is working on a portfolio strategic plan. He has been informed that there is a new governmental regulation that may impact the organization's strategy. What type of situation is being described? (Easy)

    A. Portfolio component inventory

    B. Gap analysis

    C. Enterprise environmental factors

    D. Portfolio process assets

    > The correct answer is **C**. Refer to Section 4.1.1.5 of the Standard for Portfolio Management - 3rd Edition. Review the descriptions and definition.

75. Agnes is currently working on the Develop Portfolio Management Plan process. She is currently working on a plan which will help her determine how resource capacity should be managed against resource utilization and changing demand to ensure the portfolio component mix generates maximum value. What is Agnes doing? (Easy)

    A. Portfolio resource management planning

    B. Portfolio value planning

    C. Portfolio reporting

    D. All of the answer choices

> The correct answer is **A**. Refer to Section 6.1 of the Standard for Portfolio Management - 3rd Edition. Review the descriptions and definition.

76. Marge just started working on the Develop Portfolio Communication Management Plan process. She is trying to gain an understanding of the structure of the portfolio and any interdependencies that exist between portfolio components. Where can she find this information? (Moderate)

    A. Portfolio management plan

    B. Portfolio

    C. Portfolio reports

    D. Portfolio roadmap

    > The correct answer is **D**. The portfolio roadmap shows the portfolio structure and also shows the relationship between portfolio components.
    > Refer to Section 7.1.1.2 of the Standard for Portfolio Management - 3rd Edition. Review the descriptions and definition.

77. Michael comes to you for advice. He has been working on portfolio risk management and is having trouble understanding the difference between risks and opportunities. How would you explain it to him? (Moderate)

    A. All negative risks which are not treated are missed opportunities

    B. If positive risks are not identified and treated, they become missed opportunities

    C. If negative risks are not identified and treated, they become missed opportunities

    D. All risks identified and not treated are missed opportunities

    > The correct answer is **B**. Definition from the Standard.
    > Refer to Section 8.2.1.1 of the Standard for Portfolio Management - 3rd Edition. Review the descriptions and definition.

78. Raphael has just started working on the Develop Portfolio Risk Management Plan process. He is trying to find the portfolio risk register and the portfolio issue register. Where can Raphael find this information? (Moderate)

    A. Enterprise environmental factors

B. Organizational process assets

C. Portfolio management plan

D. Portfolio process assets

> The correct answer is **D**. Risk and issue register are part of portfolio process assets.
> Refer to Section 8.1.1.2 of the Standard for Portfolio Management - 3rd Edition. Review the descriptions and definition.

79. Bethany believes she has completed the Manage Portfolio Risks process. She shows you that she has filed portfolio reports and updated the portfolio management plan. What else does Bethany need to update? (Difficult)

    A. Portfolio charter, enterprise environmental factors

    B. Portfolio process assets, organizational process assets

    C. Portfolio roadmap, portfolio charter

    D. Portfolio process assets, portfolio roadmap

> The correct answer is **B**. Outputs of Manage Portfolio Risks.
> Refer to Section 8/Figure 8-1 of the Standard for Portfolio Management - 3rd Edition. Review the descriptions and definition.

80. Bethany believes she has completed the Manage Supply and Demand process. She shows you the completed portfolio reports. You point out to her that she is not completely finished. What is she missing? (Moderate)

    A. Portfolio roadmap updates, portfolio component inventory

    B. Portfolio roadmap updates, portfolio component inventory

    C. Portfolio roadmap updates, portfolio component inventory

    D. Portfolio updates, portfolio management plan updates

> The correct answer is **D**. Refer to Section 6.2/Figure 6-5 of the Standard for Portfolio Management - 3rd Edition. Review the descriptions and definition.

81. As her supervisor, Jackie comes to you and indicates that she has finished the Manage Strategic Change process. What should you be asking her for that would indicate or demonstrate that she has completed the process? (Difficult)

   A. Portfolio charter updates, prioritization analysis, scenario analysis

   B. Stakeholder analysis, gap analysis, readiness assessment

   C. Portfolio strategic plan updates, portfolio charter updates, portfolio roadmap updates, portfolio updates, portfolio process assets updates

   D. Portfolio strategic plan updates, portfolio process assets updates, portfolio updates, stakeholder analysis

   > The correct answer is **C**. Refer to Section 4.4 of the Standard for Portfolio Management - 3rd Edition. Review the descriptions and definition.

82. Within portfolio performance management, during which processes would elicitation techniques be used? (Moderate)

   A. Develop Portfolio Performance Management Plan, Manage Supply and Demand

   B. Manage Supply and Demand, Develop Portfolio Management Plan

   C. Develop Portfolio Performance Management Plan, Manage Portfolio Value

   D. Authorize Portfolio, Manage Portfolio Value

   > The correct answer is **C**. Refer to Section 6.1/Figure 6-2 of the Standard for Portfolio Management - 3rd Edition. Review the descriptions and definition.

83. Within the context of the Manage Portfolio Value process, which of the following is a significant attribute of the weighting and scoring model which leads to portfolio component authorization? (Moderate)

   A. Revenue Growth

   B. Intrinsic Value

   C. Operating Margins

   D. Expected value

   > The correct answer is **D**. Refer to Section 6.3 of the Standard for Portfolio Management - 3rd Edition. Review the descriptions and definition.

84. Within with Manage Portfolio Value process, the scoring of a component against established criteria is an example of what type of analysis? (Moderate)

    A. Benefits realization analysis

    B. Elicitation techniques

    C. Progress measurement techniques

    D. Value scoring and measurement analysis

    > The correct answer is **D**. Refer to Section 6.3.2.2 of the Standard for Portfolio Management - 3rd Edition. Review the descriptions and definition.

85. Nicholas tells you that he is about to start the Authorize Portfolio process, but he doesn't know where to begin. What would you tell him? (Difficult)

    A. I would tell him that he needs to have enterprise environmental factors, prioritization analysis, and the portfolio management plan to start this process

    B. I would tell him that he needs to have a capability and capacity analysis, portfolio component inventory, and cost-benefit analysis to start this process

    C. I would tell him that he needs to have a portfolio charter, portfolio roadmap, and portfolio reports to start this process

    D. I would tell him that he needs to have the portfolio, portfolio management plan, and portfolio reports to start this process

    > The correct answer is **D**. Inputs to Authorize Portfolio.
    > Refer to Section 5.4 of the Standard for Portfolio Management - 3rd Edition. Review the descriptions and definition.

86. Kathryn is working on the Manage Portfolio Risks process. She is currently running a simulation where the model is iterated. What type of tool is Kathryn using? (Moderate)

    A. Sensitivity analysis

    B. Performance variability analysis

    C. Monte Carlo technique

    D. Investment choice analysis

The correct answer is **C**. Per the Standard, the Monte Carlo is the tool used for most simulations and it utilizes an iterative method.
Refer to Section 8.2.2.2 of the Standard for Portfolio Management - 3rd Edition. Review the descriptions and definition.

87. Lydia is nearly finished working on the Develop Portfolio Performance Management Plan process. During the process, there were several changes made to the benefits schedule and resource schedule. Where does Lydia need to document these updates? (Moderate)

   A. Portfolio roadmap

   B. Portfolio process assets

   C. Portfolio

   D. Organizational process assets

The correct answer is **B**. Portfolio process assets contains the benefits schedule and resource schedule.
Refer to Section 6.1.3.2 of the Standard for Portfolio Management - 3rd Edition. Review the descriptions and definition.

88. Annie has come to you for advice on the Manage Strategic Change process. She originally asked Bob who said that he thought Annie needed to understand the strategic plan better before going any further. Annie wants to know why it is so important to understand that first? (Difficult)

   A. Bob is incorrect. Understanding the strategic plan won't benefit Annie.

   B. It is important to ensure that all of the correct components within those organization areas with the highest strategic value are included

   C. It is important to go back and review the strategic plan and pay special attention to the Cost-benefit analysis

   D. Bob is correct that it is important, but it is more important for Annie to go back and re-run the prioritization analysis

The correct answer is **B**. Refer to Section 4.4.1.1 of the Standard for Portfolio Management - 3rd Edition. Review the descriptions and definition.

89. Daniel comes to you for help. He has started working on the Optimize Portfolio process and has the existing portfolio reports, but is unsure how he is supposed to use them as it relates to this process. How would you advise him? (Difficult)

   A. He should look in the portfolio reports to find the approach for defining, optimizing, and authorizing portfolio components

   B. Portfolio reports are not used as part of the Optimize Portfolio process

   C. He should look in the portfolio reports to find portfolio risks associated with portfolio components as well as resource pool report data which is used to understand resource allocation

   D. He should refer to the portfolio reports for information on relevant data, tools, and templates regarding optimizing the portfolio

   > The correct answer is **C**. The portfolio reports contain risk information about portfolio components and resource pool report data.
   > Refer to Section 5.3.1.4 of the Standard for Portfolio Management - 3rd Edition. Review the descriptions and definition.

90. Craig has all of the inputs for the Manage Portfolio Risks process, but is struggling with where to begin in terms of analyzing them. What tools and techniques can Craig apply during this process? (Moderate)

   A. Weighted ranking and scoring techniques, graphical analytical methods

   B. Graphical analytical methods, prioritization analysis

   C. Prioritization analysis, weighted ranking and scoring techniques

   D. Weighted ranking and scoring techniques, quantitative and qualitative analysis

   > The correct answer is **D**. Tools and techniques of Manage Portfolio Risks.
   > Refer to Section 8/Figure 8-1 of the Standard for Portfolio Management - 3rd Edition. Review the descriptions and definition.

91. Craig is currently working on the Manage Portfolio Value process. He is running an analysis to determine alliance partner value, managerial value, and societal value to the organization. What type of analysis is Craig running? (Difficult)

   A. Comparative advantage analysis

   B. Cost-benefit analysis

C. Value scoring and measurement analysis

D. Benefits realization analysis

> The correct answer is **D**. The type of value examined is done as part of a benefits realization analysis.
> Refer to Section 6.3.2.3 of the Standard for Portfolio Management - 3rd Edition. Review the descriptions and definition.

92. Devin is currently working on the Manage Portfolio Value process. He is currently using a SWOT analysis to gather information to ensure that benefits are comprehensively and holistically taken into consideration. What tool and technique is Devin applying? (Difficult)

    A. Elicitation techniques

    B. Value scoring and measurement analysis

    C. Value measurement techniques

    D. Progress measurement techniques

    > The correct answer is **A**. As stated in the Standard, SWOT analysis is used as an elicitation technique.
    > Refer to Section 6.3.2.1 of the Standard for Portfolio Management - 3rd Edition. Review the descriptions and definition.

93. During the Develop Portfolio Management plan process, portfolio process assets should be reviewed to look for what kind of information? (Moderate)

    A. Information about ongoing and planned portfolio management tasks

    B. Performance information from a portfolio's past performance or history (for benchmarking purposes)

    C. Portfolio management decisions and open issues

    D. All of the answer choices

    > The correct answer is **D**. Refer to Section 5.1.1.4 of the Standard for Portfolio Management - 3rd Edition. Review the descriptions and definition.

94. Claire is nearly finished the Authorize Portfolio process. While she was working on this process, she needed to update the portfolio funding to reflect the funding allocated to authorize portfolio elements. Where would this information be reflected? (Difficult)

A. Portfolio process assets

B. Portfolio charter

C. Portfolio management plan

D. Portfolio reports

> The correct answer is **D**. This is type of information that would be reflected in a portfolio report.
> Refer to Section 5.4.3.3 of the Standard for Portfolio Management - 3rd Edition. Review the descriptions and definition.

95. Environmental Factors include which of the following? (Easy)

A. Government standards

B. Legal constraints

C. Industry standards

D. All of the answer choices

> The correct answer is **D**. Refer to Section 3.2 of the Standard for Portfolio Management - 3rd Edition. Review the descriptions and definition.

96. Environmental Factors include which of the following? (Easy)

A. Existing human resources

B. Infrastructure

C. Personnel administration

D. All of the answer choices

> The correct answer is **D**. Refer to Section 3.2 of the Standard for Portfolio Management - 3rd Edition. Review the descriptions and definition.

97. Christy is working on portfolio performance management. She is currently conducting a scenario analysis and quantitative and qualitative analysis. Which process is Christy engaged in? (Difficult)

    A. Manage Portfolio Value

    B. Develop Portfolio Management Plan

    C. Manage Supply and Demand

    D. Develop Portfolio Performance Management Plan

> The correct answer is **C**. The two tools and techniques describes are done only during the Manage Supply and Demand process within portfolio management.
> Refer to Section 6/Figure 6-1 of the Standard for Portfolio Management - 3rd Edition. Review the descriptions and definition.

98. Benjamin is currently working on the Develop Portfolio Communication Management Plan process. He is presently conducting interviews on the effectiveness of communication. What tool and technique is Benjamin applying? (Moderate)

    A. Elicitation techniques

    B. Prioritization analysis

    C. Stakeholder analysis

    D. Communication requirements analysis

> The correct answer is **A**. Interviews are an elicitation technique.
> Refer to Section 7.1.2.2 of the Standard for Portfolio Management - 3rd Edition. Review the descriptions and definition.

99. Blake approaches you for advice. He has recently been working on portfolio risk management. He is trying to understand the difference between risks and issues. How would you explain the difference to him? (Moderate)

    A. If negative risks are not identified and treated, they become issues

    B. All negative risks are issues

    C. If positive risks are not identified and treated, they become issues

    D. All positive risks which are not treated are issues

100. Blake is working on the Optimize Portfolio process. He is currently working on developing histograms, pie charts, and risk vs. return charts. What stage of the process is he in and what he is doing? (Difficult)

    A. Blake is applying tools and techniques with a graphical analytical method

    B. Blake is gathering inputs including the portfolio roadmap

    C. Blake is applying tools and techniques with a qualitative analysis

    D. Blake is applying tools and techniques with a SWOT analysis

> The correct answer is **A**. Histograms, pie charts, and risk vs. return charts are all graphical analytical methods.
> Refer to Section 5.3.2.4 of the Standard for Portfolio Management - 3rd Edition. Review the descriptions and definition.

101. Stakeholder analysis is performed to assess which of the following? (Moderate)

    A. Level of influence

    B. Level of interest

    C. Level of urgency

    D. All of the answer choices

> The correct answer is **D**. Refer to Section 7.1.2.1 of the Standard for Portfolio Management - 3rd Edition. Review the descriptions and definition.

102. Carl is about to start working on the Manage Portfolio Value process. What should he have to start working on this process? (Moderate)

    A. Portfolio, portfolio management plan, portfolio reports

    B. Portfolio charter, portfolio roadmap, portfolio

    C. Portfolio reports, portfolio charter, portfolio management plan

D. Portfolio roadmap, portfolio management plan, portfolio reports

> The correct answer is **D**. Refer to Section 6.3/Figure 6-7 of the Standard for Portfolio Management - 3rd Edition. Review the descriptions and definition.

103. Kayla is currently conducting portfolio review meetings and just recently completed utilizing elicitation techniques. Which portfolio governance process is Kayla working on? (Moderate)

   A. Provide Portfolio Oversight

   B. Develop Portfolio Management Plan

   C. Authorize Portfolio

   D. Define Portfolio

> The correct answer is **A**. The two tools and techniques describes are done during the Provide Portfolio Oversight process.
> Refer to Section 5.5 of the Standard for Portfolio Management - 3rd Edition. Review the descriptions and definition.

104. While implementing a particular technique during the Develop Portfolio Performance Management Plan process, Steve is regularly consulting with stakeholders and key subject matter experts through planning meetings and brainstorming sessions to develop measures and ensure that the correct items are being measured to ensure optimal resource performance. What technique is Steve using? (Moderate)

   A. Capability and capacity analysis

   B. Portfolio management information system

   C. Facilitation techniques

   D. Elicitation techniques

> The correct answer is **D**. Elicitation techniques involves brainstorming sessions, planning meetings, interviews and surveys.
> Refer to Section 6.1.2.1 of the Standard for Portfolio Management - 3rd Edition. Review the descriptions and definition.

105. Examples of Organizational Process Assets used as inputs to planning for risk management include all of the following except: (Moderate)

A. Organizational chart

B. Vision and mission statements

C. Organizational strategy and objectives

D. Organizational risk tolerance and lessons learned

> The correct answer is **A**. Refer to Section 8.1.1.3 of the Standard for Portfolio Management - 3rd Edition. Review the descriptions and definition.

106. When developing the portfolio management plan it is important to be guided by the: (Moderate)

A. Management Plan

B. Financial Plan

C. Project Plan

D. Strategic Plan

> The correct answer is **D**. Refer to Section 5.1.1 of the Standard for Portfolio Management - 3rd Edition. Review the descriptions and definition.

107. When new strategic direction is given during the Manage Strategic Change process, what needs to be considered before and during portfolio changes? (Moderate)

A. Executives and key stakeholders' expectations and communication requirements

B. Cost-benefit analysis, prioritization analysis

C. Previous strategic direction provided by Executives, Readiness assessment

D. None of the answer choices

> The correct answer is **A**. Refer to Section 4.4.1.1 of the Standard for Portfolio Management - 3rd Edition. Review the descriptions and definition.

108. Funnel charts, bubble charts, histograms, burn-down charts, burn-up charts, and other types of diagrams are all stored where? (Moderate)

A. Portfolio reports

B. Portfolio management plan

C. Portfolio

D. Portfolio roadmap

> The correct answer is **A**. Refer to Section 6.2.3.3 of the Standard for Portfolio Management - 3rd Edition. Review the descriptions and definition.

109. Glenn is currently involved in the Authorize Portfolio process. He is describing to you a tool and technique he is currently applying which identifies which portfolio components have been assigned resources. What is Glenn describing? (Difficult)

    A. Portfolio management information system

    B. Portfolio component inventory

    C. Portfolio component categorization techniques

    D. Portfolio authorization technique

> The correct answer is **A**. This tool is used to indicate which portfolio components have been assigned resources.
> Refer to Section 5.4.2.2 of the Standard for Portfolio Management - 3rd Edition. Review the descriptions and definition.

110. Jenny has been asked to make a determination as to how prepared the organization is to perform the steps needed to bridge the gap between the "as-is" portfolio state and the "to-be" state. What is she being asked to perform? (Moderate)

    A. Readiness assessment

    B. Cost-benefit analysis

    C. Stakeholder analysis

    D. Gap analysis

> The correct answer is **A**. Refer to Section 4.4.2.3 of the Standard for Portfolio Management - 3rd Edition. Review the descriptions and definition.

111. A tool and technique for managing strategic change is a readiness assessment. Why is this important? (Moderate)

    A. Determines the if, when, what and how of implementing change

B. Determines the if, when, what and how of implementing a plan

C. Determines the if, when, what and how of implementing strategy

D. None of the answer choices

> The correct answer is **A**. Refer to Section 4.4 of the Standard for Portfolio Management - 3rd Edition. Review the descriptions and definition.

112. In order to assess stakeholder influence, which of the following questions may be asked? (Moderate)

    A. Which of the stakeholders are considered leaders, influencers, or early adopters?

    B. Is their role as a stakeholder recognized by the organization?

    C. What are the interrelationships among the stakeholders?

    D. All of the answer choices

> The correct answer is **D**. Refer to Section 7.1.2.1 of the Standard for Portfolio Management - 3rd Edition. Review the descriptions and definition.

113. In order to assess stakeholder influence, which of the following questions may be asked? (Moderate)

    A. Which stakeholders are known to resist change?

    B. Who are the members of the governing body?

    C. What level of authority does each stakeholder have affecting the portfolio and the organization?

    D. All of the answer choices

> The correct answer is **D**. Refer to Section 7.1.2.1 of the Standard for Portfolio Management - 3rd Edition. Review the descriptions and definition.

114. Resource capability and capacity management analyze which of the following: (Moderate)

    A. Resource types and schedules

    B. Strategic objectives

C. Portfolio value assessments

D. All of the Answer Choices

> The correct answer is **A**. Refer to Section 6.1.2.4 of the Standard for Portfolio Management - 3rd Edition. Review the descriptions and definition.

115. Stephanie is working on the Develop Portfolio Performance Management Plan process. She has setup an automated tool to collect information in order to support the portfolio management process. What type of tool and techniques has Stephanie setup? (Moderate)

A. Portfolio management information system

B. Portfolio component inventory

C. Elicitation techniques

D. Capability and capacity analysis

> The correct answer is **A**. An automated or manual tool used to collect data is a PMIS.
> Refer to Section 6.1.2.2 of the Standard for Portfolio Management - 3rd Edition. Review the descriptions and definition.

116. Stephen has received a list of risks. This list of risks includes concerns regarding portfolio components' cost, time and, scope. What organizational level likely provided these risks to Stephen? (Moderate)

A. Executive Management

B. Operations Management

C. Portfolio Manager

D. Program or Project Teams

> The correct answer is **D**. Costs regarding portfolio components' cost, time, and scope come from program and project teams.
> Refer to Section 8 of the Standard for Portfolio Management - 3rd Edition. Review the descriptions and definition.

117. In portfolio component categorization technique, which of the following are examples of "increased profitability" considerations? (Moderate)

A. Cost reduction and avoidance

B. Revenue increase

C. Revenue generation

D. All of the answer choices

> The correct answer is **D**. Refer to Section 5.2.2.2 of the Standard for Portfolio Management - 3rd Edition. Review the descriptions and definition.

118. Laura Ann is approached by a senior manager during the Provide Portfolio Oversight process who is inquiring about a proposal they made concerning a change in funding allocation. Where can Laura Ann find this information? (Difficult)

A. Portfolio

B. Portfolio process assets

C. Portfolio management plan

D. Portfolio reports

> The correct answer is **A**. Proposals for a change in funding allocation would be documented in the portfolio.
> Refer to Section 5.5.1.1 of the Standard for Portfolio Management - 3rd Edition. Review the descriptions and definition.

119. Andre is currently working on the Manage Portfolio Value process. He is currently using earned value as part of value scoring and measurement analysis to evaluate the portfolio. What type of technique is Andre using? (Difficult)

A. Progress measurement technique

B. Cost-benefit analysis

C. Portfolio efficient frontier

D. Comparative advantage analysis

> The correct answer is **A**. Earned value is provided by the Standard as an example of a progress management technique used during the Manage Portfolio Value process.
> Refer to Section 6.3.2.2 of the Standard for Portfolio Management - 3rd Edition. Review the descriptions and definit

120. George is approached by a key stakeholder who wants George to be able to drill down on the expected benefits for a particular portfolio while also detailing how they will be measured. Where can George tell the stakeholder his concerns are typically addressed? (Moderate)

   A. Portfolio management plan

   B. Portfolio charter

   C. Portfolio reports

   D. Portfolio performance management plan

> The correct answer is **D**. One of the most important components of the portfolio performance management plan is benefits realization.
> Refer to Section 6.1.3.1 of the Standard for Portfolio Management - 3rd Edition. Review the descriptions and definition.

121. In risk management, which is the most difficult to quantitatively or qualitatively evaluate? (Difficult)

   A. Risk probability

   B. Risk impact

   C. Risk importance

   D. Risk interdependencies

> The correct answer is **A**. Refer to Section 8 of the Standard for Portfolio Management - 3rd Edition. Review the descriptions and definition.

122. Courtney comes to you for advice. She understands that there is a strategic management process but is unsure of what stage in the process she is in. She is currently doing a scenario analysis and analyzing capacity. What phase is she in? (Moderate)

   A. Develop Portfolio Strategic Plan

   B. Manage Strategic Change

   C. Define Portfolio Roadmap

   D. Develop Portfolio Charter

123. Which of the following is NOT considered a primary activity for portfolio management? (Select the best answer)

    A. Identifying and aligning organizational priorities

    B. Managing the details of programs and projects

    C. Managing risk, communication and resources

    D. Determining a governance and performance management framework

    The correct answer is **B**. Refer to Section 1.2 of the Standard for Portfolio Management - 3rd Edition. Review the descriptions and definition.

124. Measures must be meaningful. The guideline dictates that the performance measures must be "Realistic". What does this indicate? (Moderate)

    A. Target is achievable given the organization's human resource capacity and it can be challenging but is achievable.

    B. Target is achievable given who the portfolio manager is assigned to it.

    C. Target is achievable given the organization's financial resources and it can be challenging but is achievable.

    D. Target is achievable given the organization's capabilities and capacity - can be challenging but achievable.

    The correct answer is **D**. Refer to Section 6.1.2 of the Standard for Portfolio Management - 3rd Edition. Review the descriptions and definition.

125. Betsy has nearly finished the Develop Portfolio Communication Management Plan process. During the process, there were several changes made to portfolio risks and issues. What should Betsy update to reflect this change? (Moderate)

    A. Portfolio management plan

    B. Portfolio roadmap

    C. Portfolio charter

D. Portfolio process assets

> The correct answer is **D**. Changes to portfolio risks and issues should be reflected in portfolio process assets.
> Refer to Section 7.1.3.2 of the Standard for Portfolio Management - 3rd Edition. Review the descriptions and definition.

126. What are enterprise environmental factors? (Easy)

   A. The portfolio's plans, policies, procedures, and guidelines

   B. Factors within the organization which do not have an impact on the portfolio strategy and plan

   C. Factors which may consist of corporate, environmental, and governmental variables that contribute to the Develop Portfolio Strategic Plan process

   D. None of the answer choices

> The correct answer is **C**. Refer to Section 4.1.1.5 of the Standard for Portfolio Management - 3rd Edition. Review the descriptions and definition.

127. What are the tools and techniques used to develop a portfolio charter? (Easy)

   A. Interdependency analysis, capability and capacity analysis

   B. Prioritization analysis, gap analysis

   C. Scenario analysis, cost-benefit analysis

   D. Scenario analysis, capability and capacity analysis

> The correct answer is **D**. Refer to Section 4.2 of the Standard for Portfolio Management - 3rd Edition. Review the descriptions and definition.

128. What are the inputs to the Develop Portfolio Charter process? (Moderate)

   A. Cost-benefit analysis, portfolio strategic plan, scenario analysis

   B. Portfolio process assets updates, capability and capacity analysis, enterprise environmental factors

   C. Portfolio strategic plan, scenario analysis, portfolio process assets

   D. Portfolio strategic plan, portfolio process assets, enterprise environmental factors

The correct answer is **D**. Refer to Section 4.2 of the Standard for Portfolio Management - 3rd Edition. Review the descriptions and definition.

129. What are the inputs to the Develop Portfolio Performance Management Plan process? (Moderate)

A. Portfolio roadmap, portfolio reports, portfolio charter

B. Portfolio management plan, portfolio process assets, organizational process assets, enterprise environmental factors

C. Portfolio roadmap, portfolio charter, organizational process assets, enterprise environmental factors

D. Portfolio management plan, portfolio process assets, organizational process assets, portfolio reports

The correct answer is **B**. Refer to Section 6/Figure 6-1 of the Standard for Portfolio Management - 3rd Edition. Review the descriptions and definition.

130. What are the purposes of the Portfolio Communication Management processes? (Easy)

A. To further develop the portfolio management plan and align it with organizational strategy

B. To implement communication policy into the portfolio charter

C. To develop the portfolio communication management plan and to manage portfolio information

D. None of the answer choices

The correct answer is **C**. Refer to Section 7 of the Standard for Portfolio Management - 3rd Edition. Review the descriptions and definition.

131. What are the inputs to the Develop Portfolio Communication Management Plan process? (Moderate)

A. Enterprise environmental factors, portfolio process assets, portfolio reports

B. Portfolio charter, portfolio, portfolio reports

C. Portfolio charter, portfolio management plan, portfolio reports, portfolio process assets

D. Portfolio, portfolio roadmap, portfolio management plan, portfolio reports, portfolio process assets

> The correct answer is **D**. Refer to Section 7/Figure 7-1 of the Standard for Portfolio Management - 3rd Edition. Review the descriptions and definition.

132. What does the strategic alignment analysis focus on? (Difficult)

    A. Gaps and changes to the organization strategy and objectives

    B. Portfolio roadmap

    C. Where there are gaps in focus , investment or alignment with the portfolio

    D. New or changing organization strategy and objectives

> The correct answer is **A**. Refer to Section 4.1 of the Standard for Portfolio Management - 3rd Edition. Review the descriptions and definition.

133. What does the portfolio structure identify? (Easy)

    A. It identifies the portfolio, subportfolios, programs, and projects based on organization areas

    B. It identifies the Portfolio strategic plan and Portfolio charter

    C. It identifies strategies and priorities, and portfolio components are grouped to facilitate effective management

    D. All of the answer choices

> The correct answer is **A**. Refer to Section 4.2 of the Standard for Portfolio Management - 3rd Edition. Review the descriptions and definition.

134. What does the score measure in a scoring model? (Moderate)

    A. Whether or not each percentage was calculated correctly

    B. Whether or not each criterion is met

    C. Whether or not each weight is correct

    D. Whether or not each category is similar

135. What does the portfolio communication management plan define? (Moderate)

    A. All communications needs, establishes communication requirements, specifies frequency, and identifies recipients for information associated with the portfolio management process

    B. It defines policies and practices for optimizing portfolio value including revenue growth and increased operating margins

    C. It identifies the stakeholders, determines the different individuals and groups, and determines their concerns, interests, and influence

    D. None of the answer choices

136. What information does the portfolio management plan provide as it relates to the Develop Portfolio Management Plan process? (Moderate)

    A. It provides stakeholder expectations and requirements, governance model, strategic change framework, planning, procurement, and oversight processes including direction for performance, communication, and risk management

    B. It contains portfolio-related documents such as the portfolio charter and portfolio strategic plan

    C. It provides stakeholder expectations and requirements, governance model, strategic change framework, planning, procurement, and oversight processes with the primary objective to maximize profit

    D. All of the answer choices

137. What is the purpose of the Authorize Portfolio process? (Easy)

    A. To provide critical information of portfolio components that is required by portfolio oversight

B. To optimize and balance the portfolio for performance and value delivery

C. To evaluate portfolio components based on ranking criteria, dependencies, and goals

D. To activate selected portfolio components by allocating resources to develop component proposals or execute portfolio components

> The correct answer is **D**. Definition from The Standard.
> Refer to Section 5.4 of the Standard for Portfolio Management - 3rd Edition. Review the descriptions and definition.

138. What is/are the process(es) in both the knowledge area Portfolio Governance Management and the Authorizing and Controlling Process Group? (Moderate)

A. Authorize portfolio

B. Optimize portfolio

C. Provide portfolio oversight

D. Provide portfolio oversight AND authorize portfolio

> The correct answer is **D**. Refer to Section 3.1 of the Standard for Portfolio Management - 3rd Edition. Review the descriptions and definition.

139. What is the portfolio manager generally responsible for updating and adding to the portfolio process assets? (Easy)

A. Performance measurement criteria

B. Specifications and work instructions

C. Proposal evaluation criteria

D. All of the answer choices

> The correct answer is **D**. Refer to Section 3.2 of the Standard for Portfolio Management - 3rd Edition. Review the descriptions and definition.

140. What is contained in Portfolio Reports? (Easy)

A. Project dashboard

B. Project management plan

C. Program status report

D. None of the answer choices

> The correct answer is **D**. Refer to Section 3.2 of the Standard for Portfolio Management - 3rd Edition. Review the descriptions and definition.

141. What is capability and capacity analysis? (Moderate)

   A. Performed to understand how much work is able to be performed based on the resources available

   B. Performed to understand the ability to finance the work to be performed

   C. Performed to understand how much work is able to be performed

   D. Performed to understand how much work is able to be performed based on the resources available as well as the ability of the organization to source and execute the selected portfolio

> The correct answer is **D**. Refer to Section 4.2 of the Standard for Portfolio Management - 3rd Edition. Review the descriptions and definition.

142. What is the purpose of a cost-benefit analysis as it relates to defining the portfolio roadmap? (Easy)

   A. It quantifies estimated costs and benefits and lists qualitative considerations of alternative portfolio components for evaluation

   B. It helps to identify dependencies the portfolio has in relationship to the portfolio environment

   C. It allows the portfolio manager to compare strategic objectives and prioritize objectives

   D. None of the answer choices

> The correct answer is **A**. Refer to Section 4.3.2.2 of the Standard for Portfolio Management - 3rd Edition. Review the descriptions and definition.

143. What is the purpose of conducting gap analysis? (Moderate)

   A. To ensure continuity and aligns key stakeholders' expectations with the changing strategy and resulting portfolio realignment

B. To enable management of the portfolio and demonstrates a clear path from the "as-is" to the "to-be" state

C. To compare the current portfolio mix and components with the new strategic direction and the "to-be" organizational vision

D. None of the answer choices

> The correct answer is **C**. Refer to Section 4.4.2.2 of the Standard for Portfolio Management - 3rd Edition. Review the descriptions and definition.

144. What is involved in the integration of portfolio management plans during the process of developing the portfolio management plan? (Moderate)

A. In involves eliciting requirements from a variety of sources utilizing different methods

B. It involves assigning performance review roles and responsibilities across each program, projects, or operational component

C. It involves referencing subsidiary plans which are always developed prior to starting the integration of portfolio management plans

D. It involves the development of subsidiary plans and the analysis of those plans to ensure they are aligned for consistency

> The correct answer is **D**. Refer to Section 5.1.2.3 of the Standard for Portfolio Management - 3rd Edition. Review the descriptions and definition.

145. What is the purpose of using a scoring model to evaluate portfolio components? (Easy)

A. It makes the portfolio components comparable for evaluation purposes.

B. It is used to satisfy regulatory and compliance requirements

C. It is used to as part of process improvement

D. None of the answer choices

> The correct answer is **A**. Refer to Section 5.2.2.3 of the Standard for Portfolio Management - 3rd Edition. Review the descriptions and definition.

146. What is the purpose of the Provide Portfolio Oversight process? (Easy)

A. To activate selected portfolio components by allocating resources to develop component proposals or execute portfolio components

B. To optimize and balance the portfolio for performance and value delivery

C. To evaluate portfolio components based on ranking criteria, dependencies, and goals

D. To monitor the portfolio to ensure alignment with organizational strategy and objectives

> The correct answer is **D**. Refer to Section 5.5 of the Standard for Portfolio Management - 3rd Edition. Review the descriptions and definition.

147. What is the purpose of the portfolio performance management plan? (Moderate)

A. To explain how portfolio value is defined and to detail how portfolio components are allocated for resources

B. To optimize and balance the portfolio for performance and value delivery

C. To activate selected portfolio components by allocating resources to develop component proposals or execute portfolio components

D. None of the answer choices

> The correct answer is **A**. Refer to Section 6.1 of the Standard for Portfolio Management - 3rd Edition. Review the descriptions and definition.

148. What is a potential goal in managing supply and demand? (Moderate)

A. Ensure resource capacity is optimally allocated against resource requirements

B. Ensure resource capacity is optimally allocated against demand based on known organizational priorities and potential value

C. Minimize both unused resources and unmet demands

D. All of the answer choices

> The correct answer is **D**. Refer to Section 6.2 of the Standard for Portfolio Management - 3rd Edition. Review the descriptions and definition.

149. What is resource leveling? (Easy)

A. A technique used to assess criteria and to discern the weight assigned to different benefits and outcomes

B. A technique used to analyze the various inputs to determine how portfolio value is impacted by change

C. A technique used to indicate whether resource capacity has been optimally matched against resource demands and highlights areas that need adjustment

D. A technique which strives to smooth performance levels by managing bottleneck areas and communicating delayed schedules

> The correct answer is **D**. Refer to Section 6.2.2.2 of the Standard for Portfolio Management - 3rd Edition. Review the descriptions and definition.

150. What is the goal in defining portfolio value? (Moderate)

A. To deliver the maximum value possible aligned with strategic objectives and with limited consideration on risk

B. To deliver the maximum value possible aligned with strategic objectives and with an acceptable level of risk based on the level of risk tolerance

C. To deliver the maximum value possible aligned with financial objectives and with an acceptable level of risk based on the level of risk tolerance

D. To deliver the acceptable value at acceptable risk

> The correct answer is **B**. Refer to Section 6.3 of the Standard for Portfolio Management - 3rd Edition. Review the descriptions and definition.

151. What is the best rationale to institute portfolio risk management? (Difficult)

A. Manage interdependencies of risks among the portfolio components

B. It is the right thing to do

C. Manage the financial impact of portfolio components

D. Manage the execution details of portfolio components

> The correct answer is **A**. Refer to Section 8 of the Standard for Portfolio Management - 3rd Edition. Review the descriptions and definition.

152. What is portfolio risk? (Easy)

    A. It is the process of identifying risk while trying to maximize financial profit

    B. It is an uncertain event or condition that, if it occurs, has a positive or negative effective on one or more project objectives

    C. It is an uncertain event or condition that, if it occurs, has only a negative effective on one or more project objectives

    D. None of the answer choices

    > The correct answer is **B**. Refer to Section 8 of the Standard for Portfolio Management - 3rd Edition. Review the descriptions and definition.

153. Matt is working on the Develop Portfolio Risk Management Plan process. He is currently in the process of trying to better balance risk by reallocating the portfolio in instances where it has deviated away from organization strategy. What is Matt doing? (Moderate)

    A. Outcome probability analysis

    B. Portfolio risk exposure chart

    C. Rebalancing methods

    D. Investment choice

    > The correct answer is **C**. Refer to Section 8.1.2.3 of the Standard for Portfolio Management - 3rd Edition. Review the descriptions and definition.

154. What role do portfolio process assets play in the Develop Portfolio Charter process? (Easy)

    A. They allow the portfolio manager to identify corporate, environmental, and governmental variables that may contribute to and constrain the process

    B. They allow the portfolio manager to understand the ability of the organization to source and execute the selected portfolio

    C. They allow the portfolio manager to leverage the portfolio's plans, policies, procedures, guidelines and any other documentation of stakeholder relationships, scope, benefits, and portfolio goals

    D. None of the answer choices

155. What role does the portfolio play in the Manage Strategic Change process? (Moderate)

   A. It is used to evaluate strategic objectives, prioritize objectives, and perform strategic assessments again current enterprise portfolios

   B. It does not play a role in the process

   C. It is used to understand the portfolio structure, scope, constraints, dependencies, and resources

   D. It is the means to the "to be" vision

   The correct answer is **D**. Refer to Section 4.4.1.3 of the Standard for Portfolio Management - 3rd Edition. Review the descriptions and definition.

156. What should be the primary focus when selecting a communication strategy? (Moderate)

   A. The primary focus should be on satisfying the most important information needs of stakeholders so that effective decisions are made and organizational objectives are met

   B. The primary focus should be on communicating as frequently as possible with all stakeholders

   C. The primary focus should be on communicating only the essential information to senior and executive level stakeholders

   D. None of the answer choices

   The correct answer is **A**. Refer to Section 7 of the Standard for Portfolio Management - 3rd Edition. Review the descriptions and definition.

157. What tends to happen during the early stages of developing a portfolio? (Easy)

   A. The portfolio may evolve as more details are obtained such as dependencies, timelines, and strategic changes

   B. The portfolio tends to have a limited amount of change

   C. The portfolio may evolve due to internal factors only

D. None of the answer choices

> The correct answer is **A**. Refer to Section 4.1.3.2 of the Standard for Portfolio Management - 3rd Edition. Review the descriptions and definition.

158. What type of stakeholder information is collected in a stakeholder matrix? (Moderate)

    A. Stakeholder expectations

    B. Stakeholder roles

    C. Stakeholder interests

    D. All of the answer choices

> The correct answer is **D**. Refer to Section 7.1.2.1/Table 7-2 of the Standard for Portfolio Management - 3rd Edition. Review the descriptions and definition.

159. Portfolio Review Meetings are: (Moderate)

    A. Recurring, formal, scheduled around significant milestones

    B. Random, informal, scheduled around significant milestones

    C. Random, formal, scheduled around significant milestones

    D. Recurring, informal, scheduled around significant milestones

> The correct answer is **A**. Refer to Section 5.5.2 of the Standard for Portfolio Management - 3rd Edition. Review the descriptions and definition.

160. Portfolio process assets that refer to portfolio communication requirements include all of the following except: (Moderate)

    A. Allowable communication media

    B. Communication technology available

    C. Record retention policies and security requirements

    D. Information technology policy

> The correct answer is **D**. Refer to Section 7.2.1.5 of the Standard for Portfolio Management - 3rd Edition. Review the descriptions and definition.

161. In the Manage Strategic Change process, what vehicles are used to plan and execute the strategic change? (Moderate)

A. Portfolio strategic plan, portfolio management plan

B. Portfolio charter, portfolio roadmap

C. Portfolio management plan, portfolio roadmap

D. Portfolio strategic plan, portfolio charter

> The correct answer is **A**. Refer to Section 4.4 of the Standard for Portfolio Management - 3rd Edition. Review the descriptions and definition.

162. In the Authorize Portfolio process, which of the following does not get updated? (Moderate)

A. Portfolio Process Assets

B. Portfolio Management Plan

C. Portfolio Reports

D. Portfolio Charter

> The correct answer is **D**. Refer to Section 5.4.3 of the Standard for Portfolio Management - 3rd Edition. Review the descriptions and definition.

163. In the process Develop Portfolio Risk Management Plan which of the following is not an input? (Moderate)

A. Enterprise environmental factors

B. Portfolio management plan

C. Portfolio and Organizational Process Assets

D. Project Charter

> The correct answer is **D**. Refer to Section 8.1 of the Standard for Portfolio Management - 3rd Edition. Review the descriptions and definition.

164. Patti is currently working on the Manage Portfolio Value process. She is currently performing analysis to determine earned value, assessed value, and measuring portfolio performance. What tool and technique is Patti applying? (Moderate)

A. Elicitation techniques

B. Benefits realization analysis

C. Benefits realization analysis

D. Value scoring and measurement analysis

> The correct answer is **D**. All of the analysis tools described in the question are performed within value scoring and measurement analysis.
> Refer to Section 6.3.2.2 of the Standard for Portfolio Management - 3rd Edition. Review the descriptions and definition.

165. Scott comes to you as his supervisor and indicates that he has finished the Develop Portfolio Management Plan process. He hands you a copy of the changes he made to the portfolio strategic plan. What is Scott missing? (Difficult)

A. Portfolio roadmap, portfolio process assets updated, portfolio management plan

B. Elicitation techniques, portfolio organizational structure analysis, integration of portfolio management plans

C. Portfolio management plan, portfolio process assets update

D. Portfolio charter, portfolio management plan

> The correct answer is **C**. Refer to Section 5.1 of the Standard for Portfolio Management - 3rd Edition. Review the descriptions and definition.

166. Gary is performing analysis to understand how much work can be performed based on the resources available as well as the ability of the organization to source and execute the selected portfolio and to determine the constraints generated by skill set limitations. What analysis is Gary performing? (Moderate)

A. Resource analysis

B. Interdependency analysis

C. Prioritization analysis

D. Capability and capacity analysis

167. Tony is working on defining the portfolio roadmap. He has been approached by an executive level stakeholder who has expressed concern about cost as it relates to certain portfolio elements. How should Tony proceed? (Moderate)

    A. Tony should run an interdependency analysis

    B. Tony should refer to the portfolio charter

    C. Tony should run a prioritization analysis

    D. Tony should run a cost-benefit analysis

    The correct answer is **D**. Refer to Section 4.3.2.2 of the Standard for Portfolio Management - 3rd Edition. Review the descriptions and definition.

168. Dwayne is the portfolio manager. During the Develop Portfolio Risk Management Plan process, Dwayne developed new risk checklists and new risk categories. What needs to be updated as a result of the change? (Difficult)

    A. Organizational process assets

    B. Portfolio management plan

    C. Portfolio reports

    D. Portfolio process assets

    The correct answer is **A**. Risk checklists and risk categories are part of organizational process assets.
    Refer to Section 8.1.3.3 of the Standard for Portfolio Management - 3rd Edition. Review the descriptions and definition.

169. A typical "what-if scenario": (Moderate)

    A. Tracks impacts of portfolio management decisions on resource capacity

    B. Tracks impacts of portfolio management decisions on portfolio assets

    C. Tracks impacts of portfolio optimization decisions on resource capacity

    D. Tracks impacts of portfolio optimization decisions on portfolio assets

The correct answer is **C**. Refer to Section 6.1.2.4 of the Standard for Portfolio Management - 3rd Edition. Review the descriptions and definition.

170. A typical tool for communication is: (Moderate)

A. Email

B. Meeting

C. Dashboard

D. All of the answer choices

The correct answer is **D**. Refer to Section 7.1 of the Standard for Portfolio Management - 3rd Edition. Review the descriptions and definition.

Chapter 10. Pullouts of Exam Aids

This exam aids here are pre-formatted to be on one sheet of paper, which you can carry and study. Remember, by registering, I will send you the Excel versions of these aids.

Exam Aid 1: Scoring Sheet

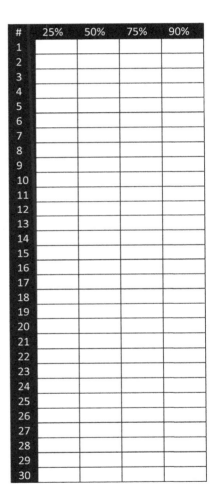

#	25%	50%	75%	90%
1				
2				
3				
4				
5				
6				
7				
8				
9				
10				
11				
12				
13				
14				
15				
16				
17				
18				
19				
20				
21				
22				
23				
24				
25				
26				
27				
28				
29				
30				

#	25%	50%	75%	90%
31				
32				
33				
34				
35				
36				
37				
38				
39				
40				
41				
42				
43				
44				
45				
46				
47				
48				
49				
50				
51				
52				
53				
54				
55				
56				
57				
58				
59				
60				

#	25%	50%	75%	90%
61				
62				
63				
64				
65				
66				
67				
68				
69				
70				
71				
72				
73				
74				
75				
76				
77				
78				
79				
80				
81				
82				
83				
84				
85				
86				
87				
88				
89				
90				

Knowledge Area	Process Groups		
	Defining Process Group (8)	Aligning Process Group (6)	Authorizing & Controlling Process Group (2)
Portfolio Strategy Management (4)	Develop Portfolio Strategic Plan	Manage Strategic Change	
	Develop Portfolio Charter		
	Develop Portfolio Define Roadmap		
Portfolio Governance Management (5)	Develop Portfolio Management Plan	Optimize Portfolio	Authorize Portfolio
	Define Portfolio		Provide Portfolio Oversight
Portfolio Performance Management (3)	Develop Portfolio Performance Management Plan	Manage Supply and Demand	
		Manage Portfolio Value	
Portfolio Communication Management (2)	Develop Portfolio Communication Management Plan	Manage Portfolio Information	
Portfolio Risk Management (2)	Develop Portfolio Risk Management Plan	Manage Portfolio Risk	

Legend:	Define (No Shade)	Align (Light Gray)	Authorize & Control (Darker Gray)

Note: Due to copyright restrictions, I cannot send this table electronically to you. But I will include an electronic "shell" in which you can practice.

Knowledge Area	Processes	Inputs	Tools and Techniques	Outputs
Portfolio Strategic Management	Develop Portfolio Strategic Plan	1. Org strategy and objectives 2. Inventory of work 3. Portfolio Process Assets 4. Org Process Assets 5. Enterprise environmental factors	1. Portfolio Component Inventory 2. Strategic Alignment Analysis 3. Prioritization Analysis	1. Portfolio Strategic Plan 2. Portfolio
	Develop Portfolio Charter	1. Portfolio Strategic Plan 2. Portfolio processes assets 3. Enterprise environmental factors	1. Scenario Analysis 2. Capability and Capacity Analysis	1. Portfolio Strategic Plan Updates 2. Portfolio Charter 3. Portfolio Process Assets Updates
	Define Portfolio Roadmap	1. Portfolio Strategic Plan 2. Portfolio Charter 3. Portfolio	1. Interdependency Analysis 2. Cost/benefit Analysis 3. Prioritization Analysis	1. Portfolio Roadmap
	Manage Strategic Change	1. Portfolio Strategic Plan 2. Portfolio Charter 3. Portfolio 4. Portfolio Roadmap 5. Portfolio Management Plan 6. Portfolio Process Assets	1. Stakeholder Analysis 2. Gap Analysis 3. Readiness Assessment	1. Portfolio Strategic Plan Updates 2. Portfolio Charter Updates 3. Portfolio Updates 4. Portfolio Roadmap Updates 5. Portfolio Management Plan Updates 6. Portfolio Process Assets Updates
Portfolio Governance Management	Develop Portfolio Management Plan	1. Portfolio Strategic Plan 2. Portfolio Charter 3. Portfolio Roadmap 4. Portfolio Process Assets 5. Org Process Assets 6. Enterprise environmental factors	1. Elicitation Techniques 2. Portfolio or Org Structure Analysis 3. Integration of Portfolio Management Plans	1. Portfolio Strategic Plan Updates 2. Portfolio Management Plan 3. Portfolio Process Assets Updates
	Define Portfolio	1. Portfolio Strategic Plan 2. Portfolio Charter 3. Portfolio 4. Portfolio Roadmap 5. Portfolio Management Plan 6. Portfolio Process Assets	1. Portfolio Component Inventory 2. Portfolio Component Categorization Techniques 3. Weighted Ranking and Scoring Techniques	1. Portfolio Updates 2. Portfolio Roadmap Updates 3. Portfolio Management Plan Updates
	Optimize Portfolio	1. Portfolio 2. Portfolio Roadmap 3. Portfolio Management Plan 4. Portfolio Reports 5. Portfolio Process Assets	1. Capability and Capacity Analysis 2. Weighted Ranking and Scoring Techniques 3. Quantitative and Qualitative Analysis 4. Graphical Analytical Methods	1. Portfolio Updates 2. Portfolio Roadmap Updates 3. Portfolio Management Plan Updates 4. Portfolio Reports 5. Portfolio Process Assets Updates
	Authorize Portfolio	1. Portfolio 2. Portfolio Management Plan 3. Portfolio Reports	1. Portfolio Authorization Techniques 2. Portfolio Management Information System	1. Portfolio Updates 2. Portfolio Management Plan Updates 3. Portfolio Reports 4. Portfolio Process Assets Updates
	Provide Portfolio Oversight	1. Portfolio 2. Portfolio Roadmap 3. Portfolio Management Plan 4. Portfolio Reports 5. Portfolio Process Assets	1. Portfolio Review Meetings 2. Elicitation Techniques	1. Portfolio Updates 2. Portfolio Management Plan Updates 3. Portfolio Reports 4. Portfolio Process Assets Updates
Portfolio Performance Management	Develop Portfolio Performance Management Plan	1. Portfolio Management Plan 2. Portfolio Process Assets 3. Org Process Assets 4. Enterprise Environmental Factors	1. Elicitation Techniques 2. Portfolio management Information System 3. Capability and Capacity Analysis	1. Portfolio Management Plan Updates 2. Portfolio Process Assets Updates
	Manage Supply and Demand	1. Portfolio 2. Portfolio Management Plan 3. Portfolio reports	1. Scenario Analysis 2. Quantitative and Qualitative Analysis 3. Capability and Capacity Analysis	1. Portfolio Updates 2. Portfolio Management Plan Updates 3. Portfolio Reports
	Manage Portfolio Value	1. Portfolio Roadmap 2. Portfolio Management Plan 3. Portfolio Reports	1. Elicitation Techniques 2. Value Scoring and Measurement Analysis 3. Benefits Realization Analysis	1. Portfolio Management Plan Updates 2. Portfolio Reports 3. Portfolio Process Assets Updates
Portfolio Communication Management	Develop Portfolio Communication Management Plan	1. Portfolio 2. Portfolio Roadmap 3. Portfolio Management Plan 4. Portfolio Reports 5. Portfolio Process Assets	1. Stakeholder Analysis 2. Elicitation Techniques 3. Communication Requirement Analysis	1. Portfolio Management Plan Updates 2. Portfolio Process Assets Updates
	Management Portfolio Information	1. Portfolio 2. Portfolio Management Plan 3. Portfolio Reports 4. Portfolio Component Reports 5. Portfolio Process Assets	1. Elicitation Techniques 2. Portfolio Management Information System 3. Communication Requirements Analysis 4. Communication Methods	1. Portfolio Management Plan Updates 2. Portfolio Reports 3. Portfolio Process Assets Updates
Portfolio Risk Management	Develop Portfolio Risk Management Plan	1. Portfolio Management Plan 2. Portfolio Process Assets 3. Org Process Assets 4. Enterprise Environmental Factors	1. Weighted Ranking and Scoring Techniques 2. Graphical Analytical Methods 3. Quantitative and Qualitative Analysis	1. Portfolio Management Plan Updates 2. Org Process Assets Updates 3. Portfolio Assets Updates
	Manage Portfolio Risks	1. Portfolio 2. Portfolio Management Plan 3. Portfolio Reports 4. Portfolio Process Assets 5. Org Process Assets 6. Enterprise Environmental Factors	1. Weighted Ranking and Scoring Techniques 2. Quantitative and Qualitative Analysis	1. Portfolio Management Plan Updates 2. Portfolio Reports 3. Portfolio Process Assets 4. Org Process Assets Updates

KA	Processes	Description	A. Portfolio	B. P. Charter	C. P. Mgmt Plan	D. P. Report	E. P. Roadmap	F. P. Strategic Plan	G. Ent Enviro	H. Org Process	I. P. Proess Assets	Tools and Techniques	Description	A. Portfolio	B. P. Charter	C. P. Mgmt Plan	D. P. Report	E. P. Roadmap	F. P. Strategic Plan	G. Ent Enviro	H. Org Process	I. P. Proess Assets
Strategic Management	D.P. Strategic Plan (3, 2)	GHI * Org strategy & objectives * Inventory of work							x	x	x	1. P. component inventory 2. Strategic alignment analysis 3. Prioritization analysis	A, F	x					x			
	D.P. Charter (3, 3)	FG, I						x	x		x	1. Scenario analysis 2. CCA	B, F, I		x				x			x
	Define Port. Roadmap (3, 1)	AB, F	x	x				x				1. Interdependency analysis 2. Cost/benefit analysis 3. Prioritization analysis	E					x				
	M. Strategic Change (6, 6)	ABC, EF, I	x	x	x		x	x			x	1. Stakeholder analysis 2. Gap analysis 3. Readiness assessment	ABC, EF, I	x	x	x		x	x			x
Governance Management	D.P. Management Plan (6, 3)	B, EFGHI		x			x	x	x	x	x	1. ET 2. P. or Org structure analysis 3. Integration of portfolio management plans	C, F, I			x			x			x
	Define P. (6, 3)	ABC, EF, I	x	x	x		x	x			x	1. P. component inventory 2. P. component categorization techniques 3. WRS	A, C, E	x		x		x				
	Optimize P. (5, 5)	A, CDE, I	x		x	x	x				x	1. CCA 2. WRS 3. QQS 4. Graphical analytical methods	A, CDE, I	x		x	x	x				x
	Authorize P. (3, 4)	A, CD	x		x	x						1. P. authorization techniques 2. PMIS	A, CD, I	x		x	x					x
	Provide P. Oversight (5, 4)	A, CDE, I	x		x	x	x				x	1. P. review meetings 2. ET	A, CD, I	x		x	x					x
Performance Management	D.P. Performance Mgmt Plan (4, 2)	C, GHI			x				x	x	x	1. ET 2. PMIS 3. CCA	C, I			x						x
	M. Supply and Demand (3, 3)	A, CD	x		x	x						1. Scenario analysis 2. QQS 3. CCA	A, CD	x		x	x					
	M. P. Value (3, 3)	CDE			x	x	x					1. ET 2. Value scoring and measurement analysis 3. Benefits realization analysis	CD, I			x	x					x
Communication Management	D.P. Communication Mgmt Plan (5, 2)	A, CDE, I	x		x	x	x				x	1. Stakeholder analysis 2. ET 3. Communication requirement analysis	D, I				x					x
	Management P. Information (4, 3)	A, CD, I P. component reports	x		x	x					x	1. ET 2. PMIS 3. Communication requirement analysis 4. Communication methods	CD, I			x	x					x
Risk Management	D.P. Risk Mgmt Plan (4, 3)	C, GHI			x				x	x	x	1. WRS 2. Graphical analytical methods 3. QQS	CD, G			x	x			x	x	
	M. P. Risks (6, 4)	A, CD, GHI	x		x	x			x	x	x	1. WRS 2. QQS	CD, G, I			x	x			x	x	
	Count:		10	4	12	8	7	5	6	5	12		Count	7	2	13	7	4	4	0	2	12

Index

abbreviations, 14
acronyms, 14
Aligning Process Group, 61
Authorize Portfolio, 11
Authorizing & Controlling Process Group, 61
benefit realization category
    sample, 113
Benefits and Values, 110
black swans, 144
Book registration, 399
business execution, 2
    framework, 40
Capability Maturity Heat Map, 78
Change
    control, 94
    strategic, 94
Communication and stakeholder management, 128
communication plan, 126
Compliance, 94
Contact the Author, 399
Define Portfolio, 11
Define Portfolio Roadmap, 10
Defining Process Group, 61
Dependencies, 95
Develop Portfolio Charter, 10
Develop Portfolio Communication Management Plan, 12
Develop Portfolio Management Plan, 11
Develop Portfolio Performance Management Plan, 12
Develop Portfolio Risk Management Plan, 13
Develop Portfolio Strategic Plan, 10
discount, 399
exam aids
    blank, 373
Exam preparation
    30 Days Study Plan, 26
    5 Days Countdown, 25
Governance, 95
Inputs, Tools & Techniques, Outputs, 29, 75, 93, 109,
    127, 145
ITTO, 14, 29, 35
Manage Portfolio Risks, 13
Manage Portfolio Value, 12
Manage Strategic Change, 10
Manage Supply and Demand, 12
Management Portfolio Information, 12
Optimize Portfolio, 11
Organization Maturity, 50

Organization Operating Level, 43, 50, 148
Organization Strategy, 50
Organizational / Inter-portfolios, 148
Performance goals, 107
Performance metrics, 111
PfMP, 7, 8
    certification requirements, 15
    exam specification, 17
    Handbook, 16
    maintaining credential, 17
PfMPs
    by countries, 9
PgMP, 7
PMBOK, 7
PMO, 47
PMP, 7
Portfolio, 76, 91, 143, 146, 148
Portfolio Bubble Chart, 96
Portfolio Charter, 76
Portfolio Communication Management, 125
portfolio dashboard, 130
Portfolio efficient frontier, 111
Portfolio Information Management System (PMIS), 128
Portfolio Lifecycle Report, 114
Portfolio management information system (PMIS, 111
Portfolio Management Process Groups, 61
portfolio manager
    skills, 47
portfolio managers
    how to think, 42
Portfolio Performance Management, 107
portfolio risks, 143
Portfolio Roadmap, 76
Portfolio Strategic Management, 73
Portfolio Strategic Plan, 77
Project Management Institute, 7
Provide Portfolio Oversight, 11, 95
Risk levels, 148
Risk management, 146
Sensitivity analysis, 147
SMART, 114
SMARTIE, 114
Stakeholder matrix, 129
stakeholders, 125
study plan, 26
Supply and demand, 112
Taleb, Nassim, 144

Additional pages for notes:

Want more practice questions?

PMO Advisory has developed the largest known bank of PfMP practice exam questions. It is on target to exceed 2,000 questions and answers.

Visit our PfMP landing page at www.pmoadvisory.com/pfmp/

Do you want to attend a PfMP training class?

PMO Advisory is proud to offer:

PfMP Intelicamp (Liver Virtual) Bootcamp &

Full PfMP Preparation Course &

Onsite Portfolio Management Course

To learn more, visit the PfMP training website at

www.pmoadvisory.com/pfmp/

As a bonus, register this book at

www.pmoadvisory.com/product-registration

to receive a 30 days access to the digital test bank of over 400 questions.

How well does your organization achieve its business objectives?

What percentage of your projects are truly successful?

What is the state of business execution in your firm?

Intrigued?

Join us for the first large scale study of its kind. PMO Advisory has initiated an ongoing study into the challenge of business execution. Our premise is that most organizations today have great ideas. But benefits are often not realized due to poor execution.

All survey respondents will receive free reports and newsletters update the results.

Visit us at www.pmoadvisory.com/research/strategic-business-execution/. There, you will find the latest information on our research including a 90 minute seminar recording of Te Wu's presentation at Montclair State University. If you want to just jump into the survey, go to: www.surveymonkey.com/s/sbe01.

Remember to use the same contact information as the book registration to receive even more discounts.

How to Contact the Author

Thank you for purchasing this book, and I wish you the best of luck in your pursuit. I welcome your feedback about this book or about books and articles you would like to see from me and my company in the future. Here are the multiple ways to interact with us:

1. Book registration: http://www.pmoadvisory.com/product-registration/
2. My Email: twu@pmoadvisory.com
3. Connect with me on LinkedIn: http://www.linkedin.com/in/te-wu
4. Follow my company on
    a. Twitter: http://www.twitter.com/pmoadvisory
    b. Facebook: http://www.facebook.com/pmoadvisoryllc
5. Complete the Strategic Business Execution survey:
    http://www.surveymonkey.com/s/sbe01

By registering this book, you are entitled to the following:

1. Digital copies of the exam aids.
2. Support Group. All registered user of this book will be invited to a moderated LinkedIn forum dedicated to users of this book and our products.
3. Discount to additional practice exam and real-time PfMP exam preparation courses. Please visit us at http://www.pmoadvisory.com/pfmp/ for more information.
4. Discount to our PfMP exam preparation course. Please visit us at http://www.pmoadvisory.com/pfmp/ for more details. My company will be one of the first, if not the first, to offer extensive training and coaching programs for prospective certified portfolio professionals.

Made in the USA
Las Vegas, NV
26 July 2022